Here's what fundraising executives are saying about *Dream Builders*:

"Dream Builders is a practical tool which will prove of great value to those seeking to maximize success in major gifts fundraising. Nick Costa has contributed mightily to our fundraising literature with this important book."

William T. Sturtevant, Vice President, University of Illinois Foundation,
author of *The Artful Journey* and *The Continuing Journey*

"Nick Costa presents eight successful major gift programs, and each is an insp͏   ͏ itself. . . .
His TOP GIFTS™ formula is the key to success. It wor͏

James Greenfield, ACFRE, FAHP, editor of the ͏
The Nonprofit Handbook: Fund Raisir͏

"The TOP GIFTS™ process creates a step-by-step approach that anyone c͏   ͏w, written by an expert who has raised big gifts. . . . Helpful suggestions on restructuring your time to focus on major gifts. A great contribution."

M. Jane Williams, Partner, Schultz & Williams,
author of the landmark book *Big Gifts*

"Dream Builders is an essential piece of a professional fundraiser's literature. It demonstrates that a truly future-focused vision is attainable in fundraising and necessary for success. . . . *Dream Builders* shows us how to focus our organizations. Nick Costa clearly provides practical and essential skills for achieving results based on 'starting with your head and going with your heart.'"

William C. McGinly, Ph.D., CAE, President and Chief Executive Officer,
Association for Healthcare Philanthropy

"Harold J. Seymour wrote the classic *Designs for Fund-Raising* in 1966. Of all the texts that have come along since then, none surpasses Nick Costa's comprehensive, well organized, visionary *Dream Builders*. It's an essential tool for every fundraiser, from beginner to veteran professional."

Henry 'Hank' Goldstein, President/CEO, The Oram Group, Inc.

"Nothing happens unless first a dream."

Carl Sandburg

DREAM BUILDERS

Everything You Need to Know to Achieve Your Organization's Most Ambitious Dreams with TOP GIFTS™ Fundraising

Nick G. Costa

E³ Fundraising
Essentials, Expertise + Excellence in Fundraising

Ridgefield, Connecticut

P.O. Box 2402, Danbury, CT 06813
or www.e3fundraising.com

© 2004 by E^3 Fundraising

Except for appropriate use in critical reviews or works of scholarship, the reproduction or use of this work in any form by any electronic, mechanical, or other means now known or hereafter invented, including photocopying and recording, e-publishing, and in any information storage and retrieval system is forbidden without the written permission of the publisher.

FIRST EDITION

10 9 8 7 6 5 4 3 2 1

Costa, Nick G.
  Dream builders: everything you need to know to achieve your organization's most ambitious dreams with TOP GIFTS fundraising / Nick G. Costa

  p.cm
Includes biographical reference and index.

ISBN.0-9747590-0-7

   1. Fund raising – Handbooks, manuals, etc. 2. Leadership. 3. Nonprofit Boards.
      Costa, Nick G. II Title.

Library of Congress Control Number: 2003099710

E^3 Fundraising
Essentials, Expertise + Excellence in Fundraising
Danbury, Connecticut

www.e3fundraising.com

Printed in the United States of America

Harness the Power of TOP GIFTS™ Fundraising

Dream Builders shares the eight steps nonprofit leaders can take to achieve their organizations' dreams and vision through a focused and active planned giving and major gifts program.

TIME

Is the timing right for your organization to launch a TOP GIFTS™ program? Are you willing to commit the time needed to succeed?

OPPORTUNITIES

People give to have impact, to transform organizations, and often to be recognized. Identify those opportunities in your organization that will engage and excite your best donors. Develop programs to attract and recognize these gifts.

PEOPLE

Attract leaders. Identify the people and organizations that can make top gifts, whose actions will serve as a model for others to follow . . . people who will help you cultivate and solicit others. Understand and respond to their best aspirations.

GOALS

Establish challenging goals. Test their viability by constructing a table of gifts and matching the people and organizations that can make the gifts required.

INVOLVEMENT

Create opportunities to involve potential donors of top gifts. Build awareness and interest; find ways to communicate the impact of each gift.

FORMALLY ASK

In most cases, personally ask.

THANKS

People love to be thanked. Recognize and show appreciation to top gift donors in ways that are meaningful to them.

STEWARDSHIP

Keep your donors informed and involved. Report on—and celebrate—what you've accomplished together.

CONTENTS

A Brief Overview of the TOP GIFTS™ Workbooks

At the end of each TOP GIFTS™ chapter, you'll find these exercises, which enable you to test the concepts and strategies presented and apply them to your organization:

Timing Assessment (p. 95)
Gauge your organization's stature on four qualities (vision, value, visibility, and validity), identify areas of concern and where leadership is needed, and then assess your personal commitment to TOP GIFTS™ fundraising.

Creating the Dream (p. 119)
Select from five models for developing a fundraising vision based on your organization's needs; then select your three highest priorities. For each priority define "the five Ws and how" that news reporters use in developing a story (who, what, where, when, why, and how).

Communications Planning Chart I (p. 121)
Help inspire potential donors or investors and build clarity into your communications. Consider whether adopting a theme or logo would enhance your ability to convey your fundraising vision.

Communications Planning Chart II (p. 122)
Convert your needs into fundraising opportunities by analyzing specific projects. For each, determine the benefit to—or impact on—society, and its relevance to your vision.

Interest Survey for a New TOP GIFTS™ Program (p. 166)
Conduct an informal market survey to assess how your best prospects view your organization; identify factors that they consider important when they make TOP GIFTS™, as well as specific benefits and recognition programs that would appeal to them.

Recruiting Top Leaders (p. 183)

Elevate the stature of your TOP GIFTS™ program by enlisting the very best leadership. You'll consider five approaches to identify leadership, prepare a list of candidates to chair your program, select the recruitment team, and begin assembling people to serve on your leadership committee.

Screening for TOP GIFTS™ Donors (p. 208)

Use the four Cs (Capacity, Connectivity, Contact, and Charity) as a tool to identify and evaluate individuals who could make top gifts. Separately, screen organizations (foundations, government agencies, etc.) based on how well your needs match their funding guidelines and the level of interest demonstrated by program officers.

Creating a Table of Gifts (p. 228)

Create the table that determines the number and amounts of the gifts you'll want to secure in order to succeed.

Building TOP GIFTS™ Relationships (p. 250)

Develop a cultivation plan for the individuals and groups you need to involve so that you can secure the gifts indicated on the table of gifts you created.

Asking for a Leadership Gift (p. 262)

Prepare for your gift request by following the steps, from getting the appointment to making the ask, to sending a thank you letter.

Designing a Donor Appreciation Program (p. 272)

Lock in the ways you want to show your appreciation to donors who give at these higher levels: pacesetting, leadership, major, and special gifts.

Creating a Stewardship Plan (p. 290)

Fulfill your commitments to your donors in ways that share the spirit and joy of their philanthropy. Consider these specific elements when building your plan.

Acknowledgments

Whether building a house or fulfilling a dream, the talents of many professionals are key.

So, too, it is with writing this book, a dream of mine for more than fifteen years. I am indebted to family, friends, and colleagues, both in the fundraising field and in other professions, for their suggestions, refinements, and criticisms of this resource manual.

My personal thanks to:

- my wife, Valerie, who gave me the time and freedom to explore this topic and who researched several of the leadership donors cited;

- Jerold Panas, author and consultant, whose encouragement and introduction to Bonus Books enabled me to write the first chapters, who assisted in providing campaigns for case studies, and whose advice enabled me to overcome many challenges;

- Devon Freeny, managing editor of Bonus Books, who guided me through the publishing process;

- Jas Szygiel, friend and award-winning designer, for translating my ideas into an instructive presentation;

- June Norris and Donna Greenberg, for editing my manuscript, adding greater consistency and clarity;

- Theodore "Dick" Brickman, a trustee to several organizations and leadership donor, who suggested the workbook pages as "a way for development professionals, trustees, and other volunteers to apply your techniques and strategies";

- Robert E. Carter of Ketchum Incorporated for directing me to the Little League Baseball campaign;

- William "Bill" Endicott of Mitchell Associates for sharing examples of the company's recognition displays and enthusiasm for the focus of this book;

- Reviewers and friends: Eileen Campbell; Beverly Goldberg; James Greenfield; George "Hank" Haines; Eileen Heisman; Richard L. Jones Jr.; William McGinly; Mary Poole; Edward Sickles; William Sturtevant; M. Jane Williams; and others for reading the many drafts and making constructive comments.

Finally, special thanks to the nonprofit and business leaders listed below who contributed ideas and fundraising materials to help convey the TOP GIFTS™ process:

Cover

The Ben Franklin National Memorial, courtesy of the Franklin Institute, Philadelphia, Pa. Reprinted with permission, Kenneth E. Kirby, Executive Vice President.

Photo of Andrew & Louise Carnegie, © and courtesy of the Carnegie Library of Pittsburgh, Pa. Used with permission.

Painting of Frank Seaver & Blanche Ebert Seaver, Lawrence D. Hornbaker, Ed.D., Vice Chancellor, Pepperdine University, Malibu, Calif. Used with permission.

Youth at Library Site, Paola Muggia Stuff, Development Director, Friends & Foundation of the San Francisco Public Library, San Francisco, Calif.

Chapter One

A Partnership to Change Lives

Paola Muggia Stuff, Development Director, Friends & Foundation of the San Francisco Public Library, San Francisco, Calif.

Ken Garcia, "The Littlest Library," *San Francisco Chronicle*, San Francisco, Calif. © The San Francisco Chronicle. Reprinted with permission.

Reigniting the Passion

Stephen D. Keener, President, Little League Baseball, Williamsport, Pa.; William Piszek, Copernicus Foundation, Philadelphia, Pa.

Protecting the Future of Nursing

Richard L. Jones, Jr., President; Fitz Eugene Dixon, Jr., Life Trustee; Abington Memorial Hospital, Abington, Pa. Recognition display by Mitchell Associates, Wilmington, Del., William Endicott & Michael Amici, Design Team.

Rx: Topeka Community Theatre

Twink Lynch, Ph.D., Member, Board of Trustees, Topeka Civic Theatre & Academy, Topeka, Kans.

Comments edited from Twink Lynch, "Spotlight on Boards: The Joy of Philanthropy," *Spotlight*, American Association of Community Theatre, Lago Vista, Tex., October 1999, p. 20, 19. Used with permission, Julie Angelo, Executive Director, AACT.

From Crisis to Opportunity

David M. Erickson, President, Samaritan Inns, Washington, D.C.

Sandra Gregg, Venture Philanthropy Partners, Reston, Va. From *Effective Capacity Building in Nonprofit Organizations*, copyright owned by Venture Philanthropy Partners, written by McKinsey & Company. Used with permission.

Challenged to Lead

Lawrence D. Hornbaker, Ed.D., Vice Chancellor, Pepperdine University, Malibu, Ca.

Closer to the Cure

Janet B. Cady, President, Children's Hospital Trust, Boston, Mass.; Hal Garnick, Chair, Heart Council, Children's Hospital Trust, Boston, Mass.

Photograph of Hal Garnick, © 2001, Richard Howard Photography. Used with permission.

The Anniversary Campaign for Princeton

Robert P. Thompson, '42; Van Zanor Williams, Jr., '65, Vice President for Development; Susan C. Robichaud, Associate Director, Office of Planned Giving; V. Renee Dixon, Assistant Director, Office of Planned Giving; Princeton University, Princeton, N.J. "A Teaching President Makes His Case," edited from "President's Teaching Initiatives," *Princeton* and campaign materials. Used with permission.

Chapter Two

Frederick F. Reichheld , *Loyalty Rules!* (Boston: Harvard Business School Press, 2001), p. 10. Used with permission.

Janet B. Cady, President, Children's Hospital Trust, Boston, Mass.

James H. Brucker, Ph.D., Director of Development, Penn State College of Medicine/Hershey Medical Center, Hershey, Pa.

Belinda Foster, Special Events Manager at Stamford Health Foundation, Stamford, Conn.

Chapter Three

Photo of Andrew & Louise Carnegie, © and courtesy of the Carnegie Library of Pittsburgh, Pa. Used with permission.

Chapter Five

WealthPulse: Survey of Wealth and Giving (New York: HNW, 2001), Tables 4A & 4B: Obstacles to Giving. © 2001 HNW, Inc. Used with permission. *www.hnw.com.*

Gene Tempel, "Fundraising: Obstacles and Opportunities," *Commonfund Quarterly* (Wilton, CT), Winter 2002, p. 4–5. Used with permission.

From *Effective Capacity Building in Nonprofit Organizations*, copyright owned by Venture Philanthropy Partners, written by McKinsey & Company. Pages 21–24, 39–41, 60. Used with permission.

Anne Lowrey Bailey, "Leslie Wexner's $250-Million Foundation," *Chronicle of Philanthropy* 3, no. 11 (March 26, 1991), p. 6–9. *philanthropy.com.* Used with permission.

David S. Newburg, Ph.D., Professor of Biochemistry & Molecular Pharmacology, Program Director in Glycobiology, Shriver Center of the University of Mass. Medical School, Waltham, Mass.

Chapter Six

Russ Alan Prince & Karen Maru File, *The Seven Faces of Philanthropy* (San Francisco: Jossey-Bass, 1994).

Case Statements

Michele Steege, Partner, Steege/Thomson Communications, Philadelphia, Pa.

Edie Kushner, Director of Development, the Jewish Home of Greater Harrisburg, Harrisburg, Pa.

Evelyn Rader, Director of Development, Friends' Central School, Wynnewood, Pa.

Named Facilities, Programs & Plaques

Twink Lynch, Ph.D., Member, Board of Trustees, Topeka Civic Theatre & Academy, Topeka, Kans.

Membership/Recognition Levels

C. Edwin Davis, Director of Development, the Florida Orchestra, Tampa, Fla.

Kathleen Watson, Vice President; Melissa B. Coopersmith, Director of Major Gifts; the Kimmel Center for the Performing Arts, Regional Performing Arts Center, Philadelphia, Pa.

Campaign Giving Policies

Robert P. Thompson, '42; Van Zanor Williams, Jr., '65, Vice President for Development; Susan C. Robichaud, Associate Director, Office of Planned Giving; V. Renee Dixon, Assistant Director, Office of Planned Giving; Princeton University, Princeton, N.J.

Premium Event That Raises Sights

Anne Lowrey Bailey, "Leslie Wexner's $250-Million Foundation," *Chronicle of Philanthropy* 3, no. 11 (March 26, 1991), p. 6–9. *philanthropy.com.* Used with permission.

Planned Gifts

Lise Twiford, Director of Planned Giving, Abington Memorial Hospital, Abington, Pa.

Chapter Seven

Jerold Panas, *Mega Gifts* (Chicago: Bonus Books, 1984). Used with permission.

Russ Alan Prince & Karen Maru File, *The Seven Faces of Philanthropy* (San Francisco: Jossey-Bass, 1994).

Chapter Eight

The Ben Franklin National Memorial, courtesy of the Franklin Institute, Philadelphia, Pa. Reprinted with permission, Kenneth E. Kirby, Executive Vice President.

Chapter Nine

Harold J. Seymour, *Designs for Fundraising: Principles, Patterns, Techniques*, (New York: McGraw-Hill, 1966).

Nick Costa, "TARGETing™ Success: The Performance Report," *AHP Journal*, Association for Healthcare Philanthropy, Falls Church, Va., Fall 1991, p. 23–24. Used with permission.

Gift tables are courtesy of each of the organizations indicated. See chapter 1 for specific acknowledgments.

Chapter Ten

Photo of George Soros, Carol Thomson, Partner, Steege/Thomson Communications, Philadelphia, Pa.

Photo of Jack Farber, Thomas Jefferson University Hospital, Philadelphia, Pa.

Photo of Gordon Moore: Gordon & Betty Moore Foundation, San Francisco, Calif.

Nick Costa, "The Nursing Imperative: Can Fundraising Help Overcome the Nursing Shortage?" *AHP Journal*, Association for Healthcare Philanthropy, Falls Church, Va., Fall 2001, p. 7–14. Used with permission.

Chapter Twelve
Recognizing Dream Builders
All displays designed and fabricated by Mitchell Associates, Wilmington Del.

Children's Play Area and the Norman & Angelina Cooper Family Waiting Area: Steven A. Rum, Vice Chancellor, Medical Center Development & Alumni Affairs, Duke Children's Hospital & Health Center, Durham, N.C.; William Endicott & Robert Agosta, Design Team; Chris Hildreth, Photographer.

Richmond Ballet, Richmond, Va.; William Endicott & Steven Yarnall, Design Team; Steven Yarnall, Photographer.

The Story of Generosity: Janet B. Cady, President, Children's Hospital Trust, Boston, Mass.; William Endicott & Robert Agosta, Design Team; Peter Lewitt, Photographer.

Horizon Society and annual donors display: Ellen R. Luken, Executive Director, External Affairs, Duke University Medical Center, Durham, N.C.; William Endicott & Steven Yarnall, Design Team; Chris Hildreth, Photographer.

History of Cardiology and major donor recognition: Jane Cosper, Director of Gift Planning, American College of Cardiology, Bethesda, Md.; William Endicott & Steven Yarnall, Design Team; Barry Halkin, Photographer.

Waterfall and sculpture display: Lyle Sheldon, President, Upper Chesapeake Medical Center, Bel Air, Md.; Steven Yarnall & Erik Dressler, Design Team; Barry Halkin, Photographer.

Chapter Thirteen
Historic Plaque Display: Janet L. Hedrick, Director of Development, St. Christopher's Hospital for Children, Philadelphia, Pa. Designed by Mitchell Associates, Wilmington, Del.; William Endicott & Robert Agosta, Design Team; Peter Olson, Photographer.

Jill Kyle, Director, Fund Development: Louise & William Gerstadt, Mr. & Mrs. F. Eugene Dixon, Jr., Dixon Scholars, Dixon School of Nursing, Abington Memorial Hospital, Abington, Pa.

Chapter Fourteen
What's Your Dream?
Douglas M. Lawson, Douglas M. Lawson Associates, New York, N.Y.; author of *More Give to Live*, Alti Publishing, P.O. Box 28025, San Diego, CA.

Appendices

PART 1

Reprinted and updated from:

Nick G. Costa, "Seven Steps to Launching a Successful Annual Appeal," *NAHD Journal*, (Falls Church, Va.: National Association for Hospital Development, today known as the Association for Healthcare Philanthropy), Summer 1984. Used with permission.

PART 2

Reprinted and updated from:

Nick G. Costa, "What Is Planned Giving and How Can Trustees Help?" *Trustee* 45, no. 11 (November 1992), p. 20–23. © 1992 Health Forum, Inc. Used with permission.

PART 3

Jan Grieff, Jan Grieff Research Associates, Sinking Spring, Pa.

Editorial Notes

Is the proper spelling . . .

fundraising

fund-raising

fund raising?

Actually, all three choices are correct depending on usage. Yet fundraisers—and even the dictionaries they consult—often disagree on what is preferred in a specific instance. After much discussion with two editors, I've chosen to standardize the spelling to *fundraising*. The reason? This is the spelling that's presented most often in the dictionaries we consulted.

TOP GIFTS AND TOP GIFTS™ FUNDRAISING

Here you'll see an effort to be more precise. When I refer to the largest gifts, these are *top gifts*. By contrast, the eight-step process to secure these gifts is called *TOP GIFTS™ fundraising* or, in brief, *TOP GIFTS™*. That said, let's get started!

*V*isionaries throughout the world are not only touching the future, but shaping it as well. This book identifies the eight steps to create and fund your organization's most ambitious dreams.

"If everybody was satisfied with himself, there would be no heroes."

Mark Twain

"Your path to fulfillment is carved by your dreams, paved with your gifts and talents, and forged by your determination."

Cherie Carter-Scott, Ph.D.
If Success Is a Game, These Are the Rules

It's astounding what can be accomplished with the power of an explosive idea coupled with visionary leadership and ample funding. Consider these examples:

In the early 1900s Andrew Carnegie sought to change the world's landscape with his vision and commitment to building public libraries. In part, it was a visible sign of gratitude to his mentor, Colonel Anderson, who lent his private four-hundred-book library to boys like young Carnegie on Saturday afternoons. Later, backed by his phenomenal wealth, Carnegie established more than 2,500 libraries—1,679 in the U.S. alone.

Less than a century later, Microsoft's Bill Gates is dedicated to rewiring many of the same libraries with broadband to introduce the Internet—and the vistas it provides—to new generations.

Many investors know Jim Barksdale from his driving leadership at companies such as Netscape, Federal Express, and McCaw Cellular. But, today, part of his tireless energy—and a one-hundred-million-dollar endowment he created—are devoted to improving literacy in his home state of Mississippi, where nearly a third of the people cannot read at the eighth grade level. Barksdale's passion for literacy emerged from his trials as a third grader with reading difficulties; his parents provided a tutor.

Barksdale's vision and tenacity are so strong that he believes that each individual's economic future is tied to "the first 1000 days of a child's school life," he told the Mississippi Economic Council. "If you don't teach them to read by then, the odds go up dramatically that you'll never teach them to read." They're more likely to be high school dropouts, delinquent, because they can't participate. The bottom 20 percent of society, the "have nots," will never join the top 80 percent because they lack a principal skill: they can't read. We "talk about the digital divide. How everyone needs a computer. Folks, if you can't read, you can't use the Internet," he warns.

Nearly twenty years earlier, Eugene Lang had his own epiphany. Speaking to sixth graders at his old elementary school in East Harlem, he realized that only 25 percent of the students would graduate from high school. He told students that, in order to succeed, they must have a dream. If they graduated from high school, he said to the sixty-one students, he would pay for their college education. Since then, Lang's "I Have a Dream" program has attracted support from other philanthropists. It has spread to more than 175 classes in sixty-two cities in twenty-six states, benefiting over thirteen thousand low-income youths, whom Lang calls "Dreamers." The benefits are enormous and the data was clear from the start. Ninety percent of Lang's first class from Harlem graduated (or secured a GED) and 60 percent went on for advanced education.

But dreams and vision are not limited to education. Paul Allen's passion for music by Jimi Hendrix led him to acquire the world's largest collection of Hendrix memorabilia. With Jody Patton, Allen created the Experience Music Project, a museum located in Seattle that celebrates and explores rock 'n' roll, encourages innovation in music, and shares some of Allen's eighty thousand artifacts of Hendrix, Bob Dylan, Bo Diddley, Muddy Waters, and Kurt Cobain.

Not all leaders with vision have the ability to fund their own dreams. In 1955, minister Dr. Robert H. Schuller arrived in Garden Grove, California, with his wife and organist, Arvelia, and five hundred dollars. For his first church, he rented the Orange drive-in theater, where he preached from the roof of the snack bar. Twenty-five years later, his dream "to build a great church for God, a church that would change and save lives" was realized with the dedication of the Crystal Cathedral, constructed of more than ten thousand windows of silver-colored glass installed in a frame of white steel trusses. Although Dr. Schuller's congregation has swelled to ten thousand members, his journey and view of the horizon are ongoing. His creed, "Find a need and fill it, find a hurt and heal it," keeps him energized as he works in more than fifty services and departments that vary from CAMP (Christians and Muslims for Peace) to prison ministry, New Hope twenty-four-hour phone counseling, Victors (survivors of incest), support groups for alcoholics, and the Association to Enforce Child Support.

It would have been easy for the spirit to be crushed along with its earthquake-damaged facilities, but leaders at a California hospital are instead thriving in a period of renewal. Sister Madeleine Shonka, the hospital's beloved former president, is leading a $120 million campaign for a new pavilion that incorporates updated technology to withstand seismic activity, offers the latest in digital imaging and communications, and has a reflecting pool and chapel for relaxation and meditation. Her message is that, regardless of the challenges it faces, this hospital is here to stay and serve the community.

These visionaries, along with thousands more throughout the world, are not only touching the future, but shaping it as well. They are taking risks, innovating, and setting challenging goals. With personal funds and leadership gifts from others, they are changing lives and having a real impact.

Their inspiration is a source of motivation, enlightenment, and renewal for their charities. It is a beacon that causes others to take notice, and, in many cases, to be inspired themselves to make major donations . . . top gifts.

This book aims to identify the steps you can use to create and fund your organization's audacious dream. It's a practical manual for major and planned gift fundraising, for *without these resources, most dreams would become lost memories and lost opportunities.*

I've developed an acronym, TOP GIFTS™, that outlines an eight-step process non-profit leaders can take to secure these essential major gifts. Here is an overview of TOP GIFTS™:

TIME

Is the timing right for your organization to launch a TOP GIFTS™ program? Are you willing to commit the time needed to succeed?

OPPORTUNITIES

People give to have impact, to transform organizations, and often to be recognized. Identify those opportunities in your organization that will engage and excite your best donors. Develop programs to attract and recognize these gifts.

PEOPLE

Attract leaders. Identify the people and organizations that can make top gifts, whose actions will serve as a model for others to follow . . . people who will help you cultivate and solicit others. Understand and respond to their best aspirations.

GOALS

Establish challenging goals. Test their viability by constructing a table of gifts and matching the people and organizations that can make the gifts required.

INVOLVEMENT

Create opportunities to involve potential donors of top gifts. Build awareness and interest; find ways to communicate the impact of each gift.

FORMALLY ASK

In most cases, personally ask.

THANKS

People love to be thanked. Recognize and show appreciation to top gift donors in ways that are meaningful to them.

STEWARDSHIP

Keep your donors informed and involved. Report on—and celebrate—what you've accomplished together.

TOP GIFTS™ is more than just a process; it's a marriage of proven, "real world" experience with research from several major studies, and it can help you pinpoint your best sources of gifts, develop strategies to involve and engage these key donors, and understand what motivates their philanthropy. Because TOP GIFTS™ fundraising focuses on the small number of gifts that ensure success, it's a time management tool as well . . . a road map to follow.

I've discovered that, when people with great vision apply the TOP GIFTS™ process, they often inspire an explosive growth in fundraising and a renewed and heightened level of confidence within the organization. With success in fundraising comes newfound courage, an openness to take on even greater challenges.

I have seen the cultures of organizations become more dynamic and energized after wrestling with and winning through strategic planning. These organizations have responded with courage and creativity to almost seismic changes in their environment. They have built their capacity, emerged with a clearer focus, and frequently added depth to their services. In their victories, they've transformed missions that were once "tired" into "inspired." Their great thoughts produced great deeds and, once achieved, their horizons were broadened. Their organizations became stronger. Economically, their campaigns have exploded in scale. By focusing on top gifts, fundraisers enabled contributions to one charity to jump first from $1 million dollars a year to $3 million dollars annually; then to over $10 million dollars, and the following year to more than $16 million. This same nonprofit organization is now considering a $60 million initiative—a goal that just a few years ago would have been considered unthinkable.

The principles that make this kind of growth possible are drawn from, refined by, and validated through years of successful capital campaigns and major gifts programs. The TOP GIFTS™ formula presents these techniques in a way that guides you through a better understanding of each step. At the request of both fundraising executives and volunteers, I've created a TOP GIFTS™ workbook; you'll find pages at the end of each TOP GIFTS™ chapter to test your knowledge and progress.

To help you visualize the process and benefits that can accrue, I've featured eight organizations that have applied and succeeded in major and planned gifts fundraising. Their stories are a powerful endorsement of these techniques in action. I've called the chapter on these entrepreneurial fundraisers "Visionary Organizations: Agents of Change." Each has gone beyond the ordinary to produce extraordinary results. Their lessons offer a view of what's possible.

In the appendixes, newcomers to fundraising are provided with a highly useful reference, "Getting Started: Fundamentals of Fundraising," that defines how to launch a successful annual appeal, and three roles for trustees in creating a dynamic planned giving program. There's even a list of Internet addresses where you can consult with development professionals.

Harvey Hornstein, author of *Management Courage*, observed that "someone must challenge what is with a dream of what might be."

To those of you who are dreamers, you have my full attention, encouragement, and applause. This book was written just for you.

NICK G. COSTA
JANUARY 2004

*A*n insider's view of eight successful major and planned gifts programs, showing you how each organization realized its dreams based on the TOP GIFTS™ fundraising process.

"Even if you're on the right track, you'll get run over if you just sit there."

Will Rogers
American-cowboy humorist

"When your work speaks for itself, don't interrupt."

Henry J. Kaiser
Industrialist and father of modern shipbuilding

Protecting the Future of Nursing

America's healthcare system is facing one of its most challenging issues: a serious shortage of nurses. Nurses listen, heal, and comfort, from your doctor's office to hospitals, birthing centers, and hospice programs. They touch our lives. But the increased demand for nurses—which will grow more acute as baby boomers age—is about to collide with a dwindling supply. Nursing school enrollments have been declining, and as many as half of all registered nurses (RNs) caring for patients today will reach retirement age during the next fifteen years.

Abington Memorial Hospital Foundation (Abington, Pa.), however, may have found a local solution that could be a model for the nation. The impact of its ten-million-dollar initiative is clear: more than twenty-five million dollars in gifts have been made, and enrollment in its nursing school are at near record levels.

The board of Abington Memorial Hospital Foundation appointed a blue ribbon panel to address its serious nursing shortage. As the panel studied causes and potential solutions to the problem, it conveyed its findings to a wider audience with this simple brochure.

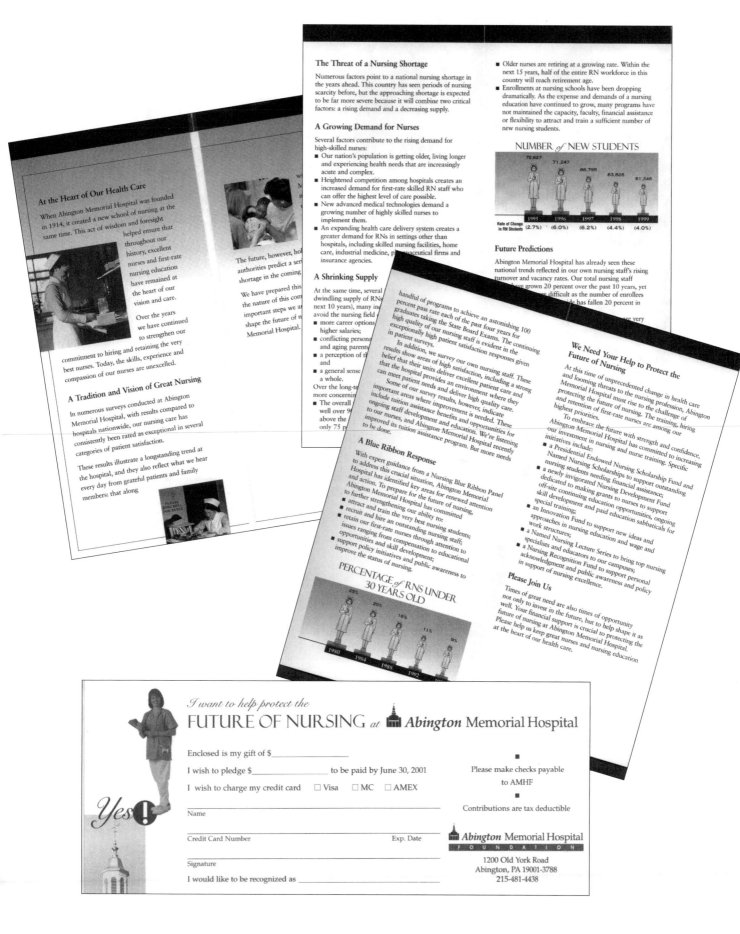

At the Heart of Our Health Care

When Abington Memorial Hospital was founded in 1914, it created a new school of nursing at the same time. This act of wisdom and foresight helped ensure that throughout our history, excellent nurses and first-rate nursing education have remained at the heart of our vision and care.

Over the years we have continued to strengthen our commitment to hiring and retaining the very best nurses. Today, the skills, experience and compassion of our nurses are unexcelled.

A Tradition and Vision of Great Nursing

In numerous surveys conducted at Abington Memorial Hospital, with results compared to hospitals nationwide, our nursing care has consistently been rated as exceptional in several categories of patient satisfaction.

These results illustrate a longstanding trend at the hospital, and they also reflect what we hear every day from grateful patients and family members: that along

---

The future, however, hol[...] authorities predict a seri[...] shortage in the coming,

We have prepared this [...] the nature of this com[...] important steps we a[...] shape the future of n[...] Memorial Hospital.

The Threat of a Nursing Shortage

Numerous factors point to a national nursing shortage in the years ahead. This country has seen periods of nursing scarcity before, but the approaching shortage is expected to be far more severe because it will combine two critical factors: a rising demand and a decreasing supply.

A Growing Demand for Nurses

Several factors contribute to the rising demand for high-skilled nurses:
- Our nation's population is getting older, living longer and experiencing health needs that are increasingly acute and complex.
- Heightened competition among hospitals creates an increased demand for first-rate skilled RN staff who can offer the highest level of care possible.
- New advanced medical technologies demand a growing number of highly skilled nurses to implement them.
- An expanding health care delivery system creates a greater demand for RNs in settings other than hospitals, including skilled nursing facilities, home care, industrial medicine, pharmaceutical firms and insurance agencies.

A Shrinking Supply

At the same time, several [...] dwindling supply of RNs [...] next 10 years), many ind[...] avoid the nursing field [...]
- more career options [...] higher salaries;
- conflicting personal [...] and aging parents [...]
- a perception of th[...] and
- a general sense [...] a whole.

Over the long-te[...] more concernin[...]
- The overall [...] well over 9[...] above the [...] only 75 p[...]

- Older nurses are retiring at a growing rate. Within the next 15 years, half of the entire RN workforce in this country will reach retirement age.
- Enrollments at nursing schools have been dropping dramatically. As the expense and demands of a nursing education have continued to grow, many programs have not maintained the capacity, faculty, financial assistance or flexibility to attract and train a sufficient number of new nursing students.

NUMBER of NEW STUDENTS

1995	1996	1997	1998	1999
75,827	71,247	66,795	63,826	61,248

| Rate of Change in RN Students | (2.7%) | (6.0%) | (6.2%) | (4.4%) | (4.0%) |

Future Predictions

Abington Memorial Hospital has already seen these national trends reflected in our own nursing staff's rising turnover and vacancy rates. Our total nursing staff [...] have grown 20 percent over the past 10 years, yet [...] more difficult as the number of enrollees [...] de has fallen 20 percent in [...]

---

handful of programs to achieve an astonishing 100 percent pass rate each of the past four years for graduates taking the State Board Exams. The continuing high quality of our nursing staff is evident in the exceptionally high patient satisfaction responses given in patient surveys.

In addition, we survey our own nursing staff. These results show areas of high satisfaction, including a strong belief that their units deliver excellent patient care and that the hospital provides an environment where they can meet patient needs and deliver high quality care.

Some of our survey results, however, indicate important areas where improvement is needed. These include tuition assistance benefits and opportunities for ongoing staff development and education. We're listening to our nurses, and Abington Memorial Hospital recently improved its tuition assistance program. But more needs to be done.

A Blue Ribbon Response

With expert guidance from a Nursing Blue Ribbon Panel to address this crucial situation, Abington Memorial Hospital has identified key areas for renewed attention and action. To prepare for the future of nursing, Abington Memorial Hospital has committed to further strengthening our ability to:
- attract and train the very best nursing students;
- recruit and hire an outstanding nursing staff;
- retain our first-rate nurses through attention to issues ranging from compensation to educational opportunities and skill development;
- support policy initiatives and public awareness to improve the status of nursing.

PERCENTAGE of RNS UNDER 30 YEARS OLD

1980	1984	1988	1992	
25%	20%	16%	11%	9%

We Need Your Help to Protect the Future of Nursing

At this time of unprecedented change in health care and looming threats to the nursing profession, Abington Memorial Hospital must rise to the challenge of protecting the future of nursing. The training, hiring and retention of first-rate nurses are among our highest priorities.

To embrace the future with strength and confidence, Abington Memorial Hospital has committed to increasing our investment in nursing and nurse training. Specific initiatives include:
- a Presidential Endowed Nursing Scholarship Fund and Named Nursing Scholarships to support outstanding nursing students needing financial assistance;
- a newly invigorated Nursing Development Fund dedicated to making grants to nurses to support off-site continuing education opportunities, ongoing skill development and paid education sabbaticals for special training;
- an Innovation Fund to support new ideas and approaches in nursing education and wage and work structures;
- a Named Nursing Lecture Series to bring top nursing specialists and educators to our campuses;
- a Nursing Recognition Fund to support personal acknowledgment and public awareness and policy in support of nursing excellence.

Please Join Us

Times of great need are also times of opportunity not only to invest in the future, but to help shape it as well. Your financial support is crucial to protecting the future of nursing at Abington Memorial Hospital. Please help us keep great nurses and nursing education at the heart of our health care.

I want to help protect the

FUTURE OF NURSING *at* 🏛 Abington Memorial Hospital

Yes!

Enclosed is my gift of $_____

I wish to pledge $_____ to be paid by June 30, 2001

I wish to charge my credit card ☐ Visa ☐ MC ☐ AMEX

Name _____

Credit Card Number _____   Exp. Date _____

Signature _____

I would like to be recognized as _____

■
Please make checks payable to AMHF
■
Contributions are tax deductible

🏛 **Abington** Memorial Hospital
F O U N D A T I O N

1200 Old York Road
Abington, PA 19001-3788
215-481-4438

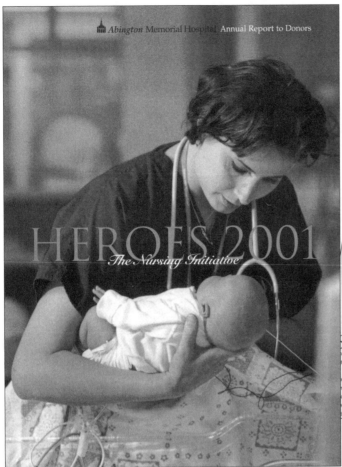

Leadership contributors to the nursing initiative were recognized in Heroes 2001, Abington's annual donor report.

TIME

Leaders at Abington saw early signs of an impending crisis: Johns Hopkins Medical Center—less than three hundred miles away—initially could not open a unit of its new cancer center because there were not enough nurses. A nearby hospital hiked wages for nursing graduates by more than 25 percent. A major Philadelphia-area health system in the midst of cost-cutting announced bonuses of up to twenty-five thousand dollars to each nurse who stayed three years. Abington had plans to enlarge its facilities. But, without nurses, would it be forced to put these plans "on hold"?

OPPORTUNITIES

Solving the problem required the leadership of the hospital and the community. A special, board-appointed blue ribbon panel was created to examine the causes of the shortage and how best to address it. Encouraging more students to enter the profession and retaining qualified nurses became its top priorities.

The panel discovered that decreasing funding to nursing education was contributing to the problem. In Pennsylvania alone, eighteen schools of nursing had closed after federal budget cuts eliminated grants for nursing education and tightened funding to hospitals. The number of Pennsylvania nursing graduates had plummeted from six thousand a year to fewer than three thousand. Fortunately, Abington Hospital had maintained its own school of nursing, but it was not immune to state and national declines: enrollment had dropped from a peak of 180 students to about 40.

The hospital surveyed its nurses to better understand how best to retain them. Two findings emerged: more funding for continuing and advanced education was needed, and an on-site daycare center would reduce the stress of juggling a career and family.

The panel organized three subcommittees (school of nursing, recruitment and retention, and fundraising). For the nursing school, three recognition opportunities emerged: gifts of one hundred thousand dollars to endow full tuition for a nursing student; and gifts of twenty-five thousand to fifty thousand dollars for partial scholarships.

PEOPLE

Leading the blue ribbon panel was hospital president Dick Jones, who, with his wife Carole, gave the first hundred thousand dollars to create the Carole and Richard Jones Jr. Presidential Endowed Scholarship. Jones's gift created excitement, eventually attracting gifts sufficient to endow full tuition for every student at the school. Fitz Eugene Dixon Jr., an investor who has owned sports teams in Philadelphia (including the Seventy-Sixers basketball team) and a philanthropist who gave Philadelphia its famous LOVE statue, was named honorary chair of the panel. Edward Asplundh, a community leader and successful businessman (Asplundh Tree Expert Company) was named vice chair; he assisted in enlisting other top leaders. Panel members were recruited for their expertise in helping find solutions and as representatives of key groups (nursing students, women's board, hospital trustees, physicians, alumni, nurses, fundraisers, etc.), as well as for their ability to make top gifts.

GOALS

An initial goal of ten million dollars was established and a table of gifts created, to focus attention on less than sixty gifts ranging from twenty-five thousand to three million dollars. When the subcommittees made their reports, however, twenty million dollars in priorities were identified and the goal increased. When the table of gifts was revised, however, less than a dozen gifts were added for the additional ten million dollars.

INVOLVEMENT

The blue ribbon panel created awareness and members openly debated challenging topics. The nursing school was losing one million dollars a year. Should it be closed or, instead, should there be a major push to increase enrollment? If so, what would be the enrollment goal? The panel endorsed the school's plan to modernize its Web site, seek news articles, and place ads to promote the full tuition assistance program (from news stories alone, fourteen hundred inquiries resulted). A new evening/weekend nursing education program was identified as a way to help people make the transition into nursing as a second career.

Leading the Way

LEADING BY EXAMPLE
Richard L. and Carole Jones

When Dick and Carole Jones made their one-hundred-thousand-dollar gift, it set a high standard for many donors to follow.

"This is the first time in all my years as a trustee with many charities that an organization's president has made such a large gift to lead the way," says Fitz Eugene Dixon Jr., a life trustee at Abington Memorial Hospital. "My wife, Edie, and I would not have made our gifts were it not for Dick and Carole Jones. Their gift made us stand up and take notice," Dixon says.

To create impact, Jones announced his family's gift at a hospital board meeting, along with a six-hundred-thousand-dollar commitment from the hospital's women's board. In a surprise announcement, Dixon pledged $250,000, which created both excitement and momentum. "It let people know we are serious about our nursing initiative," says Jones. The president then chaired a special blue ribbon panel and participated in key solicitations.

The Dixon family was one of the campaign's most ardent supporters. Mr. Dixon continued to create excitement by adding five million dollars to help endow the nursing school, provoking a standing ovation at a hospital board meeting when the gift was announced.

A number of other donors have echoed Dixon's view on the key role of Jones's leadership gift. "I want to match what you and Carole have done. I'm giving the nursing initiative one hundred thousand dollars," they often told the hospital president.

FORMALLY ASK

Panel members were solicited personally and asked to suggest names of others who could make leadership gifts; they also received regular fundraising progress reports. The panel's honorary chair, Fitz Eugene Dixon Jr., gave five million dollars—his largest gift ever—to Abington's nursing initiative in honor of his wife, Edith, and his mother, who built the original nurses' home. Another major gift of one million dollars established the Frances and Jacob Seidman Endowment Fund for the Advancement of Nursing. Among the leaders and groups who rallied to support Abington's nurses were its medical staff, women's board, department of medicine, alumni association, trustees, doctors, employees, and patients. Materials were developed to incorporate the nursing initiative into the hospital's annual fundraising appeals, attracting gifts from more than four thousand people.

THANKS & STEWARDSHIP

A recognition display with plaques was designed to honor donors of top gifts (with plaque sizes matched to amounts on the gift table). Donors could have their names attached to a full tuition package (Presidential Endowed Scholarship) or a partial scholarship (Founders Award). A sketch of the plaque display, including a key to plaque sizes and gift amounts required, was printed and used in gift requests. A reception was held to dedicate the nursing display and enable donors and scholarship recipients to meet. Donors also received thank you notes from these students. Each donor of one hundred thousand dollars or more was featured in an article and photo in the annual donor recognition report, which lists the names of contributors of one hundred dollars or more.

In less than two years, as a result of the nursing initiative and its scholarships and full tuition packages, enrollment at the Dixon School of Nursing has surged from 40 students to 171. More than twenty-five million dollars has been raised, including $1.8 million in gifts for a childcare center for children of hospital employees, and an endowment for grants to nurses for continuing education.

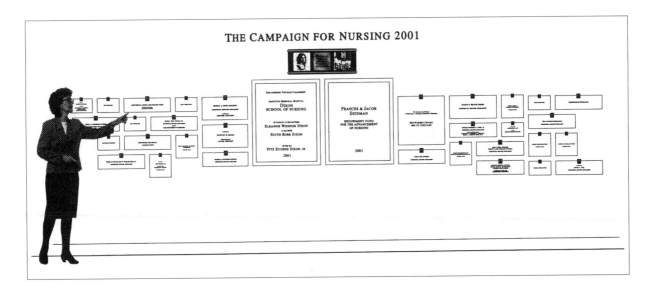

Contributors of twenty-five thousand dollars or more to the nursing initiative are recognized in this display designed by Mitchell Associates.

A Partnership to Change Lives

For more than forty years, San Francisco libraries have been able to count on the Friends and Foundation of the San Francisco Public Library for advocacy, programming, and fundraising. Its work is noticeable and effective:

In the 1970s, city budget deficits almost forced the closing of branch libraries. Yet, through its successful *Keep Libraries Alive* campaign, the Friends kept open the doors of all neighborhood branches.

In 1986, the city's fire marshal threatened to shut down the main library because of fire safety risks. The Friends championed Proposition A for a $109 million bond issue to build a new facility, then raised another $32 million with a citywide campaign, embracing San Francisco's diverse communities (including gays and lesbians, African Americans, Chinese, Filipinos, and Latinos) and affinity groups (advocates for the environment and children's interests).

Community pride launched the new Ocean View Library Campaign, with direction provided by the Friends and Foundation of the San Francisco Public Library. Here high school students visit the Ocean View Library construction site, and, later, omi Neighbors in Action celebrate the opening day parade.

LIBRARY

Open to All Possibilities

FRIENDS & FOUNDATION

AUTUMN 1999

A Publication of the Friends & Foundation
of the San Francisco Public Library

THE LITTLE LIBRARY THAT COULD

"The little library that could" – the tiny branch that has endured nearly 100 years of inadequate funds and insufficient space – is finally getting a permanent home. Thanks to dedicated professionals and loyal patrons who believe in their library, the new Ocean View Branch will be a reality for the 21st century!

The storefront library at 111 Broad Street.

"This is one of the most important and positive steps to be taken in the Ocean View in more than 40 years," says Royce Vaughn, president of the Ocean View Merced Ingleside (OMI) Business League.

According to Dr. Willis Kirk, chairperson of the community-based New Ocean View Library Development Committee, "The new library is a giant step in rejuvenating the neighborhood. We are asking people throughout the City to help us engineer changes that will help our children and revitalize (Ocean View's) commercial district."

Considerable support has already come from City Hall in the form of a $1.7 million construction fund pledged by Mayor Willie Brown last year. Mr. Vaughn and Dr. Kirk were among the coalition of OMI community leaders and librarians who met with Mayor Brown at one of his lively Saturday morning sessions in late 1998.

"It didn't take long to get his attention," says Mr. Vaughn. "We just asked him how we were going to keep our kids off drugs and the streets. How were we going to cajole them into the library if we didn't have one for them to use?"

The mayor was particularly impressed by the group's tenacity and their willingness to tackle a major part of the fundraising effort.

"He was right on target," says Will Reno, a longtime Ocean View businessman who was also part of

the successful meeting with the mayor. "He told us that he agreed with our cause and he just laid it out, plain and simple: 'You will get your library during my administration!' He was just great."

Mayor Brown has proved true to his word and the walls of the new library are going up right now, and the library is scheduled to be completed by Spring, 2000.

However, the hardest work is only just beginning. The neighborhood fundraising committee and the Friends & Foundation of the Library are currently raising additional money to furnish the new library with computers, bookshelves for expanding collections and important interior improvements. The goal is $267,000.

"You know, this really is a wonderful cause," says Darcus Thomas, who served as Ocean View Branch Manager from 1994 to 1997. "The old site was so cramped and far too small to accommodate all the needs of this kind of a community. Ocean View is a very lively neighborhood with a diverse population, in need of multi-language books and videos and a broad range of children's materials.

"We have all kinds of people out here," says Mrs. Thomas. "We want to build a place where they can all be

continued on page 6

AUTUMN 1999

"Our community is dedicated to building a first-rate library for the youth of Ocean View. I applaud the fundraising efforts of the neighborhood committee and the Friends & Foundation of the Library, and encourage San Franciscans to give generously to this worthy cause. Remember, educational opportunities are the key to the future."

Mayor Willie Brown, Honorary Chair, Campaign for the New Ocean View Library

REMY CHARLIP'S WORLD

OPENS OCTOBER 13 AT THE LIBRARY

"What you learn doing art or being creative is that by putting two things together you get something new," says Remy Charlip, children's author and artist. "When you put your whole self into a song, a dance, a drawing, painting or sculpture, and make things with your own hands and body, you have an experience that affects every aspect of your life."

Welcome to Remy Charlip's World, where children's fantasies come to life through words, song, dance and art. Beginning in September, Remy Charlip, creator of 29 children's books and an innovative performer, leads a series of book and mural making playshops for children ages 6 - 11 years. The playshops take place at different branch

libraries, and are part of *Remy Charlip's World: Books into Theater/Theater into Books*, a major children's exhibit sponsored by the Friends & Foundation of the Library.

Remy's exhibit, which will include artwork produced at the playshops and illustrations from his book, opens in the Jewett Gallery at the Main Library on October 13 and runs through December 13.

Please join us for the opening reception and book signing on Wednesday, October 13. A performance by Remy and children from the San Francisco Arts Education Project takes place following the reception at 7 p.m. in the Koret Auditorium. All events are free and the public is invited to attend.

The Main library - San Francisco's Most Novel Event Space

Private dinners, holiday parties, corporate receptions in the Library? Absolutely!
The Main Library is fast becoming one of San Francisco's premier event spaces.
Seven unique spaces are available for private events when the building is closed to the public.

Rental fees are tax deductible to the fullest extent allowed by law and are used to support a variety of library services.

"Friends" provided the framework for fundraising, including identifying naming opportunities (to encourage and recognize higher-level gifts) and visibility for the campaign in its publication.

☐ **Browsing Area**
Gift Level
$20,000

This area will contain new books such as fiction, non-fiction, mysteries and other book genres. A collection of current popular audio-visual material will also be located in this section for patrons looking for recently released videos and CDs.

☐ **First Floor Stairwell**

This grand stairwell will provide patrons with direct access to central location, the stairwell will be both a major functional building's design.

☐ **Main Entrance / Lobby**

The Main Entrance/Lobby is the central entrance for the ne area the patrons see upon entering the building. Because through it all day, display cases will be located here to high public announcements.

☐ **Reference & Circulation Area**

The reference/circulation area will have chairs and furnitu collection and working with library staff at the circulation will be one of the most trafficked, because of traditionally branch.

☐ **Reading Area**

The Reading Area will be used by those patrons looking individual assignments, away from the hustle and bustl This area will be comfortably furnished with new chairs serve as a modern, state-of-the-art facility in a once n

---

MAIN FLOOR

☐ **Children's Area**
Gift Level
$25,000

The Children's Area will be a primary resource for children of Ocean View, serving school children, parents and teachers with an extensive collection of materials for children at all reading levels. Also included will be materials in several languages as well as a folk and fairy tale collection. Events and activities coordinated by library staff will take place here during open hours.

Another feature of the area will be the *Childrens' Electronic Discover Center* with more than thirty-five video games and education software programs designed to engage and challenge young minds, stimulating their desire to learn. Designed specifically for San Francisco, the C.E.D.C. encourages initiative and creativity by enabling a child working in a geography program, to quickly incorporate a spelling or math program.

☐ **Adult Area**
Gift Level
$20,000

The Adult Area is comprised of diverse book collections, CDs, audio-video material, newspapers, magazines and periodicals. The space is designed to accommodate more than 10 adults who come to the Library for research, studying and quiet reading. On a given day, you can expect to see them pursuing a current novel, sitting with a paper, drafting a resume or correspondence to friends, and completing job applications.

☐ **Teen Area**
Gift Level
$20,000

This area will be used by the many teens in the neighborhood who are studying, researching class assignments and investigating career prospects. Important reference and book collections are housed in this area as are audio cassette books, CDs, newspapers, magazines and periodicals. New chairs and tables will give teens a comfortable working environment.

More recently, the Friends spearheaded the successful *Yes on A* campaign for a $106 million bond offering to renovate, relocate, or build twenty-four branch libraries. Its success is built on partnerships. "The Friends began in 1961 with very little, except a wonderful sprit of determination to improve the San Francisco Public Library. As a group, we had no money, no power, and remarkably little experience to guide us," wrote Marjorie Stern, a founding member. "Since we had to turn our minuses into pluses, we discovered what a marvelously effective and very precious commodity citizen commitment can be."

That commitment is seen in the $267,000 campaign for San Francisco's *smallest* branch—the Ocean View Library—spurred by the vision and tenacity of community leaders. More than $490,000 was raised.

TIME

It was hard for San Francisco Mayor Willie Brown to argue with Ocean View community leaders in 1998. Their community's needs had to become a priority. With a history of drugs and violence, and employment and educational testing scores well below city averages, the neighborhood needed help. The community demanded that Ocean View's small, 575-foot, storefront library be replaced with a large facility. "It didn't take long to get his attention," says Royce Vaughn, president of the Ocean View Merced Ingleside (OMI) Business League. "We just asked him how we were going to keep our kids off drugs and the streets. How were we going to cajole them into the library if we didn't have one for them to use?"

The mayor agreed, providing $1.25 million for construction. The next step was to raise funds to outfit the facility. Contributions would make the difference, and allow Ocean View to update lighting, bookshelves, computers, and furniture for such areas as the children's library and reading rooms.

OPPORTUNITIES

The reasons for expanding the library were clear, compelling, and urgent. "In this neighborhood where many people are struggling to survive and the streets are not safe, there is something truly positive for this community: its library. Amid the empty storefronts, the library is a place for residents of all ages to read and learn. After school, it is a safe haven for children of parents who have to work. It provides books to two nearby elementary schools and a Head Start program whose own

☐ **Children's Book Collection** — Gift Level $15,000

This collection, one of the largest at Ocean View, includes videos, audio-book sets, picture books, Young Reader Books, holiday books, board books, paperbacks and magazines. Children use this collection to learn to read and form a lifelong relationship with the library. Teachers from neighboring elementary schools and head-start programs come in weekly to check out books to use in the classroom. Teachers, parents and caregivers also use library visits their children to read and check out books on their own.

☐ **Children's Chinese Lang. Collection** — Gift Level $5,000

This collection of Chinese language materials for children includes works by authors throughout the Chinese-speaking world as well as translated works in other languages to Chinese. The collection is comprised of materials for pleasure-reading and research. Children are able to read and learn in their native language while learning English.

☐ **Homework Reference Collection** — Gift Level $5,000

This collection is made up of reference materials to assist the many students that reside in the Ocean View community. Encyclopedias, dictionaries and bound periodicals allow students to research almost any topic for class assignments. In combination with information access through the Internet, students from neighboring high schools, City College and San Francisco State University are able to increase their knowledge on all topics including science, history, and literature. The library staff makes sure that all materials are updated, so that students have access to the most recent information on a topic.

eer/Job Collection — Gift Level $10,000

ed collection helps patrons investigate career and job ssisting small business owners and those who want to start their . This resource provides Ocean View with the most recent blications, detailing education requirements. Books on resume hat to include on job applications; and how to win an interview the key materials found in this important collection.

nting Collection — Gift Level $5,000

ngtime parents find this collection valuable for parenting tips There are books and videos devoted to pregnancy, caring for ildhood development and how to be an effective parent to a n important resource and is set up to answer the many e with being a parent; topics range from nutrition to toilet-

☐ **Children's Spanish Lang. Collection** — Gift Level $5,000

This collection of Spanish language materials for children includes works by authors throughout the Spanish-speaking world. Materials for pleasure-reading and research are found in this small but growing collection of children's books. The new Ocean View Library will accommodate more books; currently, the library rotates books from the Main Library and Bernal Heights Branch.

Interest Collection — Gift Level $15,000

s at the branch, the materials found in this n history, culture and literature. It is a vital e researchers/readers as well as w library this collection will be expanded to the demands of the community and will be ction in the system.

e Collection — Gift Level $15,000

uage books covers all subjects, including nish language countries and translations of . The branch collection is currently dditional Spanish Language books from s branch. The new library will be able to rent size to more effectively serve the w. Expanding this collection is a high

ollection — Gift Level $15,000

es now make up this expanding all subjects. Included are works by other parts of Southeast Asia as well to Chinese. This collection reflects ts from China and other Chinese- oubled in size in the new building.

reading resources are limited. And, despite its tight space, it offers events for the community. Residents really love this library, yet the storefront library was too small," recalls Friends development director Paola Muggia Stuff, who served as coordinator and grant writer to the campaign.

The campaign recognized all donors, for gifts large and small. Names would be listed on a donor wall, and the size of the listing would be based on the amount of the gift and campaign giving categories.

Friends staff identified naming opportunities to spur larger gifts. "There's always a dialogue of how to provide naming opportunities in a public space. Some people argue against it," Muggia Stuff says, yet the public good won out. "For gifts of five thousand dollars or more, we have areas and collections we can designate with a plaque." A printed list of opportunities provided a brief description of each and suggested gift amounts, including: Storytelling/Program Room ($50,000); Children/Teen Computers ($25,000); Children's Area ($25,000); Teen, Adult, or Browsing Areas ($20,000 each); African-American Interest, Spanish Language, or Chinese Language Collections ($15,000 each); Career/Job Collection ($10,000); Reading Area, Homework Reference Collection, or Parenting Collection ($5,000 each).

PEOPLE

With the neighborhood already mobilized to lobby the mayor, individuals stepped forward to lead the library's campaign. "The children need a safe place to go. I'm going to see to it that they get it," says Will Reno, owner of a barbershop in Ocean View who joined the New Ocean View Library Development Committee.

Community leaders included such visible people as Dr. Willis Kirk, a former college president who served on other boards and chaired the New Library Development Committee; Royce Vaughn, president of the OMI Business League; Darcus Thomas, former SFPL librarian; and Will Reno, known for his work with the Southwestern Neighborhood Improvement Group, who provided space behind his barbershop to the development committee and community groups to hold meetings.

GOALS

When the initial $267,000 goal was met, it was raised to $300,000. "The development committee worked closely with library and Friends staff. With more funds, we continued the dialogue, asking the community, 'What do you want to accomplish now?' 'Should we improve the book collections or are there other, more important needs?'" says Muggia Stuff.

INVOLVEMENT

The community owned the project from the start and was involved in all aspects of the campaign. Yet each team member brought strengths to the project. Library staff could articulate specific needs and make presentations. Friends staff offered campaign counsel and implemented an effective corporate and foundation solicitation strategy.

FORMALLY ASK

The community's commitment to a project that could change lives so quickly was a message that inspired gifts at all levels. Yet Friends staff recognized that large gifts were key. Grant proposals were prepared and submitted to its best potential supporters. "Foundation donors felt their gifts would make a tangible difference and last for generations. There's something special about knowing that your gift will be there for the long term," says Muggia Stuff. Of the $490,000 raised, more than $450,000 was given by foundations and corporations.

Thanks & Stewardship

Events from the groundbreaking to the dedication and ribbon-cutting ceremonies celebrated the importance of the project and campaign. Children marched in the opening day parade and drew pictures on the theme "What the Ocean View Library means to me."

The success of the New Ocean View Library Campaign can be seen every day at the new facility, which boasts 2,175 square feet, a state-of-the-art computer training room, an expanded book collection, and a children's storytelling room. The Friends share the story on their Web page and encourage donors through membership programs, volunteer opportunities, newsletter, calendar, and events. Perhaps one donor said it best: "Books and children: what a great combination. From childhood on, I have loved books and have considered libraries a spiritual haven. It is wonderful to know that the Ocean View Library is serving so many children so well."

Conveying a Message of Hope

As most fundraisers will tell you, "The case statement is a written document communicating your needs, your plans or dream for the future, and your organization's capacity to make it a reality." Yet the "case" can appear in many formats, as varied as a printed brochure, a newspaper article, a video, and a PowerPoint presentation.

For the New Ocean View Library campaign, it was this article by Ken Garcia in the *San Francisco Chronicle*. "The Littlest Library" gave the campaign wide exposure and boosted its fundraising.

"What struck me was that this library was so tiny, probably the smallest library I had ever seen," says Garcia.

"This place was just falling apart. It was being kept alive by the love of a few people. The library was in a neighborhood that time had forgotten and was long neglected," he points out.

"It's amazing how many people will rally around a library. . . . It [the library campaign] only needed a little spark in order to make good things happen," he says.

Giving the library's needs, the wide exposure had almost instant impact.

"I discovered we were preaching to the converts," Paola Muggia Stuff says of the media's impact on corporate and foundation leaders. "The article was read by the people who sit on the boards that were reviewing our proposals."

Individuals responded as well. Gifts poured in not only from San Francisco, but also from many areas of California and place as distant as Seattle and Kansas.

San Francisco—Something good happens every day at 111 Broad St., which is worth noting, because so much bad happens almost every day around it.

The address is in a neighborhood called Ocean View, a funny name for a place that offers a better glimpse of the freeway. And, until recently, it was a place that both time and government forgot largely because it is a lower-income area populated primarily by African American families.

Any place neglected as long as Ocean View would naturally show the signs of such indifference, and for years it has come in the form of open drug dealing, violence, and a general climate of fear. It is a place where parents worry about the safety of their children and have sought sanctuaries for them wherever they could. Havens like the one at 111 Broad St.

At that address is the Ocean View Library, all 575 square feet of it. It is so small that any visiting elementary class can fill it, which happens several times a day during the school year. It is by far the smallest public library in the City and County of San Francisco, and it has been since it opened in 1932 during the Great Depression.

What happened in that library over the past year has become a great source of joy in a neighborhood. The reading and storytelling and tutoring programs offered amid the clutter of books proved so popular and successful that neighborhood advocates realized what might happen if they got a real library. A library with computers, and classroom space, a reading room, and a kitchen where the Xerox machine didn't double as the table and the encyclopedias weren't located on a shelf next to the microwave.

And through the efforts of a number of community activists, several dedicated librarians, and an electorally shrewd mayor, a brand new library is going up not far from 111 Broad St. It is being touted as the key to the neighborhood's renaissance, a symbol of Ocean View's rejuvenation. And if that seems too flowery a thought, then it would be safe to say that you haven't been to the area lately.

About six weeks ago, Ocean View got its first pizza parlor, the first new business in the community in years. It is a few doors down from the library, which is to say, it is now perched down from the liquor store, RC's Package House, the Vali of Dolls Hair and Nail Salon, Herman's Fish and Poultry Store and Furlough's Tonsorial Parlor, which as any kid with a dictionary can tell you, is a fancy name for a barber shop.

New business came to Ocean View about as often as tourists, and the sense that it was a neighborhood no one cared about could be seen at the library, where the children wrote about their gloomy existence. How else to explain the fact that kids acted out drive-by shootings in the puppet shows and wrote poems titled "The World is Coming to an End."

But the fact that dozens of kids kept coming to the library gave many residents hope, and some time back they began lobbying for a new library. They wrote letters. Sent petitions. Called. And on Saturdays, once a month, when the mayor had his early morning meeting with citizens, a group from Ocean View would show up to plead the case for a new building.

After much lobbying, the mayor relented. Good politics or good heart? Likely both. But credit Willie Brown with finding $1.25 million in city money to build the new library. Now it's up to the community to raise $267,000 to furnish the site with tables, desks, bookshelves, lighting and computers. It's a lot of money for the community to raise, but after spending some time there, I can't think of a more worthy cause.

Certainly not after meeting Dorothy Coakley and Kathleen Au.

Coakley is the new librarian at Ocean View, Au her assistant in title only. Together, they have managed to turn the once-neglected library into the neighborhood's busiest after-school program, and by far, the most creative use of a 575-square-foot space in the city. In a building so dilapidated that leaking pipes have formed a permanent pond in the backyard, they now run what city officials call "the little library that could."

"The kids know they're loved here, which is why we see them every day," Coakley told me as we toured her tiny oasis the other day. "We get a lot of children who have known a lot of tragedy in their lives. This place has been an island of sanity for them—the first place where they ever had access to books."

Coakley is an impassioned leftie who spent more than a decade trying to inspire patrons at another once-neglected library in Bernal Heights. Au for the past five years was the glue that has bound the book center together. They can laugh now about the quirky nature of 111 Broad St.—the fact that the two tiny makeshift reading rooms are so out of compliance with workplace safety rules that the governing agencies just shrugged and said they could use them anyway.

When an electrical fire broke out a few months ago, an inspector was so shocked at the makeup of the wiring, that he asked, incredulously, if children were actually allowed in the building.

"Yes," Au said. "But only since the 1930s."

They share an office smaller than a walk-in closet and a tiny kitchen that serves as the reference room. Those everyday necessities like fax machines were donated by individuals, as were a fair share of the books.

Yet it took a new direction for the city's library administration, headed by Regina Minudri, Donna Corbeil and Susan Hildreth, to make the new building a reality. And when the new branch opens next spring, it will have roughly four times the space, modern amenities, handicapped access and a community meeting room.

No pond. No safety hazards. Even enough space for some public art.

All they need now is money. Nothing big mind you. Ocean View knows the value of things small. You can join me in sending a check to The Friends & Foundation, Main Library, Civic Center, San Francisco, CA 94102. Re: Ocean View Library 2000.

"We try to work with what we have and a lot of beautiful things have happened here," Coakley said. "We're turning lights on here and they're staying on."

Bright lights. Small city.

Reigniting the Passion

After becoming number one in their respective fields, how many organizations would launch a strategic planning process and the first capital campaign in their history?

That's the story of Little League Baseball (Williamsport, Pa.), the world's largest youth sports organization, with nearly three million players in 50 states and 103 countries.

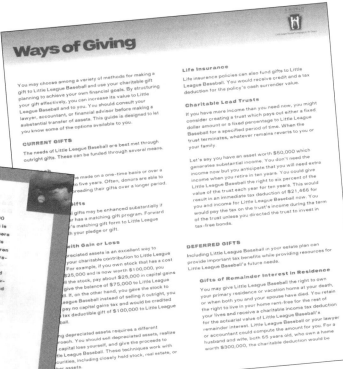

"I used to think I couldn't live without baseball," says former U.S. Senator Bill Bradley, of the impact Little League has had on his life. Little League's campaign case statement reminds readers of those memories, and illustrates how "Little League promises to become an even more powerful force in the lives of children," in the words of campaign chair Howard Pastor. The campaign's purposes are well defined in this attractive booklet and on the individual cards that fit neatly into a pocket. Information on the cards addresses the campaign, naming opportunities, ways of giving, and leadership.

TIME

In 1999, "We were struggling with fundraising for our new European headquarters in Poland, which promotes Little League in Europe, Africa, and the Middle East," says Stephen D. Keener, Little League president and CEO. "Board members naturally were concerned because, in addition to our European Leadership Center, there were other initiatives. We debated how to best move forward."

OPPORTUNITIES

According to Bill Piszek, who was involved in those discussions, "Board members started asking themselves, 'What is our dream? Where do we want to be in ten years? How can we build on what we've accomplished?' Little League Baseball is more than a youth sports organization; it's about helping more kids and bringing families closer together. We identified five priorities:

1. "enhancing the Urban Initiative, which promotes baseball as an alternative to negative influences, such as drugs and gangs, and unites families;

2. "increasing education programs for players and volunteers (in such topics as prevention of the use of tobacco, drugs, and alcohol, and child abuse prevention);

3. "improving communications at all levels of Little League through technology;

4. "building new facilities in Williamsport to host our Little League World Series; and

5. "expanding availability of Little League in the United States and internationally."

PEOPLE

Keener recalls: "Edward J. Piszek, a trustee of the Little League Foundation [and founder of Mrs. Paul's Kitchen], decided the organization could use some outside help. Without fanfare, he offered to underwrite the cost of hiring a fundraising consulting firm to help with strategic planning and fundraising. Ed suggested that we place our most important initiatives under one fundraising umbrella."

"We're a family that likes to see leverage," says Ed's son, Bill Piszek. "We thought we could prime the pump with our gift." Not only was Ed Piszek recruited to the foundation's board, but baseball legend Stan "the Man" Musial joined the Little

League Poland Foundation Board of Trustees. Peter O'Malley, former president of the Los Angeles Dodgers and longtime Little League booster, had already stepped up to the plate as president of its foundation. Both boards accepted ownership of the new campaign. A stronger leadership team roster was put into place.

GOALS

The cost of achieving the organization's five priorities totaled twenty million dollars, which became its goal for *A World of Opportunity—Little League Baseball Capital Campaign for the Future.*

The fundraising consultant developed a table of gifts. But an interesting phenomenon occurred: At its core, Little League is about values, doing one's best but with a uniting spirit of teamwork. Some major donors, as members of the team, did not want the size of their gifts to stand out. Little League responded by listing many donors' names together in one category. However, to succeed, Little League president Steve Keener and board members needed to focus on major gifts. Their success is reflected in the fact that the campaign's top five gifts and contributions from Little League board members represented more than half its goal.

INVOLVEMENT

Keener talked with potential donors to learn their interests. A longstanding tradition has been to invite donors to its World Series, where the spirit of Little League can be best felt. Little League's annual award, induction into its Hall of Excellence, was presented to President Bush, who also attended the World Series, giving added exposure to Little League and its values. To gain more viewers, a later broadcast (6:30 P.M.) was arranged, and additional games were televised. The network also agreed to air a public service message for the campaign each night. Board members networked and personally delivered the campaign's dreams to potential donors.

FORMALLY ASK

The prestige and leverage of board members opened doors for the campaign, adding to the roster of Little League supporters. "We have a number of high-profile leaders on our boards who were willing to ask business associates to consider supporting the campaign. In many cases, we had only twenty minutes to make our case. My message became very direct: 'I need your help and here's why,'" explains the Little League president.

Charting Its Future

On the cover of this Case for Support *booklet, the Little League Pledge conveys what the sport—and campaign—are all about.*

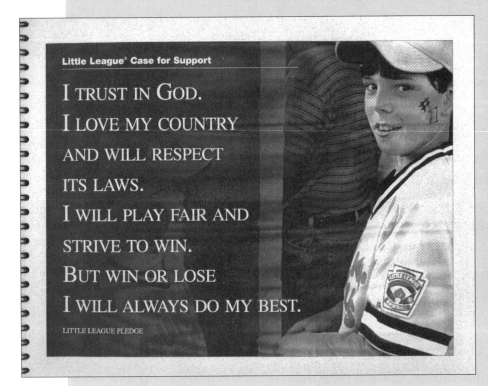

Little League® Case for Support

I TRUST IN GOD.
I LOVE MY COUNTRY
AND WILL RESPECT
ITS LAWS.
I WILL PLAY FAIR AND
STRIVE TO WIN.
BUT WIN OR LOSE
I WILL ALWAYS DO MY BEST.

LITTLE LEAGUE PLEDGE

Although Little League Baseball, Inc., has always been sure of its values, it was less certain of its priorities for the future. By investing in strategic planning, the organization was able to define five major initiatives for its future, enlist top business leaders to communicate its mission, and successfully secure major gift support. Several gifts of one million dollars or more resulted after Little League translated its needs into messages that matched the giving interests of its best potential donors.

Messages were tailored to each audience. The Little League International Board of Directors, for example, made a successful pitch to its state representative and then-governor Tom Ridge for a three-million-dollar government grant, citing the visibility, tourism, and economic benefits that the Little League World Series brings to Pennsylvania. The Conrad N. Hilton Foundation, long a champion of alleviating suffering among children, gave an impressive one million dollars to the Urban Initiative, a program that was attractive to many contributors who wanted to help inner-city kids. Little League Baseball Foundation gave three million dollars, with additional gifts from both boards totaling two million.

THANKS & STEWARDSHIP

Outside the new stadium in Williamsport is a recognition wall listing more than five hundred major contributors. The new stadium in Kutno, Poland (located one hundred miles west of Warsaw), part of the European Leadership Center, was named in honor of Stan Musial. In a surprise announcement, a second stadium was dedicated in honor of Ed Piszek, whose faith and funds ignited the planning and fundraising process.

"The campaign has really energized our Boards. When we started, we didn't know if we could reach twenty million dollars. In fact, there were some who doubted it. Today, there's more of a 'can do' attitude, a greater confidence in what we can accomplish for Little League," says Piszek. "The campaign has lived up to its theme, 'A World of Opportunity,' both for our future and the youth we serve."

Rx: Topeka Civic Theatre

When Twink Lynch was preparing her master's thesis in theater, she focused on a local community group whose future was so tenuous that she entitled her paper "Is There a Doctor in the House? Rx: Topeka Civic Theatre (TCT)."

"For more than thirty years, TCT was an itinerant group of theater gypsies, staging three shows a year: talent looking for a home," she recalls. At times, its finances were perilous. "In 1970, the theatre's total assets were two hundred dollars in the bank and forty-five members paying two dollars a year." Yet, despite its challenges, the theater company put on quality plays and, in doing so, captured the hearts of many in the Topeka, Kansas, area.

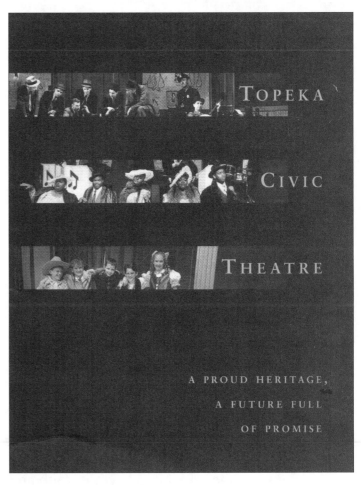

Its future, however, would change dramatically in the 1970s when Carmie Wolfe, an English teacher who had a passion for the arts, left forty thousand dollars of her estate to the theater. With the charitable windfall, an artistic director was hired who encouraged the theater to raise funds to buy a building. "It was a warehouse on the wrong side of the river and the wrong side of the tracks," Dr. Lynch says with some humor, yet "it gave us another life entirely. We had a home and now could do things like dinner theater. The place was so small [135 seats] that dinner was first served on the stage and you had to run outside if you wanted to get from one side of the stage to the other. It was a funny little place, but the community loved it. Five years later [1979], we knew we had outgrown the warehouse but nobody felt we could afford a larger space."

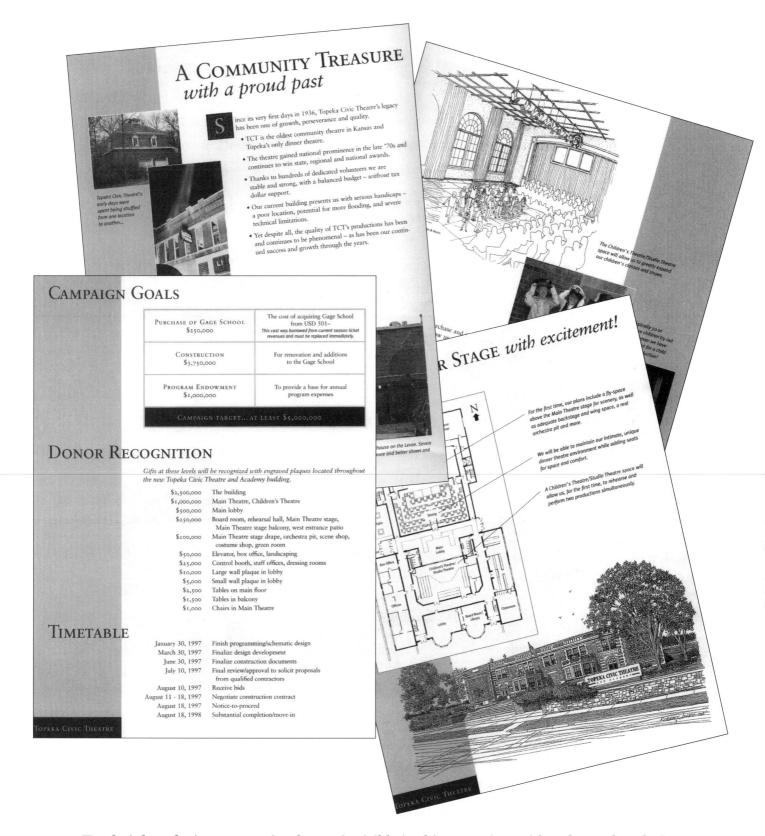

A COMMUNITY TREASURE
with a proud past

Since its very first days in 1936, Topeka Civic Theatre's legacy has been one of growth, perseverance and quality.

- TCT is the oldest community theatre in Kansas and Topeka's only dinner theatre.
- The theatre gained national prominence in the late '70s and continues to win state, regional and national awards.
- Thanks to hundreds of dedicated volunteers we are stable and strong, with a balanced budget – *without* tax dollar support.
- Our current building presents us with serious handicaps – a poor location, potential for more flooding, and severe technical limitations.
- Yet despite all, the quality of TCT's productions has been and continues to be phenomenal – as has been our continued success and growth through the years.

Topeka Civic Theatre's early days were spent being shuffled from one location to another...

The Children's Theatre/Studio Theatre space will allow us to greatly expand our children's classes and shows.

CAMPAIGN GOALS

PURCHASE OF GAGE SCHOOL $250,000	The cost of acquiring Gage School from USD 501– *This cost was borrowed from current season ticket revenues and must be replaced immediately.*
CONSTRUCTION $3,750,000	For renovation and additions to the Gage School
PROGRAM ENDOWMENT $1,000,000	To provide a base for annual program expenses

CAMPAIGN TARGET... AT LEAST $5,000,000

DONOR RECOGNITION

Gifts at these levels will be recognized with engraved plaques located throughout the new Topeka Civic Theatre and Academy building.

$2,500,000	The building
$1,000,000	Main Theatre, Children's Theatre
$500,000	Main lobby
$250,000	Board room, rehearsal hall, Main Theatre stage, Main Theatre stage balcony, west entrance patio
$100,000	Main Theatre stage drape, orchestra pit, scene shop, costume shop, green room
$50,000	Elevator, box office, landscaping
$25,000	Control booth, staff offices, dressing rooms
$10,000	Large wall plaque in lobby
$5,000	Small wall plaque in lobby
$2,500	Tables on main floor
$1,500	Tables in balcony
$1,000	Chairs in Main Theatre

TIMETABLE

January 30, 1997	Finish programming/schematic design
March 30, 1997	Finalize design development
June 30, 1997	Finalize construction documents
July 10, 1997	Final review/approval to solicit proposals from qualified contractors
August 10, 1997	Receive bids
August 11 - 18, 1997	Negotiate construction contract
August 18, 1997	Notice-to-proceed
August 18, 1998	Substantial completion/move-in

TOPEKA CIVIC THEATRE

...STAGE with excitement!

For the first time, our plans include a fly-space above the Main Theatre stage for scenery, as well as adequate backstage and wing space, a real orchestra pit and more.

We will be able to maintain our intimate, unique dinner theatre environment while adding seats for space and comfort.

A Children's Theatre/Studio Theatre space will allow us, for the first time, to rehearse and perform two productions simultaneously.

Topeka's love for its community theater is visible in this campaign, with a theme that depicts A Future Full of Promise. Even this publication was made possible by firms that donated creative services, film, and printing as a way to help the campaign succeed.

TIME

In 1993, flooding of the Mississippi, Missouri, and Kansas rivers created such pressure that it produced geysers in the theater's basement, and the local fire department had to flood it to equalize the building's pressure. While the community stood by the theater with one hundred thousand dollars in gifts to address the problem, the theater's long-range planning committee and board grappled with issues, studying the group's mission, goals, and resources for answers. "Some people thought that, even with the repairs, the warehouse wasn't safe. As a community theater, our mission is to reach out to all ages, but our facilities were constrained. We offered minimal programs for children and none for seniors. How could we expand our programming without adding space?"

The Little Tin Box

With his one-million-dollar gift to Topeka Civic Theatre, Irv Sheffel had a critical impact. Had his gift not been made, the group would never have realized its dreams for a new theater and expanded programming designed especially for children and seniors (from ages four to eighty-four and beyond).

How could an individual who lived so modestly be able to make such a large gift, many in Topeka wondered. Before a standing-room-only crowd on opening night for the new facility, here's how Irv Sheffel answered them.

"Some of my friends have been curious about how I saved enough money to make my pledge. I have been secretive about this, but now I will tell all. Some of you may remember the popular musical *Fiorello* about Fiorello LaGuardia, the great mayor of New York City. One of the most memorable songs was 'The Little Tin Box,' about how some of the city officials had saved money to buy expensive cars, yachts, and large mansions. By strange coincidence, I also had a little tin box. When I sold *Saturday Evening Posts* in the 1920s for five cents, I made one and a half cents profit on each copy, and I placed the one and a half cents in the tin box. Then I added the four cents from each *Ladies Home Journal* sale, the nickels from selling lemonade, quarters from caddying and coins from relatives. Lo and behold, when I opened the box I found that the coins had mated over the years and produced new generations of coins. You *do* need the right temperature for the box in order to produce the best results.

"I know my pledge is listed as a contribution, but from my point of view it is one of the best *investments* I have ever made. It brings far greater pleasure than any investing I have done for

OPPORTUNITIES

An opportunity for a new theater surfaced as five school buildings were put on the market, including "a beautiful brick school built in 1929 with 4.5 acres of land. With the new building we could do eight main stage shows a year, offer classes for all ages, a studio and children's theater program, and launch three performance groups [Laughing Matters, Senior Class for those over fifty, and WTCT Players, which presents old radio scripts such as *The Shadow* and *Fibber McGee*]. We could buy the school for $250,000 but to build a main stage and update the building's heating, wiring, and other systems would cost as much as $7.2 million. Yet, there was a growing 'can do' attitude on the board, so we hired a firm to do a planning study to see how much we could raise," says Dr. Lynch. The

personal gain. It will bring lasting benefits, not just to me and my family, but to individuals of all ages throughout our community. It will stimulate creativity among the children and adolescents who attend the academy. They will learn more about why people behave the way they do, and about themselves. Some of them will enjoy being onstage, some will prefer to be backstage, and some may write and produce plays. They will all enjoy becoming part of a supportive extended family. . . .

"Since it won't be possible to take the little tin box with me, why not enjoy trying to empty it while alive instead of leaving it in the form of bequests after death? This way I can see and enjoy the results."

A New Generation

"So how do you thank such a donor—a humble man who lives quietly and initially wanted his gift to be anonymous?" Dr. Lynch asks. "Besides naming the theater in his honor (incidentally, we asked him for the wording and he chose 'The Sheffel Theatre' to honor his deceased first wife, Beth, his deceased daughter, Anita, and his lovely new wife, Peggy), we also gave him another 'little tin box' with a few coins in it to start him on his next million dollars! He loved it! God bless him and all the mega-givers all over the country who have helped so critically in making some of our impossible dreams come true."

group also developed naming opportunities to encourage larger gifts, including a theater seat ($1,000), named classrooms, rehearsal hall, children's theater, main auditorium, offices, even the roadway to the facility. Finally, "As a favor to one of our board members, Kevin Kline performed *An Evening of Shakespeare*. We charged five hundred dollars a person and raised $119,000 net from that one event. He electrified the audience."

PEOPLE

Tim Etzel (a business leader and board member) and his wife, Carole, joined with retired newspaper owners John and Ruth Stauffer to co-chair the campaign for the new theater. A Campaign Cabinet was created to enlist leadership for the pre-announcement or silent campaign, challenge gifts, leadership gifts, board and staff gift solicitation, public relations, donor recognition, and evaluation committees. Etzel was among those who looked at the stature and dedication of the theater's board and said, "We can do this."

GOALS

At the time, no local organization had ever raised the level of funding that TCT needed. While the architect was able to scale back plans for a five-million-dollar project, which included one million dollars for a permanent endowment, initial results from the fundraising study could only justify a $3.5 million campaign, "not enough to make the new theater a reality," Dr. Lynch says. Fortunately (see "The Little Tin Box," pages 32–33) a donor stepped forward with a one-million-dollar gift, enough to justify a five-million-dollar campaign, then the largest campaign goal ever for a local Topeka-area organization.

INVOLVEMENT

The theater has a history of involving the community, dating to the seven parties referred to as Warehouse Wackery that raised funds to purchase its original building, along with its twenty-five-member board, theater events and new campaign cabinet and committees. These longstanding relationships were helpful to the theater in getting a special permit to allow it to be located in a residential area. "We invited neighbors of the school to a show at the warehouse, shared our architectural plans with them, and talked about how we would convert the former outdoor playground area to ensure adequate parking. [Some neighbors worried that theater patrons might clog their neighborhood streets.]" To reach the challenging goal, everyone's involvement was essential, including the six hundred production volunteers (actors, ushers, stage hands, etc.) who gave one hundred thousand dollars.

Formally ask

All leadership and major gifts were personally solicited and a five-hundred-thousand-dollar challenge grant from the Mabee Foundation created an urgency to give. "Officials at the Mabee Foundation told us that in order to meet the threshold for the grant application to be considered [at least two million dollars raised toward the goal], we needed to raise another five hundred thousand dollars in five days. This challenge gave us a reason to ask for the largest gifts: each gift could make a huge difference. Then, after qualifying for the grant, we only had a year to raise the matching funds. It was 'all or nothing.' If we didn't raise all five hundred thousand dollars, we wouldn't receive a penny of the foundation's funds. The challenge grant gave us extra leverage." The Etzels, Stauffers, and Lynchs each gave one hundred thousand dollars, which not only fueled the campaign but also had a positive impact on solicitations. "We were able to say, 'This is what we've done. We hope you will too,'" says Dr. Lynch. Another strategy was to focus on recognition opportunities to encourage top gifts: "We have a great opportunity in the new children's theater, which we'd like to name after you," Dr. Lynch recalls saying to one potential donor. For most of the major gifts, two or three board members or volunteers participated in each personal solicitation.

Thanks & Stewardship

Donors were thanked several ways, from listing all names in the program book of the opening production to placing an attractive recognition display at the entrance of the theater with the names of donors giving five thousand dollars or more. When she reflects on the $5.22 million raised, Dr. Lynch says, "We didn't have development staff or even fundraising software when we started." Today, she's an enabler, helping other community theaters reach their potential. "I don't think you can become what you're capable of becoming, unless you dream of what's possible," she says.

From Crisis to Opportunity

The crack cocaine epidemic of the mid-1980s inflicted lasting damage on the poorest neighborhoods of Washington, D.C. It was not just the soaring murder rate; equally disturbing was an explosion in the city's population of drug addicts, many of them homeless.

The bulk of the city government's response was targeted on funding twenty-eight-day treatment programs administered by local hospitals. Scant attention was paid to people once they had graduated from treatment, with the all-too-predictable result that many soon slipped back into their old patterns of drug addiction and homelessness.

Where government may have failed, however, the nonprofit sector saw opportunity. In 1986, David Erickson, a District-area social activist, created a new nonprofit organization called Samaritan Inns, which focused on rebuilding the lives of addicted, homeless people who had completed treatment programs. Samaritan Inns provided them with assisted living, then housing and support to improve their chances of finding employment and successfully reintegrating into society. Erickson's model worked and Samaritan Inns grew robustly. In 1995, its twenty-three-member staff was serving 280 people a year with an annual budget of $750,000. Its success, however, was about to collapse.

In 1996, the District government discontinued funding most twenty-eight-day treatment programs, virtually cutting off Samaritan's access to a steady stream of people completing rehabilitation programs. The entire enterprise was now at risk. What to do?

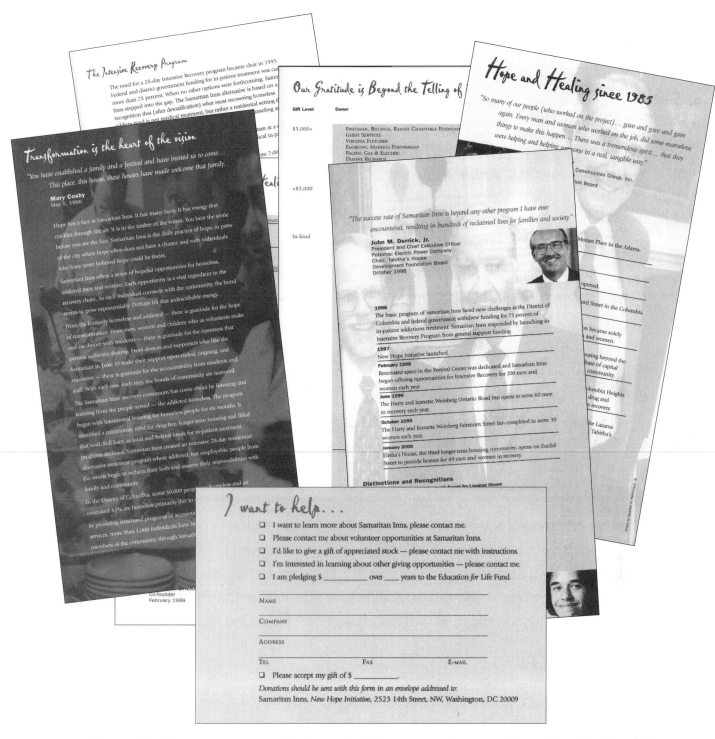

In the words of its supporters, a driving principle at Samaritan Inns is making "so few dollars do so much good . . . reclaiming lives for families and society . . . [and developing] long-term solutions for the homeless." The organization's commitment to making every dollar count is clear from this booklet—it serves many roles, from dedicating the success of its New Hope Initiative *campaign, to recognizing campaign leadership, listing donors names by giving categories, providing a stewardship report, offering a brief history, and even soliciting the next gift.*

TIME

Erickson and his staff did not panic; instead they explored the full variety of options to respond to the crisis. These options ranged from partnering with another organization, to paying someone else to provide rehabilitation services, to going into the rehabilitation business themselves.

OPPORTUNITIES

Samaritan Inns decided to in-source the rehabilitation program, allowing it to control services from diagnosis to rehabilitation to independent living. While there was opportunity in this crisis, Samaritan Inns faced the enormous challenge of building organizational capacity to meet the demands of its new strategy. It had no experience running intensive treatment programs and needed to add staff with those skills. It did not have either the systems or infrastructure required to manage an endeavor of this scale. And it needed money—lots of money. *New Hope Initiative* was the theme for addressing each of these gaps.

PEOPLE

To tackle immediate funding needs, a short-term development board was established to raise money within Washington, D.C., business circles. Fundraising got a further boost from a pro bono consulting project that qualified the "social return on investment" of Samaritan Inns. This project provided a rigorous, quantitative, third-party endorsement of the organization's results, making the entire program more attractive to individuals, as well as corporations and foundations.

GOALS

Erickson describes himself as "extremely detail-oriented," so it is not surprising that he mapped out his own table of gifts for the campaign and included in his case statement a well-thought-out plan for both building facilities and phasing in staff and services. "It reassured potential donors," he says of its purpose. The results? *New Hope Initiative* campaign raised $6.3 million to underwrite the cost of new facilities, which included a five-hundred-thousand-dollar Kresge Foundation Challenge Grant. By 2001, Samaritan Inns was operating a comprehensive, three-phase program to combat addiction and homelessness, composed of an intensive rehabilitation facility, five temporary assisted-living facilities, and three single-room-occupancy facilities.

INVOLVEMENT

"We built a board of business leaders with a clear commitment to the campaign; they were not distracted by other board responsibilities. We had the benefit of a prominent individual who helped us organizationally—by providing us entry to other leaders, who in turn introduced us to peers in their business networks. That's how our development board grew, through relationships. The fact that we were asking people to serve for a limited period—two or three years for the campaign— also made it attractive," Erickson says.

FORMALLY ASK

Samaritan Inns found a receptive audience in foundations, "which are naturally clear about their interests. I learned that it's always person-to-person with individuals and corporations. . . . We talked about our work: reclaiming people, how we could bring back their gifts, ability, and talents to our larger community. For CEOs of national and multinational companies, our big job was to build in accountability to the process to keep them informed and engaged, yet respectful of the limits on their time. . . . We offered naming opportunities, such as naming a household suite for a gift of one hundred thousand dollars or more, but I don't think that made a difference to most donors."

THANKS & STEWARDSHIP

From simple onsite lunches ("in keeping with our culture," says Erickson) to the dedication of its buildings, Samaritan Inns offered donors the opportunity to feel the spirit of its work and see the quality of its programs. Opening celebrations, along with a "Celebration" report, reinforced what these top gifts made possible. One of the true hallmarks of its success, however, is the loyalty of its board members. When more than six hundred applicants applied for the eighty units of housing funded by the campaign, Erickson recognized that his work was not over. To meet the need, fundraising had to continue. Yet he had promised his development board that their terms would end with the recently completed campaign. "I personally met with each board member, thanked them for serving and explained the challenges we faced. Every board member wanted to continue to be involved." Perhaps A. James Clark, a board member and business leader who enlisted his peers and committed two million dollars to the campaign, said it best. "I've never seen a program in an inner city like Washington with so few dollars do so much good."

Making the Case

Many human-service agencies find it challenging to demonstrate their accountability to business leaders. Samaritan Inns responded to these concerns in two ways. First, it presented its case in economic terms with a cost-benefit analysis. The analysis demonstrates that a gift to Samaritan Inns has a greater economic return than investing in Microsoft stock during its growth years (see "Annual Return" in the image below).

After Samaritan Inns gained credibility as a cost-effective organization, its staff and development board was then able to convey its mission. Frequently, potential donors came onsite to view the transitional housing or inns, meet board and staff leadership, and watch a videotape of interviews with men and women who had completed rehabilitation. One former client, Phillip, tells how today he is able to give back to society and provide for his daughter after the death of her mother. Shortly after being released from prison on drug charges, Phillip entered Samaritan Inns for rehabilitation.

"Today, I pay property taxes, state taxes, federal taxes. I pay my babysitter, my rent, electric bill, and car insurance. . . . I thought my past [of drug and alcohol use] was my great time, but these are the great times," Phillips says of his family life. Five years after being drug-free, Phillip is a responsible father and married. Samaritan Inns, he says, "turned me into a new man."

SAMARITAN INNS'
NEW HOPE INITIATIVE:
By Any Measure, An Extraordinary Investment

SAMARITAN INNS
COMBATING HOMELESSNESS
REBUILDING LIVES.

Over the past four years, the international management consulting firm of McKinsey & Company has undertaken a series of analyses of the costs, benefits and returns of the work of Samaritan Inns. These results show that, by any measure, Samaritan Inns' New Hope Initiative is an extraordinary investment.

The government has historically paid $6,720/month per person, for medically-oriented substance abuse treatment. Samaritan Inns' alternative 28-day residential program costs less than $1,850/month —*savings of nearly 75%*.

The foundation of the Samaritan Inn's approach is a 28-day residential Intensive Recovery Program designed to enable homeless and addicted men and women to address their addictions and begin their journey back. More than 90% of those who participate complete the program.

$6,720	vs.	$1,850	=	75%
Government Per Month Per Person		Samaritan Inns Per Month Per Person		Savings

McKinsey & Company found that an investment in three new Inns will yield a 219% annual return to society—equivalent to a $1 investment worth $3.19 just one year later. This return is in the form of savings to the community from the *direct* costs that would otherwise be incurred to support homeless and addicted men and women. This return outpaces even extraordinary investment opportunities such as Microsoft stock during the last 5 years (~50% avg. annual return to shareholders).

The second building block of the Samaritan approach is a six month transitional housing program (the "Inns") which enables men and women to take what they have learned in the Intensive Recovery Program and practice it in the real world. Nearly 80% leave this phase clean and sober, with a job and housing.

$1		$3.19	=	219%
Investment Today	→	1 Year Later		Annual Return

Avoiding the direct *costs* of homelessness is just one part of the savings equation. Capturing the *benefits* that these men and women have to offer our community is another part. According to the McKinsey & Company calculus, the opportunity benefit of these men and women at this third stage–in employment earnings alone–is *triple* the annualized costs of the New Hope SRO.

The capstone of the Samaritan Inn's approach is affordable, drug-and alcohol-free longer term single-room occupancy (SRO) housing that provides a structure that nurtures and reinforces the positive behavior of work, sobriety, and responsibility that were developed during residency at the inns. Over 90% move-on from our SRO's clean and sober and employed — and, according to a recent follow-up survey, they stay that way.

Employment Earnings Alone	>	3	X	New Hope SRO Annualized Costs

Compiled & Printed by Arthur Andersen

Challenged to Lead

Many organizations talk about "friend-raising" as central to their fundraising, but few can match the success of Pepperdine University in Malibu, California.

During its recent *Challenged to Lead* campaign, Pepperdine's friends—individuals who were never students of the university—contributed a remarkable $181 million, more than half the $353 million raised. Their loyalty and impact over the years has been far-reaching, transforming what was once a small college into a world-class university.

Two forces are behind Pepperdine's dynamic growth: defining and spreading the word about its unique, values-driven educational mission in southern California; and attracting leadership to identify and cultivate those it calls its "army of friends."

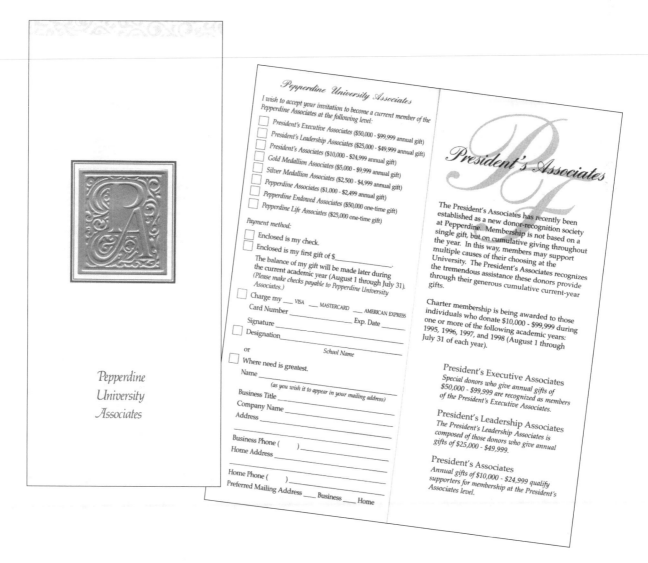

Pepperdine
University
Associates

Pepperdine University Associates

I wish to accept your invitation to become a current member of the Pepperdine Associates at the following level:

☐ President's Executive Associates ($50,000 - $99,999 annual gift)
☐ President's Leadership Associates ($25,000 - $49,999 annual gift)
☐ President's Associates ($10,000 - $24,999 annual gift)
☐ Gold Medallion Associates ($5,000 - $9,999 annual gift)
☐ Silver Medallion Associates ($2,500 - $4,999 annual gift)
☐ Pepperdine Associates ($1,000 - $2,499 annual gift)
☐ Pepperdine Endowed Associates ($50,000 one-time gift)
☐ Pepperdine Life Associates ($25,000 one-time gift)

Payment method:

☐ Enclosed is my check.
☐ Enclosed is my first gift of $_____
   The balance of my gift will be made later during the current academic year (August 1 through July 31).
   (Please make checks payable to Pepperdine University Associates.)
☐ Charge my ___ VISA ___ MASTERCARD ___ AMERICAN EXPRESS
   Card Number _____
   Signature _____ Exp. Date _____
☐ Designation _____
   or   School Name
☐ Where need is greatest.
   Name _____
        (as you wish it to appear in your mailing address)
   Business Title _____
   Company Name _____
   Address _____

   Business Phone ( )_____
   Home Address _____

   Home Phone ( )_____
   Preferred Mailing Address ___ Business ___ Home

President's Associates

The President's Associates has recently been established as a new donor-recognition society at Pepperdine. Membership is not based on a single gift, but on cumulative giving throughout the year. In this way, members may support multiple causes of their choosing at the University. The President's Associates recognizes the tremendous assistance these donors provide through their generous cumulative current-year gifts.

Charter membership is being awarded to those individuals who donate $10,000 - $99,999 during one or more of the following academic years: 1995, 1996, 1997, and 1998 (August 1 through July 31 of each year).

President's Executive Associates
Special donors who give annual gifts of $50,000 - $99,999 are recognized as members of the President's Executive Associates.

President's Leadership Associates
The President's Leadership Associates is composed of those donors who give annual gifts of $25,000 - $49,999.

President's Associates
Annual gifts of $10,000 - $24,999 qualify supporters for membership at the President's Associates level.

SCALING THE HEIGHTS

April 3, 2001

A SILVER ANNIVERSARY TRIBUTE

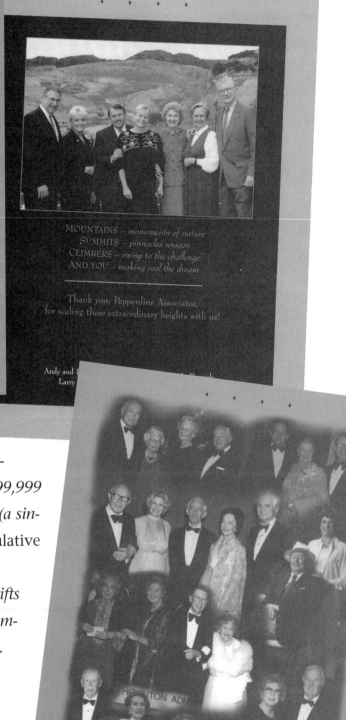

MOUNTAINS — *monuments of nature*
SUMMITS — *pinnacles unseen*
CLIMBERS — *rising to the challenge*
AND YOU — *making real the dream*

Thank you, Pepperdine Associates,
for scaling these extraordinary heights with us!

Andy and Larry

Over time, Pepperdine's recognition programs have grown to encompass recognition for annual giving ($1,000 through $99,999 annually); endowed or life membership (a single gift of $25,000 to $50,000); and cumulative annual giving ($10,000 to $99,999). *The George Pepperdine Society commemorates gifts over one hundred thousand dollars, and naming opportunities are available at that level. On its twenty-fifth anniversary, associates were recognized for "monumental commitments to the University during their lifetimes" that ranged from twenty-five hundred dollars to the ten million dollars or more given by twelve inspiring members of the Golden Wave Society.*

Pepperdine University's Challenged to Lead *campaign enlisted "people of vigor, vision and dedicated philanthropy," profiled here in its leadership booklet.*

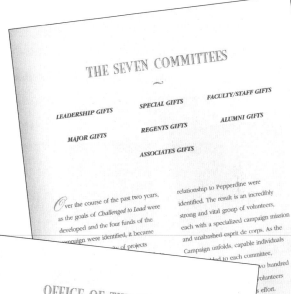

THE SEVEN COMMITTEES

LEADERSHIP GIFTS   SPECIAL GIFTS   FACULTY/STAFF GIFTS

MAJOR GIFTS   REGENTS GIFTS   ALUMNI GIFTS

ASSOCIATES GIFTS

*O*ver the course of the past two years, as the goals of *Challenged to Lead* were developed and the four funds of the campaign were identified, it became ... of projects

relationship to Pepperdine were identified. The result is an incredibly strong and vital group of volunteers, each with a specialized campaign mission and unabashed esprit de corps. As the Campaign unfolds, capable individuals ... led to each committee, ... two hundred ... volunteers ... effort.

ADVISORY COMMITTEES

*I*n addition to the seven action committees of the *Challenged to Lead* campaign, two important advisory groups will advance the campaign's mission and goals through regional and worldwide ombudsmanship and outreach activities.

WORLD ADVISORY COMMITTEE

The Honorable
GLEN A. HOLDEN, *chair*
Former Ambassador to Jamaica

More than 30 leaders from many nations—including a number of Pepperdine alumni—will form a network of global ambassadors as the campaign's World Advisory Committee, signifying the University's expanding national and international role in higher education. Their credentials include executive-level leadership in commerce, communications, the arts, education, law, medicine, politics, science, and other professions.

19

OFFICE OF THE CHAIR

JERVE M. JONES   **ROSEMARY RAITT**   **CHARLES B. RUNNELS**

*T*alent and tenacity are put to the test in a comprehensive campaign. Thus, the University tapped three individuals, each of them Pepperdine Regents, who clearly are up to the challenge. They have pledged their willingness to invest the hours, to marshal a vast corps of volunteers, and to lead by example through their own personal commitments to the goals of the Campaign and to the University they continue to serve with distinction.

Left to right: Charles B. Runnels, Jerve M. Jones, Rosemary Raitt, David Davenport, Laurence D. Hornbaker

5

TIME

Pepperdine has a history of "providential occurrences; that is, overcoming significant obstacles and becoming a stronger institution as a result," explains Larry Hornbaker, Ed.D., Pepperdine's vice chancellor. "This was true from the very beginning. In February of 1937, George Pepperdine had the vision to create a Christian college. Just seven months later, 163 students paid their tuition and became the first freshman class, housed in three buildings. Pulling the college together in a matter of months is an impressive achievement at any time, but you have to remember that this was during the Great Depression," he says.

"With the turmoil of the 1960s, there were many Americans who believed their own colleges had lost their way. Pepperdine University offered a compelling alternative. As a Christian college, Pepperdine's mission is to prepare students for lives of purpose and leadership built on strong core values. There are many conservatives who not only liked what we do, but wanted us to be even more successful in reaching students and changing society."

OPPORTUNITIES

Propelled by its mission, Pepperdine seized two opportunities: attracting a new kind of supporter (see "People," page 45) and creating ways to involve and recognize them. The university increased the size of its board (from thirteen to forty) and, for the first time, allowed non–church members to compose up to 49 percent of the membership. It created the University Board, an advisory council, to educate and involve the most promising individuals. The Associates Program was established in 1975 to honor annual contributors of one thousand dollars or more; it has grown from four hundred charter members to more than fifteen hundred today. The George Pepperdine Society (starting at one hundred thousand dollars for the Benefactors Circle) encourages continued support through cumulative giving levels. Recognition is so important that a full-time memorial manager suggests ways to commemorate high-level gifts (naming opportunities are varied: schools, chairs, fellowships, programs, etc.).

Friend-Raising at Its Best

While Pepperdine University's *Challenged to Lead* campaign enlisted record support from *all* its constituents, its "army of friends" contributed more than half the funds. These are individuals who never attended the university as students, but are dedicated to its mission. Consider the statistics below, which compare gifts from *Friends* to all gifts to the *Campaign*.

	Friends		Campaign	
Giving Level	*Donors*	*Amount*	*Donors*	*Amount*
$50 million	1	$51,695,000	1	$51,695,000
$25 million	1	$34,100,000	1	$34,100,000
$10 million	3	$30,554,000	4	$48,727,000
$5 million	3	$24,733,000	6	$46,597,000
$1 million	26	$47,156,000	53	$92,261,000
Sub-total	34	$152,443,000	65	$273,380,000
$100,000+	67	$20,390,000	167	$52,775,000
$10,000+	156	$3,545,000	515	$13,244,000
$1,000+	1,338	$4,109,000	3,422	$9,914,000
<$1,000	5,045	$741,000	25,959	$4,015,000
Grand Total	6,639	$181,228,000	30,128	$353,228,000

PEOPLE

Identifying and accessing the motivated wealthy got a boost when Dr. Charles B. Runnels, who today is Pepperdine's chancellor, took a company-paid leave of absence from Tenneco in the 1960s. Dr. Runnels joined important clubs in the area and was so successful as Pepperdine's ambassador that he became known as the "Pepperdine man." Not only did Frank Seaver and his wife, Blanche Ebert Seaver, became major supporters, but Blanche also personally persuaded her social and philanthropic friends to join her in making Pepperdine's dreams a reality.

GOALS

With each challenge came increased campaign goals. When the university acquired thirty-three acres of land for a new campus in Malibu in 1969, it needed a minimum of five million dollars for construction. Months later, before an audience of 3,100 people, Blanche Seaver announced her eight-million-dollar gift to a campaign that raised $25.6 million. In 1982, $137 million in gifts enabled the construction to continue, far surpassing the hundred-million-dollar campaign goal. In 1992, with the need for endowments as its major focus, Pepperdine launched a three-hundred-million-dollar campaign, which closed with $353 million raised.

INVOLVEMENT

Top business, entertainment, and political leaders embraced Pepperdine's view that a university could excel not only in education but also in "the formation of a life and even the transformation of the character and values" of its students (in the words of David Davenport, Pepperdine's sixth president). With such boosters as former governor Ronald Reagan and entertainer Pat Boone, Pepperdine's stature was elevated; their involvement helped attract the attention of major donors. In 1970, for example, when Pepperdine launched its campaign, a hotel accommodating 2,100 people was booked for the dinner banquet; yet more than 3,100 people responded, requiring Pepperdine to host the event at two hotels. During their presidencies, Nixon and Reagan sent cabinet officials and Supreme Court justices to address Pepperdine audiences, including those at its new law school, adding prominence to a university positioning itself to shape the minds of tomorrow's leaders.

FORMALLY ASK

Blanche Seaver and other individuals opened doors for the university's president, chancellor, and Dr. Hornbaker. "Mrs. Seaver was our angel," recalls Dr. Hornbaker. "Without Mrs. Seaver, we would never have been able to talk with many of these people. She would invite the president, the chancellor, or me to join her for private lunches and dinners with her friends. She challenged many to make their best gifts to Pepperdine. Her life was her philanthropy and Pepperdine became her number one charity." The Seavers personally gave over two hundred million dollars to Pepperdine; the Seaver College of Arts, Sciences, and Letters serves as a lasting reminder of their leadership.

THANKS & STEWARDSHIP

Pepperdine's philosophy is to make a friend. Out of that friendship will grow a gift; and we remember our many friends. "Pepperdine Associates are invited to exclusive cultural, social, and athletic events throughout the year, where they meet with faculty, students, and fellow members," its membership brochure reads. Members are treated to a black-tie reception and hear distinguished speakers (keynote speakers have included former first lady Nancy Reagan, Nobel laureate Milton Friedman, journalists Alistair Cooke and George Will, and Hall of Fame baseball coach Tommy Lasorda). Members have access to university libraries, including the rare-book and special collections. Their names are listed in the dinner program book and on a recognition display prominently displayed on the grounds of the university.

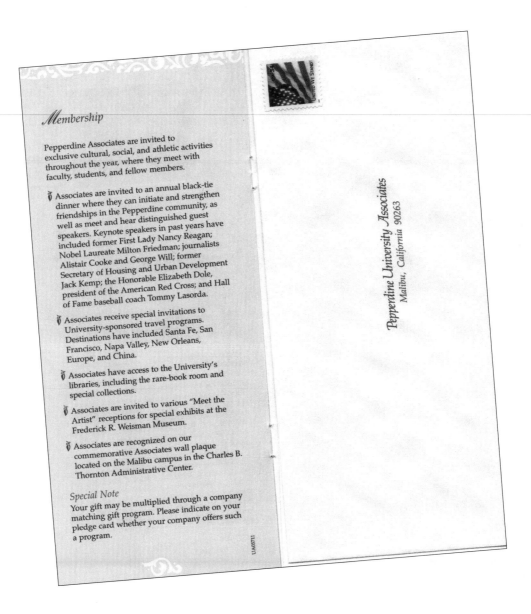

Membership

Pepperdine Associates are invited to exclusive cultural, social, and athletic activities throughout the year, where they meet with faculty, students, and fellow members.

❧ Associates are invited to an annual black-tie dinner where they can initiate and strengthen friendships in the Pepperdine community, as well as meet and hear distinguished guest speakers. Keynote speakers in past years have included former First Lady Nancy Reagan; Nobel Laureate Milton Friedman; journalists Alistair Cooke and George Will; former Secretary of Housing and Urban Development Jack Kemp; the Honorable Elizabeth Dole, president of the American Red Cross; and Hall of Fame baseball coach Tommy Lasorda.

❧ Associates receive special invitations to University-sponsored travel programs. Destinations have included Santa Fe, San Francisco, Napa Valley, New Orleans, Europe, and China.

❧ Associates have access to the University's libraries, including the rare-book room and special collections.

❧ Associates are invited to various "Meet the Artist" receptions for special exhibits at the Frederick R. Weisman Museum.

❧ Associates are recognized on our commemorative Associates wall plaque located on the Malibu campus in the Charles B. Thornton Administrative Center.

Special Note
Your gift may be multiplied through a company matching gift program. Please indicate on your pledge card whether your company offers such a program.

UA05711

Pepperdine University Associates
Malibu, California 90263

UNITED WE STAND

Closer to the Cure

"Bringing donors closer to the medicine" is how Janet B. Cady, president of the Children's Hospital Trust (affiliated with Children's Hospital Boston), describes her organization's two Philanthropic Leadership Councils, each with a unique and special focus: pediatric heart disease or developmental medicine. Along with the creation of a foundation or "trust" board focused on philanthropy, the Leadership Councils represent one of several new initiatives fueling a rapid and significant increase in giving to

HeartBeat
News for supporters and friends of the Cardiovascular Program at Children's Hospital Boston

Fall 2001   Children's Hospital Boston

Improving Children's Lives Through Translational Research

Research is at the very heart of Children's Cardiovascular Program, for it is only through research in the laboratory and the clinical setting that the care of children with complex cardiac conditions can be improved. Children's Hospital Boston, the nation's preeminent academic pediatric center, is a leader in "translational" research, which brings discoveries made in the laboratory into the clinical setting as quickly as possible for the benefit of patients.

Children's cardiac surgeon Pedro J. del Nido, MD, and his colleagues are currently involved in two major research initiatives that promise to further improve the outcomes of children with a variety of cardiac conditions. In addition, del Nido plans to launch a new, innovative program—the first of its kind in the world—that has the potential to transform the way pediatric cardiac surgery is performed by merging recent advances in the fields of medicine and engineering.

Preventing heart muscle damage

One of del Nido's research efforts is aimed at better understanding and finding preventive strategies for heart muscle damage that occurs among some children who undergo multiple cardiac surgeries, which at Children's is about one in three patients.

Cardiac surgeon Pedro J. del Nido, MD

Inotropic drugs are routinely administered immediately following heart surgery to improve the heart's function and hasten recovery, explains del Nido. While beneficial, these medications also have a downside. "In high doses and under certain conditions, these drugs [which are administered for only a few days] may have deleterious effects on the heart that can occur within minutes," says del Nido.

Del Nido and his colleagues hypothesize that these drugs trigger a natural process called apoptosis—programmed cell death—of heart muscle cells. They are currently working on confirming the specific mechanism by which this occurs and testing several ways to block apoptosis and, thereby, prevent heart muscle damage. "I think we should have a pretty good answer within the next year or two," predicts del Nido.

Reducing the need for transplantation

Heart failure, a condition in which the heart is unable to pump blood efficiently, is the main reason children require a heart transplant. Although Children's Cardiac Transplant Program is a national leader in pediatric heart transplantation, a heart transplant is never the ideal option for a child.

Del Nido and his team of investigators have been studying one of the mechanisms by which heart failure occurs in children. The hypothesis they are currently testing is that there is a "mismatch" between the heart's demand for blood (which increases as the ailing heart must work ever harder) and the number of capillaries (hair-thin blood vessels) through which blood flows to the heart.

"We believe this mismatch increases as the disease progresses, robbing the heart muscle of nutrients and eventually leading to the death of heart muscle cells and, ultimately, heart failure," says del Nido.

Based on this hypothesis, del Nido and his colleagues are investigating whether agents that trigger the formation of new blood vessels (angiogenesis, a field pioneered by

Research continued on page 2

HeartBeat

New Cardiac Intensive Care Unit

...any measure, Children's 23-...Cardiac Intensive Care Unit ...CU) is a special place. Every ...more than 1,300 patients ...around the world, some as ...two pounds and all ...ely ill, receive superb, ...-the-art care from a ...sciplinary team of dedi-...lth professionals.

...g to CICU director ...Wessel, MD, patients ...CU have access to the ...therapies, many of ...pioneered and ...hildren's. The excel-...provided in the ...resented by its low ...lly declining mortal-...at approximately ...among the lowest

...ildren's CICU is ...20 years old and ...ded. To ensure ...able to con-...most advanced, ...—some of which did not exist two decades ago—to patients and families, a new, 24-bed CICU will be constructed in Children's new clinical building. When completed in 2004, the new building located on Shattuck Street will comprise 216,000 square feet and 10 stories.

"The new CICU will enable us to provide state-of-the-art care to critically ill patients and their families well into the future," notes Patricia A. Hickey, RN, MS, vice president of Cardiovascular and Critical Care Programs at Children's. Hickey adds that the new Cardiac Catheterization Laboratories will also be constructed in the new clinical building, close to the CICU. "Having this new space will support and further enhance our efforts to offer sophisticated technologies and treatments in a family-centered environment."

Almost double the bed space

Hickey points out that the bed space (270 square feet per bed) in the new CICU will be almost double that of the existing unit's bed space. This will not only provide more room for patients' family members (including ample space for comfortable, built-in sleep benches), but also for large and often life-saving technologies, such as ECMO (extra corporeal membrane oxygenation). In addition, the unit will have spacious and comfortable consultation rooms, waiting rooms and rooms for breastfeeding mothers.

The design of the CICU, which is still being refined, reflects the input not only of staff members at every key step of the process, but also family members and former patients, who suggestions were "invaluable," says Hickey. "We paid meticulous attention to making the new unit as normal and supportive as possible for families of critically ill children," stresses Hickey. "We are thrilled about the new CICU and the continued opportunity to care for critically ill patients and their families in a new and improved facility."

The creation of the new CICU is a major priority of Children's Hospital and the many friends and supporters of the Cardiovascular Program. For information about how to support the new CICU, please contact:

Karen Ann Engelbourg
(617) 355-8863
karen.engelbourg@chtrust.org

The new, 10-story clinical building, slated to open in 2004, will include a new, 24-bed Cardiac Intensive Care Unit and sophisticated new Cardiac Catheterization Laboratories.

4

Children's. Contributions have tripled in just three years (from ten million dollars in 1997 to thirty-one million in 2000). The surge in support escalated to sixty million dollars in 2001, the year the trust launched its comprehensive five-year campaign.

At the core of its success is the Leadership Council's program design, "which brings parents who have had life-changing experience at the hospital in close touch with incredible doctors. It's a close-knit group of donors with a common orientation: they want to make a difference," Cady explains. Parents of children born with congenital heart defects, for example, "can hear from our researchers about a new cardiac

technique being developed for fetal intervention. With this new technique, babies can be born with healthy hearts. The news brought tears to the eyes of many parents who understand what a profound effect this procedure can have on a child's life. And Children's is one of only three hospitals in the U.S. doing this level of research.

"We're simply seizing on the energy and passion of parents and other donors who want to have an impact. We're going where our donors want to go."

Potential donors are encouraged to join at high levels, such as the Children's Circle of Care ($10,000). Members receive regular updates from physicians at events and private gatherings, as well as in printed reports.

TIME

When Cady arrived at Children's Hospital, "The hospital understood the increasingly important role of philanthropy. Managed care was hitting hard at the bottom lines of many hospitals in New England. Charitable gifts were viewed as an important part of our future." The hospital considered several models for involving philanthropic leaders. The choice was a distinct trust board (foundation model) that was established with a new generation of leadership. "The average age is about forty-five, with a number of leaders in the investment world as well as venture capitalists, which is a real contrast to many traditional boards."

OPPORTUNITIES

With a fresh leadership board in place, Cady focused "on taking compelling aspects of the hospital and developing a small number of high-powered groups around these interests. Children's Hospital has a large number of exciting specialties and departments. We created the Heart Council and Developmental Medicine Council as a way of bringing a relatively small group, perhaps twenty-five people, in close contact with our doctors. Each is staffed by a senior development officer—Karen Engelbourg for the Heart Council and Joan Romanition for the Developmental Medicine Council. They run these like any leadership volunteer group, with a great deal of attention on engaging participants at a high level. In a relatively intimate setting, donors receive impactful reports. They learn about a wonderful and noble cause." Cady increased her major gifts staff as well ("It's a labor-intensive process"), and had each officer specialize and gain expertise in three or five areas of clinical care and scientific research, which includes orientations in their departments by doctors, nurses, and researchers. With such an intense knowledge base, each of the nine talented major gifts officers secures two to five million dollars annually, including seven-figure gifts.

PEOPLE

"Leadership is everything," Janet believes, so an extraordinary effort was invested to find the best trust board and council members. "We screened our lists and met with physicians to review names we had identified and discuss their recommendations. Working with the physician, we'd invite people on tours and educational events. Council members also enlist new members, their friends who can make a difference. . . . After assuming leadership roles on the councils, we've had members say, 'I can do more. What else can I do?' The councils have become a source for trustee development; it's sometimes like a farm team for volunteers who want to move onto the trust or hospital board."

An Easy Decision

To Hal and Laure Garnick, the decision to become involved with the Children's Hospital Trust was easy. A family member had been touched by the hospital in a remarkable way. "After my son's care, we were so appreciative. I was actually looking for a way to connect with the hospital," Hal says.

"My son developed a high fever and a major rash upon our return from traveling. We immediately visited his pediatrician who thought it was a virus and suggested we give it a few days. The next day it became substantially worse. My son's lips were bleeding and his pupils were yellow. Our pediatrician immediately referred us to Dr. Jane Newburger, a world expert on Kawasaki Disease at Children's Hospital Boston."

According to the American Heart Association, Kawasaki Disease is a leading cause of heart disease in children. If not diagnosed and treated early, it can lead to permanent heart damage or death. Its cause is not known. Often, it takes an experienced team of experts—such as the Kawasaki Disease Program at Children's—to quickly analyze the symptoms, treat, and provide long-term follow-up, as needed. About eighteen hundred new cases are detected in the U.S. each year.

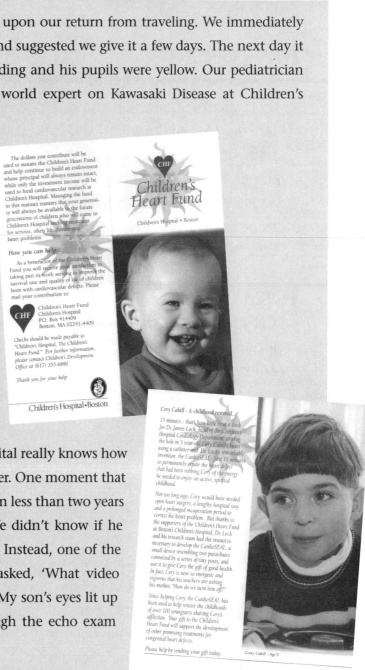

"Fortunately, with treatment, my son's health turned around quickly. There was no permanent damage. We were so appreciative, and it goes beyond the cure. You could tell that Children's Hospital really knows how to deal with kids . . . that they've got their act together. One moment that stands out in my mind is when my son, who was then less than two years old, had to take a forty-five minute echo exam. We didn't know if he would need to be sedated to get through the exam. Instead, one of the hospital's staff cheerfully turned to my son and asked, 'What video would you like to watch? *Barney*? Or *Sesame Street*?' My son's eyes lit up when he heard about the videos and smiled through the echo exam watching them."

Continued on page 55

GOALS

A five-year "minicampaign," complete with a staff-written case for support, was approved by the Developmental Medicine Council. After funding research and program needs, the Heart Council is actively raising funds for a new neonatal intensive care unit, a campaign priority. Major gift officers have goals too: cultivating and soliciting as many as 150 people, with a real focus on the top twenty to thirty individuals.

INVOLVEMENT

Reports from hospital specialists bring home the message of the crucial role played by Leadership Council members. "At several meetings a year, our physicians speak of their work and progress, and express their sincere thanks for the council's support and partnership. Council members are given deep feedback, and they know our physicians speak from their hearts. Being among high-level donors often raises an individual's sights. They may begin to say to themselves, 'I can do more. I want to be a part of this program in a significant way.' Through the Leadership Councils, they become more comfortable in making higher-level gifts."

FORMALLY ASK

Cady and her staff are known for being well prepared, and that preparation includes solicitations. "Our solicitations are usually by a physician and a major gifts officer or by a council member with major gifts staff. The gift requests are well prepared so each professional knows what to say and there are few, if any, surprises."

THANKS & STEWARDSHIP

Children's hosts an annual Heart-to-Heart event for donors, and each participant receives a small gift. "Heart Council members are key to the event's success, and are listed on the invitation and in the program book. But our volunteers and donors are in it for the impact . . . to be closer to the medicine and the cure, rather than for personal recognition." Yet Children's is not about to forget showing its gratitude. Leadership Council members receive several letters of thanks (often from the president, board chairman, key physician, etc.). And perhaps their most important feedback is to see their gifts in action in the faces of children and in the advances of caregivers and scientists.

Continued from page 53

Something We Wanted to Do

It was a friend who introduced Hal to the staff at the Children's Hospital Trust. Hal and Laure took a tour of the hospital, then joined the Heart Council. "It was something we wanted to do. We get the greatest satisfaction from knowing that we're helping. When you tour the intensive care unit (ICU), you see there are children who are really having a difficult time. But, with the care they receive, you discover that 98 percent of the kids come out fine."

Hal says he was ready to "roll up my sleeves" to help Children's, and he is now chair of the Heart Council and a member of the real estate committee of the board. "The Heart Council is in the process of raising several million to help fund the new cardiac ICU. We're also funding important research projects." Hal is using an approach that has worked well for the council, and includes "networking with friends, inviting them to a few functions. Council members also may host a dinner in their homes, with doctors and researchers describing their work to eight to ten couples. The dinners are followed up with a call to each couple to say, 'Thank you for attending. Would you like to take a tour of the hospital?' The most important step is for them to see the hospital. They may also be invited to our Heart-to-Heart dinner. The events let you get the lay of the land, or determine someone's level of interest. I've learned that even a relatively small, first-time gift can lead to a larger gift. One of my friends started by giving twenty-five hundred dollars, for example. Later, he made a six-figure gift. Often I ask people to join the Children's Circle of Care [$10,000 annually]. Another friend surprised me by responding with a six-figure gift!"

He says, as a volunteer, "The Children's Trust staff is great. They always send you a thank you note after you've brought friends for a tour or hosted a dinner. Or they may call you the next day. They make you feel appreciated."

The best potential donors, Hal says, "Are parents who have a child who has had terrific results at Children's. The Circle of Care adds to that common bond. We're not only 'doing a good thing,' but we're doing it together. With many people involved, it's easier and it's fun."

"The doctors, researchers, and staff at Children's are focused on the best interests of the kids. The Heart Council is a volunteer effort to give them what they need."

The Anniversary Campaign for Princeton

Drawing on its strong traditions and values, Princeton University announced a comprehensive campaign in November 1996, which five years later triumphantly exceeded its original goal by a remarkable 52 percent! *The Anniversary Campaign*, commemorating 250 years since the founding of the university, established new records for giving to Princeton: $1.146 billion raised, including gifts from 78 percent of its undergraduate alumni.

Embracing both the richness of its traditions and its potential to "stand as a model of the very best in liberal education, scholarship and research," The Anniversary Campaign for Princeton reached out to its alumni through existing events and publications, as well as new venues. The campaign was announced during a three-day sprint known as the Eventful Days. The alumni newsletter, Princeton, *maintained its focus on education and campus life, while weaving in campaign news.*

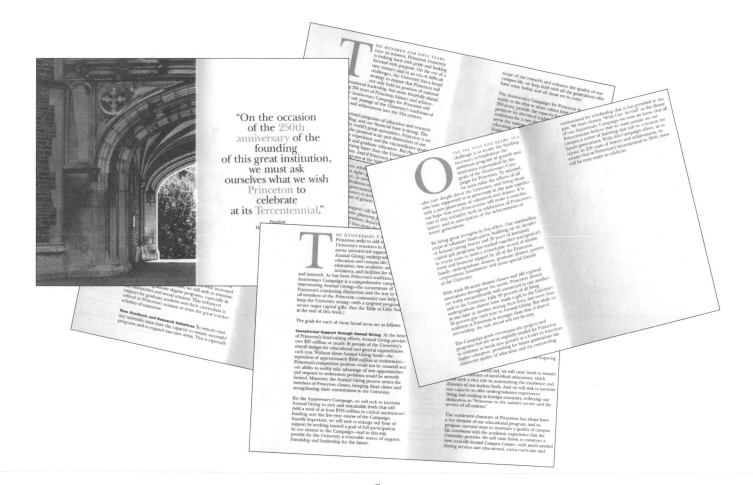

"On the occasion of the 250th anniversary of the founding of this great institution, we must ask ourselves what we wish Princeton to celebrate at its Tercentennial."

"Every text is at the mercy of its readers."

"Language alone protects us from the scariness of things with no names. Language alone is meditation."

"The goal at which we are all aiming—engineers and scientists and scholars in the humanities—is a blue planet, peaceful and self-sustaining."

Small booklets (approximately five by seven inches in size) brought messages on Teaching, Learning, *and* With One Accord *(the campaign's theme), and were presented to alumni during visits by campaign volunteers and staff.*

6:04am

Generations of student carriers have distributed The Daily Princetonian, founded in 1876.

The student body needs its sleep, but at Princeton, sleep is a priority often deferred. For many students, days end late and begin early. Their time on campus is a precious thing, not to be dreamed away, and the first orange rays of morning light that stream across Old Nassau carry with them both promise and urgency. The days of learning in this luminous realm glide by as swiftly as the delivery of yesterday's news.

10:50am

Professor Alan Blinder '67, former vice-chairman of the Federal Reserve, teaches Economics 101, The National Economy, in McCosh 50.

Special hours of learning remain indelible in memory, like the image of a renowned professor delivering a powerful lecture in the resonant hugeness of a historic hall.

1:19pm

Professor Alain Kornhauser '71 advises a senior whose engineering thesis analyzes traffic patterns.

As the academic day resumes, it carries forward a learning process firmly rooted in the wisdom of the past and yet constantly evolving and expanding into the future.

Hands-on laboratory experience is as crucial in the fast-opening new field of molecular biology as it is in chemistry, which has been taught at Princeton since 1795.

Professor Daniel Kammen leads a seminar on science, technology and public policy.

The anniversary was a rallying point both for the campaign and for reuniting with fellow Princetonians through "regional conferences and celebrations from New York to Los Angeles and Hong Kong; in colloquia on topics ranging the habitability of the earth to the future of higher education; and in a splendid 250th Opening Ceremony," a lead article in the *Princeton* proclaimed. "This place has an atmosphere that grabs many of us and never lets go."

Yet amid the anniversary celebrations, the campaign enabled the university to think seriously about its future. "On the occasion of the 250th anniversary of the founding of this great institution, we must ask ourselves what we wish Princeton to celebrate at its Tercentennial," said Harold T. Shapiro GS'64, the university president who served during the historic campaign.

Here's how the university answered that question through its *Anniversary Campaign.*

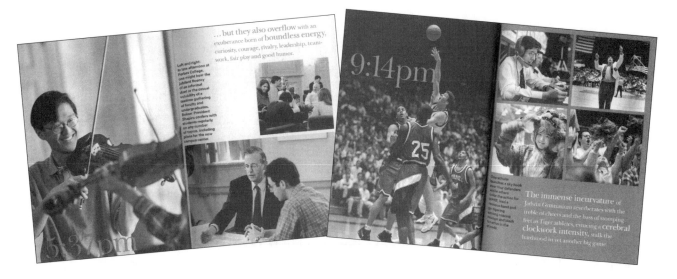

TIME

The milestone anniversary marked a time to re-invigorate the university and its "tradition of shared stewardship—of going back and giving back," said campaign co-chair Dennis Keller at the kickoff dinner, highlighting the need to link "Princetonians from generation to generation . . . and get us to our final campaign goal." Traditions pervade *The Anniversary Campaign*, from its theme, With One Accord—words taken from the first verse of the university's song, "Old Nassau"—to the campaign's color, bright orange, which dates to 1867 when student George Ward produced badges of orange ribbon for students to wear at a baseball game against Yale.

OPPORTUNITIES

Through a rigorous strategic planning process, the university developed "a broad strategy to ensure that Princeton will not only hold its position of national and international leadership, but move forcefully ahead," proclaimed President Shapiro. With five campaign priorities (see Goals, page 62), the university was able to inspire and engage donors to contribute major and planned gifts through such programs as the Presidential Teaching Initiatives (with naming opportunities for Endowed Professorship at $2.5 million; Endowed Preceptorship for the most promising junior faculty at $1 million; Endowed Museum Curatorship at $1.5 million; Endowed University Fellowship for one of Princeton's best graduate scholars at $750,000; etc.). Gifts to scholarship and fellowship endowment funds under $50,000 were also encouraged, but do not bear the donor's name (giving opportunities include Endowed Undergraduate Student Aid Fund at $50,000; Book Acquisition Fund at $25,000; Student Carrel at $10,000; etc.).

PEOPLE

Top leadership was the hallmark of the campaign. Included within its well-orches-
trated campaign organization were regional chairs and committees seeking leadership gifts (see Formally Ask). Reunion giving was the touchstone for "going back
and giving back." The pacesetting gift, announced at the kickoff, was a record-setting one-hundred-million-dollar commitment from Gordon Y. S. Wu '58 (at the
time the largest gift to Princeton and the biggest by a foreign national to a U.S.
university). Wu heads Hopewell Holdings, one of Hong Kong's largest development
groups. In a speech that brought tears to many attending the kickoff celebration
and culminated in a standing ovation, Wu said, "I knew I had received a tremendous subsidy from people who had come to Princeton before me. Now I feel it is a
solemn duty to create more opportunities to benefit the next generation, just as
we have benefited from our predecessors."

A Teaching President Makes His Case

A Princeton tradition is that the university's president
teaches and, for more than a decade, Harold T. Shapiro
has carried it out with passion.

Known for faculty of the highest caliber, Princeton's
teaching has become synonymous with excellence. It is
understandable then that the largest component of the
campaign is Undergraduate Education and Campus
Life, $317 million in support for innovation and excel-
lence in teaching, aid for students, and enhancements
in the quality of campus life. More than one hundred
million dollars of these projects are known as
Presidential Teaching Initiatives, with the university's
president committed to raising fifty million of this goal.

President Shapiro, who led The Anniversary
Campaign for Princeton, *assumes a crucial role
in fundraising to ensure continued excellence in
teaching (left). He also is seen leading a student
seminar (opposite).*

"I've decided to personally carry the torch for a renewed burst of support for Princeton's central and enduring commitment to out-standing undergraduate teaching."

"Our strategic planning process has emphasized our determination to be second to none, both in the quality of our scholarship and research at Princeton, and in the quality of our teaching program," Shapiro explains. After skillfully guiding the campaign to success, he later retired from the University's top post.

Included in the Presidential Initiatives are:

• A 250th Anniversary Fund for Innovation in Undergraduate Education, essentially a twenty-five-million-dollar "venture capital fund for new ideas in teaching";

• Four 250th Anniversary Visiting Professorships for Distinguished Teaching endowed at a total of twelve million dollars, with one faculty member each in the humanities, social sciences, natural sciences, and engineering;

• The Center for Teaching and Learning, a thirteen-million-dollar investment in a state-of-the-art center with technologies and expert consultants to help faculty develop new materials and methods. The center will support mentoring, an electronic classroom configured for hands-on learning, an expanded language laboratory, a multimedia computer cluster, and a writing center with work stations.

• Society of Fellows in the Liberal Arts, a fourteen-million-dollar endowment to attract highly talented young people to Princeton and give them research and teaching experience.

Visionary Organizations: Agents of Change

GOALS

Seven hundred fifty million dollars was established as the initial goal ($300 million for endowment [40 percent], $228 million for construction [30 percent], and $222 million for term funding [30 percent]). Three years into the campaign, backed by strong support from alumni, the university seized on new opportunities and increased the goal to nine hundred million dollars. As defined by President Shapiro, the campaign's five core priorities were:

1. *Unrestricted Support Through Annual Giving* over five years ($150 million goal), which provides nearly 10 percent of the university's budget each year and is "at the heart of Princeton's fund-raising efforts";

2. *Undergraduate Education and Campus Life* ($317 million) "in support for teaching, aid to students, and essential enhancements of the quality of life on our campus";

3. *Graduate Education* ($78 million) "for expanding student support, new interdisciplinary training, and much-needed renovations of the Graduate College . . . at a time when federal support is declining";

4. *New Academic and Research Initiatives* ($211 million) for "programs in genomics, religion, environmental science and policy, and in the humanities . . . Women's Studies, Finance and Jewish Studies"; and

5. *Facilities for Education and Research* ($144 million) to renovate libraries and academic buildings, update technology, and provide "state-of-the-art settings for academic and scholarly activities."

INVOLVEMENT

Years of planning by committees defined Princeton's core strengths, values, and opportunities. Yet the work was challenging: "a smaller inventory of objectives of the highest priority would have to be selected and presented to the Princeton community as the targets of a comprehensive fundraising campaign," said President Shapiro. That presentation came on the Eventful Days, thirty-six hours surrounding the campaign launch that featured: a press conference announcing the Wu gift; a volunteer assembly for campaign leaders; a colloquia with presentations ranging from the "history of the universe to speculations about life in the twenty-first century"; a celebratory dinner launching the campaign (with twelve hundred supporters gathering in the Jadwin Gym, which was reborn with monumental banners and black and orange tents); and food, films ("Princeton in the Nation's Cinema"), and football.

Formally Ask

Volunteers were enlisted to personally solicit about 5 percent of Princeton's alumni, "3,000 of Princeton's prospective donors—who are thought to be capable of leadership gifts: *combined* annual giving and capital gifts of $100,000 or more. These individuals will be solicited in a face-to-face meeting with a Campaign volunteer, often accompanied by a member of the development staff. In some cases, solicitation teams may also include class leaders, University Trustees, or senior members of the faculty and administration" (source: volunteer orientation materials). Volunteers received printed materials on the campaign table of needs, ways of giving, selected naming gift opportunities, and campaign policies (See chapter 6, "Opportunities II," for campaign policies). These solicitation teams were in *addition* to the several thousand volunteers already involved in Princeton's annual giving program.

Thanks & Stewardship

With more than eighty classes participating, along with donors and volunteers from around the world, campaign communications and stewardship were paramount. *Princeton, With One Accord*, an existing broadside newsletter prepared by Princeton's Office of Development Communications, kept alumni informed not only of campaign progress but also of general university news, which "touched every aspect of life on Princeton's campus—from renovating such collegiate Gothic landmarks as Cleveland Towers, to launching ambitious multidisciplinary efforts such as the new Lewis-Sigler Institute for Integrative Genomics," one front-page article reports. Other stories kept readers grounded in the campaign's purpose, seen through renowned faculty ("Tyson's Stellar Teaching Illuminates Astrophysics"), sports achievements ("Tiger Track Team Captures Third Triple Crown"), alumni success ("Two More Princetonians Named to MacArthur Genius Awards"), and new and renovated buildings on campus.

Invest more of your time and energy where they will have the greatest return.

"The shell must break before the bird can fly."

Alfred Lord Tennyson

"Potential just means you ain't done it yet."

Darrell Royal
Football coach at the University of Texas

Y ou've seen it before, perhaps dozens of times. Nonprofit leaders and fundraising executives so entrenched in meetings, phone calls, mail appeals, special events, and other labor- and time-intensive activities that they don't have a minute to think about creating and funding their long-term goals. Fundraisers are being eaten alive, consumed by the daily string of crises, golf outings, galas, mailings, or other activities through which they seek smaller gifts.

TOP GIFTS™ fundraising challenges that lifestyle and calls for new thinking. It dares you to set ambitious goals, to seek the extraordinary, to reach your full potential . . . to be more effective and successful. TOP GIFTS™ is based on:

- defining and embracing a compelling vision,

- recruiting and involving the very best leaders, and then

- developing, soliciting, and recognizing major and planned gifts at the highest levels.

It's one of the most efficient and effective ways to raise money. While other approaches to fundraising do have value, there's nothing like major and planned gifts (or top gifts!) to fuel your total giving. Just compare the results (or "Net Proceeds") on page 67. If you seek to increase your fundraising by only ten thousand dollars, as few as three solicitations can surpass hundreds or even thousands of requests by special events or direct mail.

Crossing the TOP GIFTS™ Chasm

Taking the "next step" in fundraising, from entry-level giving such as direct mail to TOP GIFTS™ fundraising, is crucial, but many fundraising executives never make that leap. It's as though there is a deep chasm, with direct mail and special events weighing them down on one side . . . and major and planned gifts seemingly out of reach on the other.

To realize your organization's dreams you must develop the courage—and the commitment—to create a TOP GIFTS™ program. For most organizations, it's a logical next step or a progression from success in direct mail and special events. Here's why.

In his book *Loyalty Rules!* management consultant and author Frederick F.

What does it take to raise $10,000?

	Cost	Solicitations	Gifts	Net Proceeds
Direct mail: Acquire	100% or $10,000	Up to 40,000	400 @ $25 each	$0
Direct mail: Renew	20% or $2,000	2,000	400 @ $25 increase	$8,000
Special Events	50% or $5,000	300	100 tickets @ $100	$5,000
TOP GIFTS	3% or $300	3	1 @ $10,000	$9,700

Where should you be committing more of your time?

> TOP GIFTS™ fundraising has the lowest cost, highest return

Direct mail: To acquire $10,000 in gifts from new donors when your average gift is $25, you'll need 400 new donors. And consider yourself lucky if you break even after expenses. In other words, it will cost you at least $10,000 for printing, postage, and mailing services to raise $10,000. If you have a 1 percent response, considered acceptable, you'll need to mail to 40,000 people just to get those gifts. If your mailing does better—say, 1.5 percent of your list responds—you're still mailing to more than 26,600 people to net 400 new donors. Renewing and upgrading donors is less costly, but you'll still need hundreds of people on your list to increase their gifts in order to reach $10,000 in new funds.

Special events: One of the major factors in special-events fundraising is cost. Most fundraisers believe that, if you net half of the proceeds, you've done well. At $100 per ticket, that's 100 tickets to total $10,000 before expenses. If one out of three people contacted purchases a ticket, that's 300 solicitations. After you deduct expenses, you'll need 600 solicitations to net $10,000!

TOP GIFTS™: Wouldn't it be wonderful to use an easier approach that has dramatic results? You can raise $10,000 by asking just one individual! Granted, not every solicitation is a success, so you may have to ask as many as three individuals. But the cost is nominal. If you take each of these individuals to lunch, you might invest $300 for expenses. This means making three solicitations for one top gift, compared to mailing to as many as 40,000 people for a direct mail acquisition, or upgrading 400 of your current donors, or asking 300 people to buy a ticket for your special event. It's easy to see where you should be investing more of your time and energy.

Reichheld makes the point that, in business, "the high cost of acquiring customers renders many customer relationships unprofitable during the early years." The same can be true for direct mail fundraising or even special events, in which "profit" can be small to nonexistent early in the relationship. Reichheld sees businesses profiting when they can develop loyal customer relationships. "In later years, when the cost of serving loyal customers falls and the volume of their purchases rises . . . [many of these] relationships generate big returns." Were a business to fail to develop its customer relationships, it would not be realizing its full potential. The same can be said of a development program that has yet to encourage its best donors (and potential major contributors) to make the large gifts that will secure and expand the organization's horizons.

Case Studies & Strategies

Countless organizations experience dramatic changes in gifts raised after committing resources to TOP GIFTS™.

Janet Cady achieved such remarkable success in fundraising that her program was featured among the top four hundred charities in *The Chronicle of Philanthropy*. And for good reason: as president of the Children's Hospital Trust, Boston, she catapulted

Too Busy for the Major Gift?

When James H. Brucker, Ph.D., began as director of development at Penn State College of Medicine/Hershey Medical Center, he could see the potential for major gift fundraising. By developing and growing relationships, major donations could bring energy and excitement, and fulfill Penn State's most ambitious dreams.

Yet, Brucker says, "Cultural changes *can* be necessary when introducing a major gift focus to a development office. This was brought home to me soon after coming to Hershey. I met with a local donor who said his foundation could give us fifty thousand dollars, *if* we could deliver a proposal to him the following day. I went back to my office, put together the proposal, and went to find a staff assistant to help get it out. I had a difficult time because all of the staff was stuffing packets for a road run the following day that would net the medical cen-

giving from ten million dollars annually to over thirty million in just three years (see "Closer to the Cure" in chapter 1). "My staff has had to grow in order to create and build the relationships needed for a successful major gifts program," she says. "I now have nine major gifts officers totally dedicated to serving donors who want to help us realize our dreams in research and care."

Your leadership may be required to change the culture in *your* office. Take a lesson from Jim Brucker (see the sidebar "Too Busy for the Major Gift?").

Six Strategies to Refocus Your Attention

What can you do to shift your focus and invest more of your time in major and planned gifts? Here are six strategies to consider. Is there one or more that's right for you?

- Hire major and planned gifts staff to enable your organization to build more relationships, increasing your ability to secure more such gifts.

- Hire staff in direct mail, special events, or data administration . . . any of the other responsibilities that distract you. Free up more of *your* time for TOP GIFTS™ fundraising.

ter about two thousand dollars. I chose a person to help with the proposal, but this led to some concerns; it had never happened before, and she already had her assignments for the road run. It was not an easy transition into major gifts fundraising.

"This was a *great* lesson for our office—we dropped everything to meet the needs of a donor, even though that it meant that the routine of the office was thrown off a bit. Responding *quickly* to major gift donors is now a part of our culture. The fact that we received the initial gift of fifty thousand dollars certainly helped!" he concludes.

With Jim's leadership, tenacity and passion, the proposal *was* typed . . . *and the gift was made!* How would you and your office handle a similar gift opportunity?

- Outsource production of your mailings. Check with several charities to determine which companies provide the best value (service at the most competitive price). For even more freedom, outsource writing and design of the mailing pieces as well.

- If budget is an issue, look for a donor to underwrite costs for new staff or outsourcing. You'll be leveraging this gift many times over. Look for a forward-thinking individual who cares about the success of your organization and its future. This gift could be offered as a challenge (a concept described in more detail in chapter 6), creating leverage by matching new and increased giving to your appeal.

- Monitor your results; pare away at inefficiencies. Some organizations never delete names from their mailing lists. If an individual doesn't have a close affiliation with your organization or doesn't respond to mail appeals within three years, ask yourself if it is really worth sending them. Use the funds saved to hire staff or a consultant/company to make your programs more productive.

- For special events, establish a minimum dollar goal for each event, net of expenses. Eliminate those events that do not meet your goal.

- Add sponsorships and other approaches to dramatically increase funds raised by the event. If sponsorships already exist, determine if you can increase sponsorship fees or add new levels of sponsorships (see sidebar, *A $294,000 Difference!*, on page 71). If necessary give events two years to meet your minimum dollar goal. If the event fails the test, thank your volunteers for their limitless energy and gracefully retire the event. I know this may be difficult. For many organizations, each event often has a loyal and vocal constituency. Working with a development council or board, however, you can develop the political muscle needed to make the hard decisions. Manage your time so you and your volunteers can secure funds for your organization's most urgent and compelling needs.

A $294,000 Difference!

Improve the effectiveness of your special events by using sponsorships, advertising and other techniques to attract and secure top gifts. In this worksheet, Belinda Foster, Special Events Manager at Stamford Health Foundation (Stamford, CT) transforms a dinner which has trouble producing income to an event that is projected to net approximately $200,000 to $300,000. The secret to her success is in the revenue-generating sponsorships and ads (see Revenue, Options A and B). Unfortunately, ticket sales alone barely cover expenses.

Dinner Expenses

	Price	Number	Total
Catering	$125.00	400	$50,000.00
Valet Parking	$9.00	250	$2,250.00
Lighting	$500.00	1	$500.00
Flowers/ decorations	$150.00	40	$6,000.00
Entertainment	$4,500.00	1	$4,500.00
Invitations, Program Design	$4,000.00	1	$4,000.00
Printing	$15,000.00	1	$15,000.00
Postage	$0.24	11,000	$2,640.00
Awards	$500.00	1	$500.00
Miscellaneous	$3,110.00	1	$3,110.00

Cost per person - $222

Total Cash Expenses			*$88,500.00*

Items to be Donated

	Cost	Number	Value
			$0.00
Total Value of Donated Items			$0.00

Revenue

	Price	Number	Total
Option A			
Title Sponsor	$50,000	1	$50,000.00
Supporting Sponsors	$25,000	2	$50,000.00
Patron Table Sponsor	$10,000	5	$50,000.00
Table Sponsor	$5,000	10	$50,000.00
Ticket Sales	$250	210	$52,500.00
Full Page Ad	$1,000	20	$20,000.00
Half Page Ad	$500	30	$15,000.00
Option A Total Revenue			*$287,500.00*
Option B			
Title Sponsor	$50,000	2	$100,000.00
Supporting Sponsors	$25,000	4	$100,000.00
Patron Table Sponsor	$10,000	5	$50,000.00
Table Sponsor	$5,000	10	$50,000.00
Ticket Sales	$250	190	$47,500.00
Full Page Ad	$1,000	20	$20,000.00
Half Page Ad	$500	30	$15,000.00
Option B Total Revenue			*$382,500.00*

	Option A	Option B
Total Cash Expenses	$88,500	$88,500
Total Cash Revenue	$287,500	$382,500
Net Revenue (expense)	*$199,000*	*$294,000*

Every Donor *Is* Important

You may have heard stories about the hundred-dollar donor who later gives one hundred thousand or even one hundred million dollars to the same organization. How do these stories fit into TOP GIFTS™?

Perfectly.

Your goal should be to identify and cultivate a core group of individuals who show an interest in and confidence about making larger gifts to your organization. There's nothing like personal contact with your best potential donors to achieve this goal. What's the best way to manage your time and resources and cultivate the interests of people making smaller gifts? Ask your donors what's important to them.

Lessons from Our Hundred-Dollar Donors: I had hired an energetic and effective director of annual giving who had many ideas for encouraging donors of smaller amounts—say, twenty-five or thirty-five dollars—to give at higher amounts. Exactly what I was looking for. But some of her ideas seemed a bit lavish, such as giving each donor who increased to one hundred dollars a year a plaque with five date tabs, one to mark each year a gift was made. I didn't want to quell her enthusiasm, but I was nervous about launching an expensive program with an uncertain future. The answer? We asked small groups of donors what was important to them. Would they give us their time to help us in our decision making?

The results came from three focus groups of hundred-dollar donors. We asked several important questions. When you make a one-hundred-dollar gift to our organization, what do you expect in return? Would you be interested in receiving a gift from us, such as this plaque, to recognize your gift? How could we improve your relationship with our organization?

Their answers were wonderful! For a one-hundred-dollar gift, the donor expected a prompt response—a thank you card or letter from us within several days. (They commented how few organizations actually did this.) And they wanted to know how their gifts were being used. They liked our publications and the work we do. It was "okay to list my name in your donor reports, if you want to," but even that wasn't essential. They did, however, want *as much of their gifts as possible used to provide services.* "Don't waste our money on plaques," they said. "For a one-hundred-dollar gift, we don't expect anything like that." Most saw their gifts as "modest," and expected that we thank them modestly as well. A simple courtesy, such as sending out an acknowledgment letter in a timely manner, was all that was needed.

While they wanted us to keep our fundraising expenses to a minimum, they—much like donors of the largest gifts—truly appreciated the personal contact. Research by Tom Peters (author of *In Search of Excellence* and *A Passion for Excellence*) and others demonstrate that if you can exceed a "customer's expectations" in ways he or she values, you build a strong and resilient relationship. And it doesn't take much. From our focus groups, we learned that whenever we reached out in a personal and genuine way (such as a phone call to give an added word of thanks for a gift; a get-well card when we hear they're not feeling well; or a personal note to mark some occasion), it is both valued and appreciated. We found this to be true for donors of *all* giving amounts.

If time is at a premium, how do you accomplish this goal? The best development programs integrate "exceptional service" into the job descriptions of their staff, making it a hallmark of their programs. For example, assign your director of annual giving, another member of your staff, or, in smaller organizations, a top volunteer, the task of calling first-time contributors of one hundred dollars or more to extend those added words of thanks. Your donors will be pleased and surprised by the calls, often sharing these views with your staff and volunteer callers.

Some tasks can actually be scheduled: Each spring and fall, we send hand-signed letters from our president to donors who give one thousand dollars or more. Five hundred or more letters are generated, each with a personal salutation and an occasional P.S., to show we care. In the letter, our president talks about our organization's accomplishments, our dreams, and why the individual's interest, involvement, and support make this organization better. It makes a difference!

Invest some time in designing the *process* so you have more time for the people.

Take the Next Step . . . to TOP GIFTS™

Securing even a small number of top gifts can produce a sizable increase in what you raise. Take the next step. In the pages that follow, you'll discover that TOP GIFTS™ combines the best features of major gift fundraising, capital campaigns, and time management. TOP GIFTS™ is:

- A goal-setting process that encourages sound planning for each step of your journey;

- A tool for focusing your time and activities where you'll have the best chances of success;

- An opportunity to evaluate your organization's mission and, with success, renew and reenergize your board and staff;

- A process for identifying leadership for major and planned gifts, as well as top volunteer roles to strengthen and lead your organization (as members of your board and strategic planning or advancement committees, and in advisory roles);

- A way to optimize your organization's fundraising and program potential and communicate its most promising and urgent needs; and

- A way to recognize those donors who can transform your organization's future.

You'll Benefit Too!

On a personal note, TOP GIFTS™ fundraising offers the opportunity for a more fulfilling and rewarding career. Focusing your time on a relatively small number of potential donors enables you to create and cultivate relationships that are important to you and your organization. You'll discover that, as you get to know your best prospects and their interests, many will become not only good benefactors to—and potential leaders of—your organization, but also close and lasting friends. It's a natural and positive outcome that can make your job more exciting, satisfying, and rewarding.

## CHAPTER 3

THE PARETO PRINCIPLE

A relatively small percentage of donors can have a big impact. For many of the organizations profiled in *Dream Builders*, as few as one hundred donors were needed to reach 75 to 99 percent of their goals!

"It's not enough to be busy . . . the question is: What are we busy about?"

Henry David Thoreau

"Throw your heart over the fence and the rest will follow."

Norman Vincent Peale

TOP GIFTS™ fundraising is based on a research finding that's more than a hundred years old: the Pareto Principle.

In 1897, economist Vilfredo Pareto discovered the 80/20 rule (also called the Pareto Principle or the Principle of Least Resistance), which states that 80 percent of the benefit from most businesses or activities comes from 20 percent of its inventory or participants.

It's a simple concept that works in most areas of life. How often have you said, "On this committee, we have only a small number of people who do any work"? You're seeing a living example of the Pareto Principle. On a ten-member committee, for example, two people (20 percent) often are carrying much of the load (80 percent).

At your favorite restaurant, 20 percent of the menu items generate 80 percent of total sales. Eighty percent of your bank's business is likely to come from 20 percent of its customers. And 80 percent of the stock in this country is owned by 20 percent of all investors.

The Pareto Principle works in fundraising, too, but there's an odd—yet uplifting—twist. *A smaller percentage of your donors can have an even greater impact!* Instead of 20 percent of your donors generating 80 percent of the total funds you raise, many organizations are finding that only 5 to 10 percent of their donors are contributing 90 or 95 percent of the funds raised. When this principle is used sensibly and sensitively, it translates into more focused fundraising . . . fundraising that can leverage the best in your organization's mission and in your donors' potentials and aspirations.

Let me again emphasize the fundamental concept of the Pareto Principle:

Eighty percent of your fundraising total can come from 20 percent of gifts

and

The trend is for more money to be given by fewer donors!

Proven Time & Again

The basic concept of the Pareto Principle—that a relatively small percentage of donors can have a *big* impact—has been proven repeatedly in fundraising campaigns and annual appeals alike. For decades, the Pareto Principle has been a guiding tenet in projecting the goals and outcomes for many major fundraising campaigns.

Consider these statistics:

- The Michigan chapter of the National Kidney Foundation reports that 12 percent of its donors (131 donors) gave 83 percent of what was raised in one annual appeal;

- The Wilma Theater (Philadelphia, Pa.) revealed that 92 percent of its annual fund total came from 5 percent of its donors;

- At Abington Memorial Hospital, about sixty gifts were needed to reach a ten-million-dollar goal and, after the hospital increased its campaign goal, two donors gave the next six million dollars;

- College fundraisers know how to excel: In one survey of twenty-three colleges, 93 percent of total funds were given by 4 percent of donors; and

- Major and capital gift campaigns do incredibly well. For many of the organizations profiled in *Dream Builders*, as few as 35 to 110 donors were needed to reach 75 percent or more of their goals (see the sidebar on page 78: "What Can You Accomplish with About One Hundred Gifts . . . or Fewer?").

Adopt a Bias for Action

I'd like to share a story. I received a call one day from a newly-hired director of development, who asked if he could stop by to talk about the challenges he faced. I agreed.

"I've read your articles and attended your seminars," he said, "And I'm having trouble convincing my volunteers to use your approach. I've been on the job less than three months. I've barely had a chance to meet everyone and the trustees want

What Can You Accomplish with About One Hundred Gifts . . . or Fewer?

It truly is amazing the impact that a focused TOP GIFTS™ program can have. With about one hundred gifts, here's what some of the organizations profiled in *Dream Builders* have achieved.

Campaign, Organization	Funds Raised	# Gifts	% Goal	% Total Raised
New Ocean View Library Campaign, Friends & Foundation of the San Francisco Public Library	$485,000	60	182%	99%
A Proud Heritage, A Future Full of Promise, Topeka Community Theatre & Academy	$4,110,000	91	82%	79%
New Hope Initiative, Samaritan Inns	$6,008,000	49	125%	99%
Protecting the Future of Nursing, Abington Memorial Hospital	$9,624,000	35	96%	94%
Challenged to Lead, Pepperdine University	$298,750,000	100	99.6%	84%
With One Accord, The Anniversary Campaign, Princeton University	$564,110,000	110	75% (initial goal)	49%

These statistics underscore the importance of focusing on the small percentage of people and organizations (foundations, corporations, and government agencies) that can fuel and propel your campaign with their major gifts!

But there are differences in how you court a potential donor for a ten-thousand-dollar gift compared to a request for one hundred dollars. When planning a major gift solicitation, unlike a special-event or direct mail appeal, you're focusing on an audience of one, seeking to understand that person's interests and motivations, to create a warm relationship and match his or her interests with the needs, opportunities, and vision of your organization. In upcoming chapters of *Dream Builders*, I'll share findings from studies and comments from donors who tell us what prompted them to make large gifts (in one study, gifts of one million dollars or more) and what they look for when they're evaluating nonprofits and their needs.

to go out and ask for gifts of a million dollars or more. I told them that first I need time to plan things, to develop a vision, identify people, involve them, and cultivate their interest. *Then* we can ask. They didn't want to wait. They actually went out and asked for a million-dollar gift! Can you imagine? A million dollars," he said angrily.

"So what happened?" I asked calmly. "Did they get the gift?"

"Yeah, can you imagine that?" he said, amazed. "It's not supposed to happen that way. You said there should be a vision and a plan. That the potential donor should be involved with the organization. That we should get to know her interests. I didn't have any of that information."

In the next few minutes he explained that this million-dollar donor *had* been a board member for more than twenty years and loved the organization (no involvement?). The trustees knew that and had a project they were sure would interest her. *They* had the vision and the plan and were patient enough to wait for the new director of development to arrive before asking for the gift. When he said "wait," they were confident enough to forge ahead. . . . To take a chance. To succeed.

"What should I do?" the new director of development asked.

"Listen to your trustees and support them. They know your potential donors, your community, and your organization's needs better than you do. But you'll learn. Help them continue to search for those needs—opportunities—that can transform your organization's future. The needs and opportunities that can be shaped into requests for major gifts. Keep everyone's sights high, seek the very largest gifts possible. If you can't do that, they will continue to move forward, most likely without you. You'll be missing the most exciting kind of fundraising and you want to be part of it."

Perfection is *not* required. Remember Patton's Law: *A good plan today is better than a perfect plan tomorrow.*

What is your organization's vision, a reason why people should give money to you *today*? Does it have urgency? Are there people willing to invest in your ideas? These are among the questions we'll begin to answer.

The Most Efficient Campaign in History

There's an amusing story about the time that Andrew Carnegie was asked to give sixty thousand dollars to the New York Philharmonic Society. Carnegie was interested in seeing the society succeed, but he wanted it to begin developing other sources of gifts. So he replied that he would give half if the society could raise the rest.

The next day, society officials responded with great news: they had raised the matching funds required! Carnegie was amazed and impressed by the speed of the response. "So who matched my gift?" he asked.

"Your wife, Mrs. Carnegie," was the reply.

While certainly humorous, the story offers a lesson. By taking time to determine who cares most about your project, organization, and the people involved, you can quickly determine whom to ask for a major gift. One donor or a relatively small group of charitable investors may enable you to reach your goal.

Is the timing right for your organization to launch a TOP GIFTS™ program? Are you willing to commit the time needed to succeed?

"We are lost, but we are making great time."

World War II pilot

"The brain is a wonderful organ; it starts working the moment you get up in the morning, and does not stop until you get into the office."

Robert Frost

How you and the leadership of your organization spend your time is a prime indicator of your priorities and commitments. Stated mathematically,

Your use of time = Your commitment

The old expression "Time is of the essence" might be rephrased to read "Time *is* the essence"; where you invest your time determines the results you can expect. Some organizations have yet to invest time into shaping their vision for the future. As a result, key stakeholders in the organization (board members, managers, employees, and volunteers) lack a clear view of the organization's priorities or where they are headed in the future. Because there is no shared view, they are unable to communicate their needs effectively, and may be squandering resources and find it difficult to raise funds.

Sometimes, for these organizations, it takes a crisis or change in their environment to crystallize the actions that need to be taken not only to survive but also to grow in the years ahead.

By contrast, other organizations do not wait for a crisis. Instead, they clarify their missions (their purposes or why they exist), then define their aspirations through processes that range from brainstorming by top leaders to board retreats, strategic planning, and capacity-building programs.

The clearer your view of the horizon, the easier it will be to map strategies and the journey ahead. Take a few moments to assess your organization's readiness for a TOP GIFTS™ program by answering these questions relating to four elements: vision, value, visibility, and validity. Don't worry if you don't have "the perfect answer" for each element or question. What's important is that you begin to assess your organization, in order to determine both your strengths and areas in which you need to focus more attention. After answering questions for each element, write your assessment or overall score at the top of each section.

Then we'll use a brief exercise to focus on improving your personal commitment of time to TOP GIFTS™ fundraising.

Vision   Score_____

- How well can you describe your organization's vision for the future? Are your aspirations based on your organization's mission, purpose, goals, and resources? Write a brief paragraph (in words easily under-stood by someone not involved in your organization's work) on what you'd like to achieve during the next three to five years. Add a second paragraph that identifies how fundraising will enable you to realize some or all of your goals.

- What are the issues or obstacles blocking you from reaching your goals? Is it insufficient staff, volunteer leadership, expertise, facilities, or funding? List each item.

- Is your vision defined by:
    - ⊙ a formal planning process;
    - ⊙ a change in your environment;
    - ⊙ visionary management and/or board leadership;
    - ⊙ unmet needs?

- Is your vision understood by people in your organization? Have the people responsible for achieving these goals accepted the responsibility? Rate their level of passion or excitement for reaching these goals. Repeat the process for trustees and others who could make top gifts.

- If your vision is not clear and/or there is limited commitment to your action-plan, what would it take to build cohesion and commitment? Would your organization benefit from a new strategic planning or capacity building process (during which you assess areas that need improvement and then direct resources to them)? Is there sufficient interest and commitment to launch a planning process?

- Do you have visionary leadership? How is your top staff viewed by board members, the people you serve, and, if known, the people who could fund your dreams? How would you rate your board leadership? Do they instill confidence and command respect? Would someone's ability to give be viewed as a positive qualification (or a negative one) in your board nominating process?

Give yourself:

3 points if your organization has updated its mission statement during the past three years;

5 points if your organization has charted a clear path for its future and you can describe your plan for the future in writing;

8 points if your staff and trustees have accepted responsibility for and are excited to implement your organization's plans; and

10 points if all are committed to moving forward, the role of fundraising has been defined, and you have recruited visionary leadership and donors to your board.

Write your Vision score at the top right of this section (above).

Value   Score_____

- Who are the individuals and groups who care most about your organization and who might potentially make large gifts? If you have trouble answering this question, start by asking yourself: If we were to go out of business tomorrow, who would be negatively impacted? Which of your services have the greatest value, will be most important in the future, and would inspire people to give? How would the absence of your organization change peoples' lives?

- Is there a reason (or reasons) for someone to give now? Would a top gift help you respond to a crisis, meet an opportunity that would significantly expand your service horizons, or provide new or greater benefits to your target population?

- How easy is it for you to quantify the benefits you provide today? What are the pressures, if any, being placed upon you? For example, do you have three hundred requests a month for service with the ability to respond only to half that volume? How would additional funds (perhaps from fundraising) reduce or remove those pressures?

Give yourself:
5 points if you can identify individuals, groups, or constituencies who value your services and have the ability to give, and the services that are central to your mission;
8 points if you can define key supporters and services, and how fundraising could best enhance your organization; and
10 points if you have groups likely to support your mission, have identified key services, have a role for fundraising, and can effectively describe the benefits and improvements that can be gained through fundraising.
Write your Value score at the top right of this section (above).

Visibility   Score_____

- How visible is your organization to key leaders, including the people who could make large gifts (businesses, foundations, government agencies, and others)? Do they:
    - ⊙ know who you are;
    - ⊙ receive your publications;
    - ⊙ understand your purpose; and/or
    - ⊙ use—or know someone who uses—your organization?

- Do you have a connection with these key people through your trustees or other leaders?

- Have you differentiated yourself enough to convey your organization's role and importance (for example, are you the: largest nonprofit serving the homeless in Seattle; the museum with the largest collection of American folk art; the nursing education program with the highest percentage of graduates passing their RN boards; or the only environmental organization preserving open space in your neighborhood)?

- How well do you communicate both within and outside your organization? What communication vehicles already exist (such as meetings, newsletters, brochures, mailings, or Web page)? Are there obstacles to using these vehicles to improve awareness of your goals and fundraising efforts, or would you need to create new approaches?

Give yourself:
5 points if your organization is known by key constituencies;
8 points if key constituencies appreciate your unique roles and you communicate with them regularly; and
10 points if your organization's roles are well understood, you communicate with your audiences regularly, and you are able to use existing communications vehicles for fundraising.
Write your Visibility score at the top right of this section (page 84).

Validity   Score_____

- Is your organization willing and able to accept large gifts? Legally, are you tax-exempt? Do you meet all state and local laws for fundraising (registration, reporting, and so forth)? *Note:* If you do not have tax-exempt status or are unsure of registration and reporting requirements, please meet with an attorney specializing in charitable giving to address these needs.

- Are you open to questions about your effectiveness, ideas for improving your services, and suggestions for using donations?

Give yourself:
5 points if you are legally qualified as a nonprofit organization and meet state and local laws for fundraising;
8 points if you are legally qualified to raise funds and are open to questions and suggestions about your services; and
10 points if you meet legal qualifications, are responsive to inquiries, and publish an annual report and other document(s) that demonstrate your effectiveness and provide financial and statistical data.
Write your Validity score at the top right of this section (above).

If your organization scores well on these factors, you are in an ideal position. Organizations that excel in fundraising have clearly defined missions with boards, executives, and managers leading the process. They have focused their time by making a commitment to addressing the organization's top priorities.

If, on the other hand, your organization needs to address one or more of these items, take the actions required. Some funding organizations will assist you with grants for strategic planning, capacity building (including computerizing key functions), management development, a benefits analysis of your current services, and even a fundraising feasibility study. You must first, however, identify your organization's greatest needs.

Learn from successful organizations by committing your time where it matters most.

Are You Ready?

It's Monday morning, 8:00 A.M. You've invested time reading this book and have the best of intentions. "Today," you tell yourself, "I'm going to start developing a plan to improve my fundraising results." You have an extraordinary project, one aimed at bringing your organization to a higher level of service. And you have several volunteers in mind who can demonstrate some leadership. "I'll start by enlisting some volunteers to involve these individuals."

But then, before you know it, it's 5:30 P.M. and you have yet to make a single call to recruit your volunteers. Maybe tomorrow, you tell yourself, dragging a pile of mail from your office. You're exhausted by the many events and responsibilities you've taken on.

Sound familiar?

If it does, you're not alone. Whether you're a fundraiser, executive director of an organization, or president of a business or even a country, we all have pressures and responsibilities pulling at us, making it hard to concentrate on matters essential to our effectiveness. Consider the story about the late Dwight D. Eisenhower. When he was president of the United States, he instructed his staff to inform him only of "urgent and important matters." He quickly discovered that everything was "urgent" and devoted most of his time moving from one "crisis" to another. There was little time for the genuinely important. When Eisenhower discovered that busywork distracted him from his true business, he was able to refocus and redirect his energies where it mattered most.

Act presidential by devoting your energy where it matters most: TOP GIFTS™ fundraising.

Begin Simply

Take a major step forward by reserving at least thirty minutes a day—an hour or two, if possible—for TOP GIFTS™ fundraising. You'll then have the time to define and evaluate each of your organization's many needs, to stimulate awareness and educate people who are interested in your work, and to create and implement a major gifts fundraising plan . . . to focus on each step of TOP GIFTS™ (time, opportunities, people, goals . . .).

The best way to give yourself this time is to *schedule* thirty minutes or more each day on your calendar. Select a time when you're most productive, then write it on your calendar. Protect this time from encroachment. Begin by asking your secretary and/or co-worker not to interrupt you with phone calls or unscheduled visitors whose visits have little to do with fundraising. Close your door.

Every journey begins with a simple—but important—step. Consider this a visible sign of building commitment and success.

Your thirty minutes a day may be used for appointments to meet with key people in your organization who can help you define where fundraising can make a difference (often disguised as problems); for lunches, meetings, and activities involving individuals and families able to make large gifts; and for soliciting and recognizing major gift donors. The good news is that most of the eight steps in TOP GIFTS™ can be scheduled.

When dealing with people of influence and affluence, however, that's not always the case.

Make Your Best Prospects Your TOP Priority

You *will* need to be flexible with your schedule. When you are presented with an opportunity for a top gift, you may have to rearrange your calendar to answer a phone call or meet with a potential donor. And, given the pivotal role of a small number of key gifts, it will be time well spent. It's what you're working for.

Every day, countless transformational gifts are lost because donors do not receive the attention they are seeking and deserve. I've seen it dozens of times in my career because I was fortunate to receive these gifts after other charities had neglected to respond to someone who *wanted* to give. Here's one story of a six-figure gift that landed on my desk, just because I was there to serve.

William D. stopped by my office one day with a briefcase filled with stock certificates. "I plan to give half of these to your organization," he explained, "And the rest to my prep school." After valuing the stock and making his gift, he said he must be going. "I've called the school several times and they have yet to respond. I want to call them again today to tie up this gift." Jokingly, I said that if he had any trouble completing his gift to the school, I'd be happy to accept the remaining stock for my organization. He laughed. Then, a month later, he called and gave me the remaining stock. "I can't believe it," he said, frustrated. "I've called several times, even written to them. No one ever responded."

Be Sensitive to the Millionaire Next Door

Not everyone wears his or her wealth on his sleeve. Anyone who wants to help your organization deserves to be treated with respect and as the friend he or she truly is. I've had volunteers who donated their time to my organization later make gifts of $25,000, $250,000, $1,000,000, or more. The initial conversations usually are friend-raising versus fundraising—taking an interest in what they do, who they are, their dreams and challenges in life. Some of those dreams match the purposes of my organization, so the time invested is beneficial to our fundraising. The time and commitment of their volunteering are priceless.

But it all starts with being sensitive and respectful.

Surprises do happen, especially with planned gifts, such as charitable bequests and life income gifts. In fact, you'll receive large, outright gifts for needs that resonate deeply with the values and interests of some donors.

Some of your best gifts may come from people you'd never expect. Take for example,

- Raymond Fay, a retired chemistry teacher, never earned more than $11,400 a year. He wore clothes that were threadbare and lived in a broken-down apartment with no phone or TV. After he retired, he devoted the next twenty-six years to reading books, preparing a neat, three-by-five index card with a review of each book he read. When he died, nearly sixteen thousand cards were found in shoeboxes. He also left $1.5 million in conservative investments, and a will that directed everything he owned to the Philadelphia Library. At the time, it was the largest gift to the library in its 105-year history, a library staff member shared with me.

"You're Not My Favorite Charity"

Emma R. called one day to inquire about a program we offer that pays donors income for life. Despite her age (ninety-two), I found her to be very knowledgeable about these gifts and the way they worked. "When can you come to pick up my gift?" she asked. "How about tomorrow morning at nine o'clock?" I responded. When I arrived the next day and knocked on Emma's door, she opened it and said, "Mr. Costa, I'm so glad to see you. But I have to tell you, your hospital is not my favorite charity." Standing in the hallway of her retirement community, the best I could do was to say, "Oh?"

Yes, she replied, "I contacted Timothy's Missions [fictitious name]. I'm a great fan of Rev. Timothy, who has an evangelical television program. On his TV show, he advertises a toll-free number to call to learn more about these gifts. I called and no one responded. Then I got his magazine and filled out a coupon asking for information about this way to give. That was a month ago and I still haven't gotten a response. I called you yesterday and you're here. So you get my gift. Come on in. . . ." Emma made three of these gifts during the next year, all to a hospital that's "not my favorite charity."

What I haven't told you is that I had a meeting already scheduled that morning with my hospital's president. He understands the importance of service to individuals who are motivated to give. He was willingly to postpone our appointment so I could meet with Emma.

Hopefully, you'll respond and be available when your top gift contributors are ready to give.

- Osceola McCarty, an African-American woman who took laundry into her home and washed it on a simple scrub board to earn a living, made international headlines when she announced her charitable bequest to a southern university. Ironically, Ms. McCarty had never even stepped onto the college's campus prior to making the gift and would have been denied admission many years ago when she was of college age. "I just wanted to help the children," she explained. Ms. McCarty beamed when she met an African-American student who received the first scholarship (the college advanced funds so that Ms. McCarty could see the benefits her bequest will provide). Living in a simple home with few luxuries, a reporter asked, "Ms. McCarty, why didn't you use some of that money for yourself? Spend the money on something that would make you happy?" She responded, "I did."

- Stan Delp, a reading specialist in the North Penn School District (Pa.), had life-saving abdominal surgery at Abington Hospital. His neighbor, Ethel Bittle, had graduated from the hospital's school of nursing, worked as head nurse on its pediatrics unit, and later retired as acting director of the school of nursing. The two met through their local church and, eventually, joined together to endow a scholarship at the nursing school where Ethel had trained. "If you believe in something like we believe in Abington and education," says Ethel, "you become someone similar to a missionary for charitable giving." Stan agrees, adding, "My life was saved at the hospital. I'm happy to give back to the hospital." He adds, "My mother would give me my allowance as a nickel and five pennies so I could put a penny in the Sunday school offering. That principle of giving has lasted throughout my life."

Developing Relationships Takes Time

Debra Ashton, the author of *The Complete Guide to Planned Giving*, once told me, "For most organizations, the question is not 'Will we have a planned giving program?' Instead the real question is how much of a program are we willing to take on?" Debra understands that it takes time to develop a relationship on which a planned gift—or major gift—is based. The more time you invest, the more opportunities you have to build relationships and the potential for success. This time must be invested by top leadership (the president, executive director, development officer, and others). Many organizations have yet to make a commitment to hiring a fundraiser, whose chief responsibility is to attract top talent and gifts to the organization. In the absence of this professional, the executive director or president must commit to investing the time to establish and cultivate relationships that add meaning and value.

Seven Ways to Restructure Your Time

Are you having trouble scheduling at least thirty minutes a day for TOP GIFTS™? Here's how to regain control of your time.

1. Focus on the Important.

Take a lesson from Charles Schwab, who as president of Bethlehem Steel challenged consultant Ivy Lee to show him ways to be more productive. If the consultant was successful, Schwab said, he would pay him any amount within reason. Lee replied that, in less than a half-hour, he could show Schwab how to increase his productivity by at least 50 percent.

Each day, he said, prepare a list of the six most important things you need to get done, then prioritize them according to their value. Start the day by looking at the most important item on the list, then work to complete it. When the first task is done, move on to the second, moving down the list throughout the day. If you're unable to finish the list that day, Lee said, don't be overly concerned. You'll know that you directed your energy to the most important tasks.

Weeks later, Lee received a letter from Schwab, who said the technique was the most effective he had used. Enclosed with the letter was check for twenty-five thousand dollars. For the first time, Schwab later reported, he and his entire team were getting first things done first.

Building relationships is one of the most important steps leading to a top gift, and it's the "little things" that can make a big impression. Often, I carry note cards along with stamped and addressed envelopes with me when I am cultivating or soliciting potential donors. Immediately after the visit, I write a note to thank the individual either for a "wonderful gift" or for the time, then mail the card. By taking care of this task when it's fresh in my mind and having the cards readily available, I'm able to take action to make a favorable impression.

2. Just Say "No."

How much of your day is consumed with tasks that add little value to your organization or to you personally? One way to keep them off your desk is to not accept them in the first place. Practice saying "no" before you need to. Then, when you're forced to give a response, be diplomatic but firm in declining to accept new tasks.

If for whatever reason you feel you absolutely must say "yes" to a close friend or associate, define your priorities and set limits. For example, if you find yourself doing too many presentations to professional groups, tell yourself, "I'm going to limit myself to three presentations a year." Define what would be a priority. Then, when someone calls, evaluate if the presentation he or she is requesting falls within the priorities you established. Why am I tempted to accept this invitation? Is this a group that is important to me or my organization? How large an audience will I have? Will I have to invest considerable time in preparing for this presentation? If your assessment indicates that you must decline, politely say, "I'm flattered that you would ask. But I've had to limit myself to a small number of presentations a year, and I've already made several other commitments" (or, "I'm only speaking on topics that focus on major gifts"). You'll not only protect your time, but also select those presentations that are closest to your highest priorities.

3. Hire Carefully, Then Train and Delegate.

Best-selling author Robert Kiyosaki *(Rich Dad, Poor Dad)* defines leadership as bringing out the best in people. Yet many executives I know do not give their staff the opportunity to do their best. Instead, these managers and executives do most of the work themselves! They use excuses such as "It's hard to find good people" or "If I don't do it myself, it won't get done right." The reality is that many of these hard-working managers are unable to let go. In some cases, they set such high standards that it's virtually impossible for anyone else to reach them.

One cure is to hire the very best people with the required skills or, if not, people who can be trained in the tasks you want to delegate. Hire people who are personable, who have a work ethic, and who are "quick studies"—that is, people you can easily train. Hire people with qualities you admire, people who will take direction. Share your goals with them, as well as the specific tasks you use to get there. Indicate important performance standards. Be supportive. Praise them for excellent performance; coach them when the outcomes are poor. If you have the opportunity to hire, you're in an ideal situation to match the person with the tasks.

One course on interviewing points out, "Past behavior is the best predictor of future performance." When interviewing, seek information about the candidate's experiences that match the tasks or situations you require. "Tell me about a time when you were expected to carry out a major project. How specifically did you approach it?" Or, "Tell me about a time when you noticed the project was not going well. What did you do to correct the situation?" Use silence to your advantage. Give the candidate time to think to develop a response.

4. Learn How to Use Committees and Meetings Effectively.

Committees and meetings are important for building and maintaining relationships. But they also have disadvantages. On the positive side, working with committees you can create awareness, educate, build consensus and ownership, foster valuable relationships, solve problems, delegate work, and set deadlines. These are vital to the fundraising process. Without clear direction, however, committees can be unfocused and time-consuming. In politics, referring a topic to a committee can be used to delay, hide, or even kill it.

To maximize the effectiveness of a committee, define its purpose and create a job description for the chair and its members. Create an agenda for each meeting and bring members together only when work is to be done.

5. Look Back.

During the past few months, what projects, meetings, and activities were fruitless? Prune away the deadwood. Also, eliminate your name from listservs, bulletin boards, newsletters, and other contacts that add time but minimal value to your day.

6. Tame Your Desk.

To convert your desk into a productive tool, understand that it is designed as a work surface, not long-term storage. Susan Silver, author of *Organized to Be the Best*, asks that you think like an air traffic controller, with your desk as the runway. As traffic controller, you determine what papers and projects land, then clear the runways for further action. A simple storage technique is to have manila folders available and create files as needed. As this is a personal, temporary file, it's okay to write the project title on the tab, such as "Budget," then slip correspondence and memos in. While you're thinking of budgeting, schedule time on your calendar for follow-up action required.

7. Relieve Stress.

Most individuals underestimate the amount of time required to complete a project. To minimize stress (both on yourself and on others), double or triple your estimate of the time required. Break large projects into smaller, bite-size steps that are easier to delegate successfully or, as needed, complete yourself.

Look for other ways to relieve stress. For example, if you're commuting sixty to ninety minutes each way to work, are you able to move closer to shorten the drive or, perhaps, work at home one or more days a week? If paying bills each month is stressful to you, contact companies to see if they can help you simplify the process. Automatic "debits" from your checking account, online payments, or prepayments with discounts may be the answer. With two children taking music lessons, for example, I received two bills each month from the same company for instrument rentals. When I called the company, I discovered I could buy one instrument for less than a year's rental fees and receive a 15 percent discount if I prepaid six months rental expenses on the second. With two kids who love to play music (and a parent who finds the twenty-four bills a year a nuisance), I opted for these options, saving money and eliminating needless stress.

The more you can relieve stress, the healthier and fresher you'll feel, and the better able you'll be to enjoy your life and career.

TOP GIFTS™ WORKBOOK
Timing Assessment

Gauge your organization's stature on four qualities (vision, value, visibility, and validity), then identify areas of concern and where leadership is needed. Finally, assess your personal commitment to TOP GIFTS™ fundraising.

Your Organization

For each item, enter total score from the start of this chapter in the appropriate column.

	5 Needs work	8 Acceptable	10 Well positioned
Vision			
Value			
Visibility			
Validity			

Leadership

For each item above rated as "Needs work," determine what actions you need to take. Then assess how to advance those that are "Acceptable." Indicate the desired outcomes and completion dates for each action.

Action	Outcome	To be completed by
1.		
2.		
3.		

Your Commitment

Indicate your level of commitment to TOP GIFTS™

	30 minutes a day— **Good**	60 minutes a day— **Better**	Full Time with TOP GIFTS™ fundraiser—**Best**
Time scheduled on your calendar			

Your Time

Unable to commit thirty minutes or more a day? Chart specific actions you could take to regain control of your time. Estimate the time you'll save, then schedule it for TOP GIFTS™.

Action	Time Saved	TOP GIFTS™ Appointment Date
1.		
2.		
3.		

People give to have impact, to transform organizations, to be recognized. Identify the opportunities in your organization that will engage and excite your best donors. Develop programs to attract and recognize these gifts.

"It's not very difficult to persuade people to do what they already long to do."

Aldous Huxley

"The majority of large gifts I have seen were given because the gift was more than money—it was a gift of life, of education, of research, of gratitude, or any of the many different things that give meaning to our existence."

Charles F. Mai
Secrets of Major Gift Fundraising

All of us remember great dreams. Who hasn't heard the Reverend Dr. Martin Luther King Jr.'s "I Have a Dream" speech, which delivered a vision that challenged a nation? Or the words of the late President John F. Kennedy, when he committed the resources of the American people to "put a man on the moon" by the end of a decade? Or his vision of the New Frontier, which compelled millions to join the Peace Corps to serve in hamlets and villages throughout the world? These words stirred our hearts and minds to imagine that we could achieve great things. And we did.

Leaders of nonprofits have dreams and visions, too. Ed Piszek, a trustee with Little League Baseball, shared the league's dream that sportsmanship could serve as an ambassador of wholesome values, with the game extending far beyond U.S. borders to other nations, including his father's home country of Poland. He seized an opportunity by providing funds to enable Little League to work toward that dream through strategic planning and fundraising (see "Reigniting the Passion" in chapter 1).

David Erickson of Samaritan Inns changed his career (from an economics forecaster) to lead and expand the organization, enhancing its ability to offer stability to society's most fragile citizens by offering food and shelter, as well as drug rehabilitation and counseling. His goal? To help the homeless not only rebuild their lives but also give back to society (see chapter 1, "From Crisis to Opportunity").

Princeton University president Harold T. Shapiro recognized that exceptional teaching is at the heart of a great university and drew on Princeton's best traditions to fund and endow initiatives that strengthen and enhance academic excellence (see chapter 1, "The Anniversary Campaign for Princeton").

A nonprofit organization's dreams can be big or small. Yet, whether for a school or university, a homeless shelter or a volunteer fire department, they can have a big impact. Just ask Joseph Catino Jr., fire chief of the Liberty Hose Fire Company of Stockertown, Pennsylvania. Stockertown is a borough of just 687 people, but its population is rapidly growing. Catino's company realized a dream by completely funding its newest fire truck with a small number of top gifts. Catino understood how to motivate and reward business owners investing in his dream. Despite some controversy, Catino offered local businesses the opportunity to be recognized with a message on the truck. "We save kids' lives," he says with pride. Five businesses invested in his dream, covering the entire amount needed to purchase the fire truck.

Your vision, an image of your organization's best potential and the increased benefits you'll provide, is one of your greatest opportunities. In this chapter, we'll explore
the tools available to create a vision that elevates the role of your organization,
enabling it to have even greater impact.

In chapter 6, we'll explore a second kind of opportunity: programs, policies, and
techniques to consider using to make it easier for people to give, and to motivate and
recognize their best gifts. We're all familiar with buildings and programs named in
honor of donors, but you can also create sponsorships, membership programs, charter opportunities, and other strategies to trigger extraordinary gifts. By setting high
standards—often tied to a table of the highest gifts you are seeking (known as the
"table of gifts" or "gifts table")—you can give your supporters added reasons to excel
at making their largest gifts.

Create Big Dreams to Attract Big Gifts

The larger your dream, the bigger its impact, and the more compelling it will be to
potential major and planned gift donors. Indeed, research indicates that the wealthy
are seeking to leave their mark, to have an impact on an organization, often to help
you fulfill a need that might otherwise go unmet.

For example, HNW, an organization that provides data to high-net-worth marketers, reveals that the lack of a vision or perceived need is the second-highest obstacle to giving. Approximately one out of six wealthy individuals (16 percent) say that
"I have not found a compelling reason to give," a view that's even higher among
wealthy men (20 percent) and among individuals who earned their wealth from
technology (27 percent).

The need to demonstrate the benefit of giving to your organization is even more
important. Half of all wealthy say, "I am not confident that my donations will be
used in a productive way," a view that unfortunately is shared by 45 percent of the
general public. By clearly identifying your fundraising opportunities with projects
and programs that provide value to society, you'll be addressing two major concerns
of potential donors (providing a compelling reason to give, and addressing their lack
of confidence in how their gifts will be used). Equally important, you'll help build

interest in your cause by capturing the imagination of your best potential donors, and you'll lift your organization to excellence.

A Five-Step Process

You can identify your best opportunities for attracting top gifts by answering these five questions, which also represent the five steps in the identification process, each of which is described in detail on the following pages:

1. What is the best way to define your organization's most compelling needs? Among the four most effective ways are:

   - Response to a crisis, a change in your environment, or an emerging opportunity;

   - Change in leadership and/or significant event in your organization's history;

   - Priorities identified through capacity building and/or other rigorous planning process (including strategic, master, or facility planning); and

   - Equipment, project, or program need(s) considered as part of your budgeting process.

2. How will you educate and involve key constituents? Your choices include:

   - Existing board or committee; or

   - Newly formed board, leadership group, committee, or panel.

3. What are your specific fundraising priorities?

4. What techniques will you use to encourage and recognize donors?

5. What is your fundraising communications plan, including the messages you will deliver?

Step 1: Define Your Organization's Most Compelling Needs

Each organization is different. A planning process that succeeds for one organization may be resisted by another. As a nonprofit leader you'll want to assess the culture and political dynamics within your organization to determine which tool or opportunity offers you the best potential for success.

The previous section listed four ways to define your fundraising vision, and the specific steps for each approach are outlined in the table "Four Ways to Create a Dynamic Vision and Identify Fundraising Opportunities" (see page 102). More information on these possibilities can be found below.

Crisis, Change in Your Environment, or Emerging Opportunity

Many nonprofit organizations have grown stronger after confronting a crisis or a significant change in their environment. In most cases, the crisis is addressed by clearly defining the problem and its causes, then identifying specific strategies to deal with it. These strategies are prioritized and, from them, an action plan is developed to overcome the crisis and strengthen the organization. Fundraising often is one of the vehicles for making the action plan a reality. Facing a crisis can force an organization to pause, evaluate, and refocus. What is our mission, our core purpose and values? Are we living in the past or truly meeting today's needs? How has the crisis impacted our ability to survive or move forward? By stopping to consider its essence or value, an organization can make the adjustments required to realign itself with its purpose, create a common vision, and rally support.

Samaritan Inns of Washington, D.C., for example, was forced to address a change in its environment, which threatened the organization's source of clients and its viability (see chapter 1, "From Crisis to Opportunity"). Visionary leadership at Abington Hospital sought to avert a national labor shortage at the local or community level (see chapter 1, "Protecting the Future of Nursing"). Both organizations are stronger today as a result of the process and the outcomes of both planning and fundraising.

FOUR WAYS TO CREATE A DYNAMIC VISION
& IDENTIFY FUNDRAISING OPPORTUNITIES

Response to a Crisis	Change in Leadership	Planning/Capacity Building	Budget Request
1. Dynamic leader defines problem, champions cause. 2. Committee/task force takes responsibility for addressing issue. 3. Situational analysis completed, options or responses developed, goals and objectives set. 4. Action plan written, including fundraising goals. 5. Plan implemented, including identification of key potential donors and solicitation of top gifts.	*Leader Who Is Leaving* 1. Leader contacted, consents to fundraising in his/her honor. 2. Leader suggests projects that will benefit; reviewed and approved by organization's leadership. 3. Tribute committee(s) formed to plan events, raise funds. 4. Plans implemented, including identification and solicitation of top gifts. *To Recruit New Leader* 1. Development council enlisted. 2. Purpose of fundraising defined (e.g., New Ventures Fund). 3. Action plan written, including fundraising goal. 4. Council and staff implement plan including identification of key potential donors and solicitation of top gifts.	• Organization's leadership makes a commitment to strategic planning or capacity building • Planning committee established with key stakeholders represented. *For Strategic Planning* 1. Mission, vision, and values updated. Situation assessment completed. Organization's strengths, weaknesses, critical issues defined. 2. Strategies, goals, and objectives developed. 3. Action plan written, including fundraising goal(s). *For Capacity Building* 1. Specific element(s) targeted for improvement (elements are aspirations, strategy, organizational skills, human resources, systems and infrastructure, organizational structure and culture). 2. Analysis completed, options or responses developed, goals and objectives set. 3. From goals developed, identification of fundraising opportunities, goals (if any). *For Both Strategic Planning & Capacity Building* • Development council enlisted. Council and staff create fundraising plan, including identification and solicitation of key potential donors for top gifts.	1. Organization's leadership agrees to use contributions for budgeted equipment and program needs (or for needs that are unbudgeted). 2. Specific needs are targeted for consideration as a fundraising goal. 3. Development council enlisted. 4. Council selects equipment/project need for which it will raise funds, sets goal. 5. Council and staff identify key potential donors and solicit top gifts.

Supply Side Philanthropy

There are times when the need or vision will be identified by someone you serve and may emerge as—or be shaped into—a gift opportunity.

"Donors wants to be involved and to express themselves through their gifts," says Gene Tempel, executive director of the Center on Philanthropy at Indiana University, in the article "Fundraising: Obstacles and Opportunities" that appeared in *Commonfund Quarterly*. "Paul Schervish's model of supply side [versus demand side] philanthropy helps us understand the dynamics of working with many major donors today. [Paul Schervish is a professor of sociology and director of the Social Welfare Research Institute at Boston College.] In the demand side model, an institution enlists donors to support its goals or projects; in other words, it's a cause in search of donors. At the extreme, the supply side model is donors with ideas in search of institutions to implement them. The fundraiser's role is to mediate between these two positions. The . . . supply side model will likely cause organizations to behave differently. . . . The new model says, 'What would you like to do with your money, and is there a way in which it can be done through our organization?'" Tempel believes that "The key to successful fundraising . . . [is] a focus on relationship building and the ability to forge real partnerships between donors and institutions."

Supply side fundraising is embraced by many donor-advised funds and community foundations, including the Columbus Foundation (Columbus, Ohio). In chapter 10, Jim Luck, who served as the foundation's president, describes the process for identifying each donor's interest.

A practical example of supply side philanthropy could involve a hospital that has outgrown its dialysis facilities. A patient who is unable to receive treatments during daytime hours asks the hospital to double its number of treatment stations, which would enable him and others to live more normal lives. The hospital determines the costs to expand and equip a larger facility, and the patient responds by underwriting these costs.

To paraphrase an old saying, fundraising opportunities are often disguised as problems. Some organizations are not open to exploring these opportunities with potential donors and, instead, point to the formal budgeting process as the only way to prioritize needs. Others carefully evaluate the request to determine if it will enhance the organization's effectiveness. You and your organization's leadership need to determine which path you will take as you evaluate each gift opportunity to determine if the donor's view of the future is consistent with the best interests of your organization.

A Change in Leadership and/or Significant Event

You can tap into the positive relationships with a beloved leader or a milestone event for your organization to reconnect with people who have built—and/or benefited from—your organization.

Your fundraising may honor a senior staff person (president, CEO, dean for a college, etc.) or a volunteer dedicated to your organization. This individual may be retiring, or leaving your organization for other reasons (another position, health, etc.). When funds are directed to a project or program related to the individual, the reason to give can be most compelling. It could be a program or project the individual championed, one that was central to his or her career, or one endorsed by the honoree as vital to your organization's success. Both as policymakers and potential donors, your top management and board should agree that the project selected will enhance your organization's mission.

One recent success story focused on a university trustee who announced his retirement from the cable industry. With his permission, his university solicited funds to establish an endowment in his name for expanding its communications program, specifically in areas involving cable communications and the Internet. Two of his business associates made lead gifts to honor his leadership in the industries.

When a physician who was the architect of a vibrant medical education program retired, an endowment fund in his name was established to stimulate learning and protect the program from government funding cutbacks. Income from the endowment has since funded guest lectures, the purchase of handheld computer devices with software for alerting doctors to harmful drug interactions, and annual awards to recognize top medical residents . . . all carrying forward the name of this pioneering doctor.

When a top leader already has left an organization, there can be a second opportunity for fundraising. One research organization actively recruiting a new president, for example, is seeking major gifts to establish a ten-million-dollar Innovations Fund. The fund will help attract the very best candidates by giving the new president resources to set up laboratories, provide research assistants, and have dollars readily available to quickly seize opportunities that will elevate research programs.

In rarer cases, the leader need not leave in order to motivate major gifts. A donor stepped forward with a gift of $2.5 million to honor Bette E. Landman, Ph.D., president of Arcadia University, so that the new library could be named in her honor.

When a key person associated with your organization dies, some donors may express interest in creating a living tribute or memorial. Facilities or programs may be named or endowed as a way of carrying forward the individual's name. A doctor who dedicated his life to a medical education program, for example, could have a proposed conference center named in his honor. Your boardroom could be named in honor of a trustee who passes away. It's important to match the visibility of the naming with the level of funds raised and the amount of impact this individual had on your organization.

Commemorating anniversaries and other significant milestones also can encourage top gifts. Many organizations have launched campaigns—or completed them—to coincide with 25th, 50th, 75th and 100th anniversaries. Themes such as the *Diamond Campaign* (for seventy-five years) or *Centennial Fund* have promoted these milestones. On the occasion of its anniversary, an art museum solicited top gifts to purchase several key French impressionist paintings to fill a major void in its collection. Supporters saw the event as an opportunity to improve an already extraordinary collection, personally have impact on the museum, and add to the celebration.

A milestone at Princeton University, the 250th year since its founding, helped launch the largest campaign in the university's history, achieve record-setting goals and participation levels, and secure the organization's future for priorities identified through a strategic planning process (see chapter 1, "The Anniversary Campaign for Princeton").

Priorities Identified Through Strategic Planning or Capacity Building

A third source for your fundraising vision is to select priorities from a new or existing strategic plan or from efforts dedicated to capacity building. In some organizations, planning may be directed toward a master, facilities, or long-range plan. Regardless of its name, for our purposes, each planning model consists of a careful analysis of the actions your organization must take in order to maximize its success in the future. Your task is to select specific priorities and goals that best motivate your potential donors and advance your organization's aspirations.

In the largest campaigns, opportunities are often selected to meet the interests of a variety of donors. Select several priorities that are likely to be alluring to your best potential contributors. A small college, aquarium, zoo, museum, environmental organization, or other nonprofit with education programs, for example, may choose to raise $1.5 million for a new library or visitors' center; $1 million for an endowment for salaries and fellowships; and $500,000 for a new technology program that places research and information in front of students and members, all as part of a $3 million campaign. Before launching a campaign, I like to test each priority to determine the interest levels and responsiveness among potential top contributors. This can be done through informal conversations, which present the priorities as "ideas we're considering. How do you think people will respond to each of these priorities? Is there a priority that you would one day be interested in supporting?"

Involve your donors as partners in the planning process, as members of the planning committee, as sources of ideas in defining and prioritizing needs, and as potential investors through their gifts.

Capacity Building

Some nonprofits are seeking to build organizational strength and resilience through "capacity building," described by Venture Philanthropy Partners as "building up their organizational muscle . . . help[ing] nonprofits become stronger, more sustainable and better able to serve their communities." In capacity building, you select and address one or more of these seven elements: your organization's aspirations; strategy; skills; human resources; systems and infrastructure; structure; and culture. For example, your goal may be to align your organization's strategies (one of the seven elements) with your aspirations or vision. This may benefit you in at least two ways. First, you could discontinue those programs that do not contribute to your mission; and, second, you could free up resources that could be used to better respond to changes in your environment or to seize new opportunities.

Two national organizations focusing on capacity building are the Nature Conservancy, the largest private conservation group in the United States, and Second Harvest, which distributes more than four hundred million pounds of bulk food each year, aiding more than fifty thousand soup kitchens, shelters, and church programs in feeding the hungry.

A major obstacle facing the Nature Conservancy was its federation-like operation; each state office was somewhat independent. To improve its effectiveness, a commitment was made to establish a common vision and goal for its many offices. The results were dramatic. A report prepared for Ventures Philanthropy Partners assesses the social impact as follows: "The Conservancy was able to develop new organization-wide initiatives, such as Last Great Places; improve the recruiting and retention of top-talent, and conduct more coordinated and aggressive fundraising campaigns. . . . The Conservancy has improved its performance on biodiversity indicators, and its revenues, staff, and the number of offices have tripled. Membership has more than doubled. Its traditional land protection activity—both through acquisition and other protective tools, including partnerships—now exceeds a million acres a year. Thanks to the unified goals and the common vision of success."

Second Harvest addressed another of the seven elements: its organizational structure. Second Harvest seized an opportunity to grow by merging with Foodchain, the country's largest food-rescue organization (transporting perishable or prepared foods to the hungry), rather than trying to build this expertise and compete with an already successful nonprofit.

A "Messy" Process?
One planning expert describes strategic planning and capacity building as "messy," because surprises may very well occur as the organization's leaders examine long-standing core beliefs, values, and principles. To be truly visionary, organizations may be forced to embrace change—admittedly a difficult process. For example, according

to the *Chronicle of Philanthropy*, when the Ohio Center for Science and Industry was planning a simple addition to its building during the early 1990s—a project deserving of community support—questions surfaced in the strategic planning process. One leading philanthropist challenged the organization by asking, should we merely add onto our current facilities or, instead, relocate to a riverfront location under development in the state's capital? How would a totally new facility help redefine and reinvigorate the center?

"What began to evolve was a new concept for Ohio's 21st-century science-technology center. . . . It was really time to take a risk in order to engage the future in a very different way," explains Roy L. Shafer, then the center's president, who led the planning process. The donor who challenged the board to go beyond a simple expansion, later donated six million dollars to erect a temporary pavilion for the museum and to pay for its move to the new facility. By changing the focus from *a building expansion program* to *an opportunity to shape and embrace the future*, the museum rediscovered its purpose and is in a stronger position to better influence generations of visitors to come.

And how does the donor feel about this level of giving?

"When I make a gift, do I really feel terrific?" asks Leslie Wexner, business-builder of the Limited and other apparel stores. "If I don't feel terrific, I know I haven't given enough."

Needs Considered as Part of Your Budgeting

Although grand visions of the future may very well stimulate the most interest and excitement among your donors, fundraising opportunities also can be identified through your annual budgeting process. This may be a more limited view (one year) of your organization's future and the resources dedicated to achieving it.

Some organizations incorporate fundraising projections into their annual budget, then select specific items from the budget deserving of support (such as equipment items, renovation projects, research initiatives, programs, etc.). A second approach is to select priorities that did not survive the budgeting process, then use gifts to extend the organization's impact and reach. Regardless of the approach you select (budgeted versus unbudgeted), start by carefully sifting through the requests, then select several needs that are of significance to your organization and offer the best fundraising potential. You'll later review your findings with key constituencies (see "Step 2," below).

Your role is much like a portfolio manager, arranging a union between your organization's major priorities and likely investors (i.e. potential donors). In this matchmaking process, you can be most effective when you understand the interests of potential donors. Some individuals will share their giving interests with you as they tell you about their relationship with your organization. A few foundation and corporate leaders, for example, have told me that they like to create new programs that

What's Your "Elevator Pitch?"

David S. Newburg, Ph.D., is a program director at the prestigious Shriver Center of the University of Massachusetts Medical School (Waltham, Mass.). Part of his time is devoted to securing grants from corporations, foundations, and government agencies to support his research.

"When I contact a program officer for the first time, I may only have one to five minutes to pique his or her interest. I open with my 'elevator pitch,' which is a succinct description of the program or project for which I'm seeking funds and why the project is important. If there's interest, then I'll get more time to describe the project. Without the elevator pitch, however, I may never get that opportunity."

Dr. Newburg first researches each funder to learn its interests and priorities. "This is not only important to focus my time on those organizations where there's a common interest, but also helps to shape my message. It's individualized for each prospect. If a government program is interested in 'Public Health,' I want my elevator pitch to show how my research favorably impacts health. For a large corporation, my elevator pitch may focus on the research's potential for improving a product they already offer. Take time to think through the strengths and impact of your project. Identify your best potential funding sources and study their funding priorities. Define your project in terms that emphasize your funder's interests. What you propose should sound like something they want to achieve."

What if a program officer has no interest in your project? "It can still be a productive contact. I might ask 'Do you have any ideas who else might be interested in supporting this project?' Often, I'll receive a lead for another foundation or government agency that is a better fit with my research goals."

serve as models for others to follow, or to take a model program to the next level, extending its benefits to a larger audience. These opportunities can emerge during budget reviews.

Janet Cady, president of the Trust for Children's Hospital (Boston), said, "When I arrived at Children's, I was amazed at the truly significant work being done by doctors and researchers. Yet, few people were aware of it. I decided that we could be more effective in funding these programs by bringing those who were motivated to give—often parents of the children we serve—in close contact with the physicians on the frontiers of medicine" (see chapter 1, "Closer to the Cure").

A Test

As you evaluate your organization's needs—through your operating and capital budgets, your strategic plan, or problems and feedback from your customers—look for specific programs, equipment, projects, and staffing needs that offer impact. To hone your skills, take the following test.

What's Right for Your Organization?

Throughout Dream Builders, *we'll be reviewing examples of fundraising opportunities with needs ranging from as little as $267,000 to more than $1.14 billion. With such a wide range, it's clear that the amount of a major gift will vary greatly from one organization to the next. But the principles behind their successes are the same. If the amounts being discussed in any example feel too small or too big, don't be afraid to add or remove zeroes to the numbers. A campaign seeking to raise one hundred thousand dollars or one million dollars needs leadership just as much as a campaign for one hundred million dollars. If necessary, adjust the examples so they are a comfortable fit for your organization.*

Imagine that you are the executive director or vice president of development launching a new TOP GIFTS™ program for each of the following organizations. You would like to select one fundraising priority. For each organization, which project would you choose to communicate to potential donors?

Library: You have the choice between raising $25,000 for new bookcases for an entire wing or establishing a $75,000 computer center where students can learn new skills and the entire community can access information on the Internet. Which need or opportunity do you think would be more attractive to potential donors? If you were asked to make a gift, which would attract your interest and enthusiasm?

Your answer:　□ Bookcases　　□ Computer Center

Food Bank/Social Service Agency: You are facing a $100,000 deficit in your operating budget next year and an unmet goal of your strategic plan is to invest $500,000 to expand your facilities, which will enable your organization to serve twice as many people. Your board believes that fundraising is the answer to both these challenges.

Your answer:　□ Deficit Financing　　□ Expanded Facilities

Hospital: You need to replace fifty beds, but are also considering a new program to harvest and freeze blood, which will help protect your community from blood shortages.

Your answer: ☐ Beds   ☐ Frozen Blood Program

College: Your college has several plans with potential. The first is establishing a new business program in international studies, which would require endowing the salary of a new professor. Another need is to fund or endow the salary of a staff person to organize and run a mentoring program for disadvantaged children that would both give these kids a role model (the mentor) and introduce them to your college and career opportunities. Finally, the soccer coach would like a new playing field; the college has the land, but no funds to develop the field.

Your answer: ☐ New Business Program   ☐ Mentoring Program

                ☐ Soccer Field   ☐ More Than One Need

For the above examples, the best answers clearly will come from your donors. Later, I'll explain how to get their views on what interests them most. In the meantime, here are my ideas:

Library: Typically, the new computer center would excite donors more than new bookcases.

Food Bank: The building would be a better investment for gifts from several donors. However, you could easily make the case to a small number of your best prospects for major gifts to resolve the deficit. This problem must be overcome before the organization can take on more debt for facilities.

Hospital: The frozen blood program would have more appeal than replacement beds.

College: Great choices; as a donor, depending on my interests (business, education, sports), I might be enticed to support any of the three. What did you decide?

Step 2: Select & Involve Key Constituents

Nearly all the Visionary Organizations profiled in *Dream Builders* leveraged the effectiveness of their visions by engaging top volunteers, staff, and potential donors in the planning process. In nearly every case, a new group was formed or an existing group greatly expanded to provide greater access. Invite your best potential donors to take a front-row seat and participate in discussions that can favorably impact your organization. You can do the same to build awareness and shared ownership.

For some organizations, this leadership may already be on your organization's board. Others may need to recruit additional people with leadership qualities. Carefully evaluate if current board members have the interest, talent, and financial ability to lead an effective TOP GIFTS™ program. If not, it may be necessary to appoint a separate board or committee (it also may be called a foundation board,

Engaging Key Leaders

Here's how these Visionary Organizations found ways to increase the scope and depth of their fundraising leadership and donor groups. In most cases, new committees were established bearing such prestigious names as a blue ribbon panel, philanthropic leadership councils, strategic planning committee, or development board.

Abington Memorial Hospital	New blue ribbon panel formed
Children's Hospital (Boston)	New trust board, philanthropic leadership councils
Little League Baseball	New campaign committees
Oceanview Library (Friends & Foundation of the San Francisco Public Library)	New development committee
Pepperdine University	New university board Expanded size of—and opened eligibility to—existing board of regents
Princeton University	New committees for strategic planning and campaign
Samaritan Inns	New development foundation board
Topeka Civic Theatre & Academy	New campaign committees

trust, advancement committee, campaign committee, etc.) whose sole focus is setting the direction of—and implementing—your organization's fundraising plan.

The advantage of creating a new board or committee is that you will be able to select members of the team whom you believe are most capable of getting the job done. Not surprisingly, many of the Visionary Organizations created new structures to involve top leadership. These approaches are identified in the chart "Engaging Key Leaders," and discussed in more detail in chapter 7, "People."

Honoring a Leader or Occasion

If you are creating a committee to honor a leader who is retiring or departing for another reason, identify the leader's "inner circle" of friends and colleagues who can make or influence large gifts and/or serve on one or more committees. Privately, the leader may feel comfortable suggesting the names of these individuals, as well as the type of events that he or she prefers to attend and the project(s) for which he or she would encourage gifts. Your committees can assist in planning events, as well as making and soliciting the largest gifts. It's important to involve and engage the leader's circle of friends in fundraising, as many honorees feel awkward personally raising funds when they are receiving so much recognition.

A committee for an anniversary event should be multitalented, with representatives from your major constituencies (including fundraising) and individuals who enjoy the excitement intrinsic in hosting a celebration. A milestone campaign is *The Anniversary Campaign for Princeton*, which honored the 250th anniversary of the school's founding. The university not only celebrated its considerable achievements, but also sought to shape its future by initiating a rigorous strategic planning process and an ambitious campaign that is profiled in *Dream Builders*.

Step 3: Decide on Specific Fundraising Priorities

Whether you engage an existing board or establish a committee or panel, you can build a sense of ownership of your fundraising project by involving members in prioritizing your fundraising needs.

This can be done by having one or more members of your staff make a brief presentation about each of the priorities or needs you are recommending as the focus of your fundraising. Include an overview of the need, a description of who would benefit, and statistics that demonstrate the potential impact and cost.

For most organizations, the development council or campaign committee:

- analyzes a minimum of three to five programs, equipment, or other funding needs that you recommend;

- assesses the value of each to the institution;

- considers the specific requests people would most likely support; then

- selects the needs or priorities for which it will seek top gifts.

A new TOP GIFTS™ program with a limited number of potential donors may decide to select one major priority with the greatest appeal. For a major campaign with a larger base of potential donors, select several funding priorities to be able to better meet your donor's funding interests.

Step 4: Techniques to Encourage & Recognize Donors

Successful fundraisers know that they can attract larger gifts by offering opportunities for recognition and by making it easy—and attractive—to give. In chapter 6, you'll find a library of many of the most effective programs, policies, and techniques. Learn from marketers by asking your best prospects which of these programs interests them most, then tailor your messages and appeal accordingly.

Step 5: Create Your Fundraising Messages & Materials

The perception of your organization and its fundraising program can have a major impact on how much money you raise. By taking the time to create and implement a communications plan for your TOP GIFTS™ program, you can help ensure that your best potential donors are aware of your needs and have sufficient information to justify making a top gift. The amount of effort you invest depends on the amount of funding you hope to raise, the number of potential donors, and the messages and images you want to convey.

Elements of Your Communications Plan

You've probably heard stories about a highly motivated college president, healthcare CEO, sports coach, or other nonprofit executive who has called upon selected prospects and raised a million dollars or more. I recall one story in which a successful college president made his personal visits armed only with a notebook that described his vision for his institution and how forty million dollars in donations would make it all possible. His personal attention to each of his 120 or so donors made the simple notebook come alive. A year later, the funds were raised.

In another case, a CEO used a sketch of a new building with the prospect's name engraved over its front entrance to help the individual see how his family's name would assume a prominent place in the institution's history. The result: a four-million-dollar gift.

Neither of these approaches involved expensive four-color printing or costly design. They worked because their messages were focused on the individual donor, essentially tailor-made. Indeed, the simplicity of the materials—a notebook with pages that could be changed and a sketch of an architect's vision of a new building— invited the individuals to ask questions and become involved and invested in the fundraising process.

There are seven elements to an effective communications plan:

1. *Shared Goals:* Analyze what you want your fundraising communications plan to accomplish. *Certainly your foremost goal is to raise funds and the role of communications is to increase your chances of success before, during, and after the request for a top gift is made.* But it can also improve the awareness, stature, or prestige of your organization. The goals you select will impact how your messages are shaped, what you spend on communications materials, and other elements of the plan. It's best to put your communications plan in writing and circulate it for discussion and approval by your president and members of your development/campaign council.

2. *Well-Targeted Audiences:* The better you can define your audiences, the clearer your messages will be. Start by naming the *groups* that have top gift potential. These might include trustees, donors who already give above a certain level, support groups to your organization (such as alumni and auxiliaries), foundations, and others. Many of these groups could use the same communications materials (such

as a campaign theme, logo, case statement, etc.). But there may be some, such as foundations or donors of your top five gifts, who will require custom-made strategies and materials (e.g., proposals, architect's renderings). List both the groups to whom you will appeal and the TOP GIFTS™ prospects who require individual strategies.

3. *Carefully Tailored Messages:* Take time to convert your needs into giving opportunities . . . messages that speak to the audiences you've identified, that inspire your donors. Study the TOP GIFTS™ Communications Planning Charts at the end of this chapter, then develop messages and select tools that respond to the interests of your audiences. Look for audiences with special needs. For example, when Little League Baseball was seeking a three-million-dollar state government grant, it emphasized increased tourism and economic development, messages marketed differently from those used to approach foundations that establish Little League programs and facilities in the inner city to counteract drug abuse and youth gangs. What you say to a successful local businessperson may differ greatly from what you say to a donor who gives primarily to religious organizations.

4. *An Effective Strategic Action Plan:* Inventory your current communications materials (e.g., newsletters, annual report, Web page), meetings, and events to determine what roles they could assume in reaching your target audiences. For trustees, for example, you could make fundraising reports at regularly scheduled meetings, include information in board mailings, or showcase your campaign at an annual meeting. Then determine what new materials and events need to be created to meet your goals. Among the tools are: logo, case statement, campaign stationery, pledge card or letter of intent, brochures, newsletters, construction site signs, and information on Web pages. Events include a kickoff party, solicitor training sessions, cultivation meetings, and groundbreaking and dedication ceremonies. Choose the tools and events that best enable you to reach your goals and secure top gifts.

5. *Communications Timetable:* Time your communications to enhance the effectiveness of your solicitations. Begin by mapping out when you want to solicit each of your audiences, then schedule your communications so information is

received before the solicitation. You want messages from your printed materials and events to be fresh in the minds of your prospects. If, for example, you want to solicit trustees during November and December, you might have the following schedule:

August: Mail planning study results to trustees

September: Present planning study findings to board; secure board approval; name Campaign Chair and Subcommittee Chairs; secure board approval

October: Hold first Campaign Steering Committee meeting; conduct solicitation training; assign trustees to solicitors

November: Complete gift requests

During August, your fundraising materials can be prepared, including a case statement, brochure or booklet, pledge cards, stationery, and even flip charts for trustee solicitations, all in advance of your November gift requests. If multiple people are involved in implementing the communications plan, prepare a simple chart that lists, month-by-month, the required activity (e.g., write fundraising brochure) and the person responsible for the task (e.g., director, fund development). A written work schedule not only communicates responsibilities and deadlines, but also enables you to track progress, be alert to obstacles, stay focused, and move forward.

6. *Budget:* It's wise to get approval for your communications plan *before* you are actively fundraising. In that way, you will not need to devote time defending each expenditure and modifying the plan when you are actively soliciting contributions. If you decide to use a communications consultant, ask this professional to provide estimates for each new activity or event that is part of your plan.

7. *Donor Recognition:* For most organizations, donor recognition should be part of your communications plan. It signifies your organization's appreciation for a top gift and lays the foundation for future gifts. Recognition may consist of publishing a feature article and photo in your organization's publication, dedicating a plaque, or holding a recognition event (such as groundbreaking ceremony, plaque dedication, presidential reception, luncheon or dinner, etc.).

TOP GIFTS™ WORKBOOK
Creating the Dream & Communications Planning Charts

Using the thirty-minute appointments you've scheduled and other time you can make available, complete the TOP GIFTS™ workbooks for *Creating the Dream* and *Communications Planning Charts*.

Starting with *Creating the Dream*, obtain information on those sources that are relevant to your organization, then identify and rate priorities or needs that have fundraising potential. List specific priorities with the highest ratings, then research three or more projects you believe are the most important and compelling.

For each priority, briefly explain in newspaper terminology ("the five *W*s and how") *what* the need is (including costs); *why* it is important; *when, where,* and *how* you plan to address it; and *who* will benefit. This description will be most useful in your presentation for top gifts, whether you're personally asking individuals and community leaders, writing a foundation proposal, preparing a letter to confirm your request, preparing a brochure or news story, or presenting in other ways.

On your *Communications Planning Charts*, you'll shape your messages into a theme or logo, and transform your needs into opportunities for donors to have impact. The goal is to refine your messages to make them compelling, exciting, and easy to understand.

A fundraising program for scholarships for training men and women in the religious life, for example, might have the theme *Ordinary People Doing Extraordinary Things* or *Caring Lives*. An appeal for new classrooms, renovated and expanded libraries, and endowments for student scholarships and faculty salaries could be described as *Changing Lives* or *The Campaign for Greatness*. A cancer center with a major research focus may communicate *Discovery, Hope* through its theme.

Some colleges and universities have mined the wellspring of positive emotions tied to their names. Their alumni have responded to themes as direct as *The Campaign for Smith* or selected words from memorable speeches or their school songs. For example, Princeton University's song includes the words "with one accord," which was part of the theme of its $1.14 billion campaign. Princeton reinforced its theme with booklets that rekindled feelings toward the school with photos as well as its bold vision for the future. These printed pieces confidently conveyed how the campaign would ensure continued excellence.

TOP GIFTS™ WORKBOOK
Creating the Dream

Sources

For each of the following, review the priorities or needs identified. Then, assess those sources that are "Least likely" to "Most likely" to offer fundraising opportunities. List each Priority or Need with fundraising potential below.

	Least Likely				Most Likely		
Crisis/Change in Your Environment							
Strategic or Facilities Plan/Capacity Building							
Change in Leadership/Event							
Requests for Equipment, Renovations, etc.							
Problem or Need Identified by Client, Staff, Potential Donor							

Priority or Need

For each priority, briefly explain in newspaper terminology ("the five Ws and how"): what the need is (including costs), why it is important, when, where and how you plan to address it, and who will benefit as well as who will be leading the cause. Use extra pages, as needed.

1.

2.

3.

TOP GIFTS™ WORKBOOK
Communications Planning Chart 1

Would a theme and/or logo enhance your fundraising? If so, start by brainstorming key words, ideas, and images. Then follow the remaining steps outlined below.

Theme and Logo. One common approach is to develop a memorable tagline or theme for your campaign, then have it designed into a logo. A logo not only attracts attention, but also creates a unified image and can instill confidence in your campaign. You'll want to use it repeatedly in your fundraising materials.

To help guide you, here is a five-step process for developing a logo, with artwork and tips from Jas Szygiel of DesignArt:

1. Brainstorm key words, themes and images for your campaign.

In our example, the following themes emerged:

Grand Destiny
New Foundations
Shaping the Future
Foundation for the Future
Vision for the Future
Building on the Best

A steeple was most often mentioned as the image with which this organization is identified.

2. Prioritize the strongest themes.

3. Ask a designer to create sketches which best represent the campaign and organization.

For Added Impact: Personalize the theme for your organization by asking the designer to include your organization's name or trademark in your campaign logo.

Logos also can be effective for membership groups or giving societies (ex. President's Council), recognition levels, etc.

4. Seek suggestions/approval from key leaders including your development council or board.

5. Select your theme and fine-tune the final design.

TOP GIFTS™ WORKBOOK
Communications Planning Chart 2

Convert your needs into fundraising opportunities by analyzing specific projects, determining each need's benefit to—or impact on—society, and communicating its relevance to your vision.

Inspiring Messages

Every organization has needs, but what's special about yours? How would tackling this particular problem or need have impact? What difference would it make? Would it change lives? Define your

- Needs
- Opportunities
- Benefits
- Vision

Needs

A Wellness Center, for example, might have the need for an endowment to fund salaries for nutritionists, fitness specialists, smoking prevention, and cessation counselors.

Opportunities

An endowment could present the opportunity to serve new or expanded audiences through smoking prevention and cessation programs, such as the growing number of elderly who are not only living longer, but also seeking to remain healthy and active; cancer patients seeking alternative therapies; and even children and high school students.

More on Messages

Why is funding your project or need important? Can the benefit be quantified? Taking time to define these benefits now will enable you to answer questions such as "What difference will my gift make?" or "Why should I consider supporting you now?" which could be asked during a solicitation. This information also is helpful in making a written request (foundation proposal, appeal letter, etc.).

Benefits

An endowment for added staff for the Wellness Center may enable it to serve more than 500 new members, reach 10 percent more of the community, or help extend life expectancies by as much as 5 percent for those enrolling in certain programs.

Vision

The vision of the Wellness Center is to become a resource for all generations, "Building a Healthier Community" (possible theme). Another approach is to create an attention-getting name (ex. Health.Com, Vision 2010, etc.).

Convert your needs into fundraising opportunities. Then define the benefits of each and your overall vision. Refine your ideas for a theme (developed in part 1).

Needs	Opportunities	Benefits	Vision
1.			
2.			
3.			
4			
Theme(s)			

People give to have impact, to transform organizations, to be recognized. Develop programs to attract and recognize these gifts.

"I am what survives me."

Ian Percy

∽

"People respond to reward and recognition somewhat like performing seals and white mice. No part of the campaign procedure can be much more important"

Harold J. Seymour

How to Encourage the Largest Gifts

We saw in chapter 5 that you can create opportunities for top gifts by developing your needs into messages that inspire. In this chapter, we'll explore twelve opportunities to inspire major gifts in another way: by developing programs that make it easy for people to give, and that motivate and reward your donors.

Many of these are programs and techniques that focus on donor recognition. Several studies demonstrate that recognition is a powerful motivator for many donors. *The Seven Faces of Philanthropy*, for example, identifies seven donor types, and at least five of the seven seek some form of public acknowledgment or recognition when they give. Recognition can be an affirmation of the donor's personal or business success, or a confirmation of their commitment to—and often participation as a leader of—the organization that receives their support.

Naming opportunities and membership/recognition levels can elevate gift amounts. Pledges make it easier for donors to commit to large gifts. Gifts of stock or life income gifts provide financial or tax incentives.

Select the techniques that stimulate the best gifts, that you can manage effectively, and that enable you to excel. With guidance from your potential donors and discussions with your development council or board, you can zero in on the program opportunities that deliver the greatest value.

Does Your New Program Pass the "Culture Test"?

As a development communications consultant, Michele Steege, partner of Steege/Thomson Communications, has seen the very best in fundraising strategies. One essential factor for success, she believes, is that the fundraising strategies or techniques you choose be a good match with your organization's culture.

"In our office, we have a saying: 'Culture eats strategy for lunch every day,'" Steege says. "If it's not a good fit, it probably won't work." Culture impacts the way work gets done—and change takes place—in your organization.

One example she cites is a project she completed for a large, decentralized university. "With so many donors and schools, the university had gotten to the point where donors were recognized and stewarded in very different ways for similar-size gifts. We were asked to develop a donor relations plan—with the same standards for all the schools—which we did. While everyone said the plan was fantastic, it was never implemented. People were too vested in doing it their way and no one wanted to put in the political capital that change often requires."

A hallmark of organizations profiled in *Dream Builders* is that they are sensitive and responsible to their cultures. David Erickson of Samaritan Inns, for example, recognized that his organization and donors did not want their contributions spent on expensive luncheons or presentations. When hosting business leaders, he served healthy and wholesome meals (often soup and sandwiches), which kept the focus on Samaritan Inns' message and its campaign goals.

In contrast, the culture of other organizations calls for more upscale dinners with presentations by prominent leaders, educators, and entertainers.

As you review the opportunities in this chapter, ask yourself, "How well would this idea work here?" If the approach passes the "culture test," then ask yourself, "What modifications are needed to increase its effectiveness?" For some organizations, there will be resistance to any new idea. Involve key stakeholders (staff and potential donors) in your planning and decision making to build credibility and overcome concerns (see this chapter's action plans and TOP GIFTS™ workbook).

1. Case Statements

In chapter 5, we discussed four ways to create a vision that will be made possible by major and planned gifts. A *case statement* is a written document that communicates that dream and demonstrates your organization's capacity to make it a reality.

"Writing a case statement is exciting because often it's the first time an organization puts down what leaders see as its strengths and vision for the future, and what donors can do to achieve that vision," says Michele Steege, partner of Steege/Thomson (Philadelphia, Pa.), which has prepared hundreds of fundraising case statements. "The precursors to an effective case statement are good mission and vision statements, and a strong strategic plan. When the case statement is just a laundry list of needs, it usually doesn't work well with donors. You must define why your needs or projects are important and how they fit into the big-picture thinking for your organization's future."

Steege identifies four roles a case statement plays. "First, the case statement helps build clarity and consensus on the goals, often helping to resolve differences in priorities. The writing process involves thinking, organizing, and decision making. Your organization's leadership decides 'what's in' and 'what's out' of the campaign's priorities. We believe in the adage, 'The case statement is the anvil on which the campaign is hammered out.'

"Second, interviewing your organization's and campaign's leadership for the case statement helps create buy-in: they become invested and involved with the project. It's a tie-in that's different from simply reading a brochure.

"The third role of the case is to present and test your ideas during the planning or feasibility study with people you want to support your campaign. Do they believe that this project is a priority? Are they willing to invest in it? And how strong will that investment be? As it evolves, the case statement shifts from its initial role of building clarity and consensus to becoming more of a marketing tool.

"Finally, the case is a source document and training tool. It becomes a reference so that everyone presents the same messages. You can draw from it to: prepare letters, proposals, and major gift requests; to write speeches, brochures, PowerPoint presentations, or even script tours and videos. You can train your volunteers with the case

You can present your campaign messages or "case" in many ways. Here are excerpts from two popular formats. Above: a four-color booklet for the Jewish Home of Greater Harrisburg (Pa.). Page 128: a newspaper format for a new athletic center for Friends' Central School in Wynnewood, Pennsylvania. Videotapes, slides and PowerPoint presentations, newspaper articles, speeches, and reports tailored to various audiences are among the many other formats (or communication vehicles) available to deliver your messages. Materials courtesy of Steege/Thomson.

statement. It helps ensure that everyone is getting out the same messages and, as importantly, asking for gifts for projects that are a priority," she adds.

"If you are the person writing your case statement, block out a solid week or two and create some privacy for the mental energy this writing requires. Get away from your office. Development professionals are service-oriented, but interruptions when you are writing can stop your thinking. You can't answer calls from your donors and work through your case statement at the same time.

"Next, think about your audience. Do they like concise, analytical writing with lots of statistics or, instead, will they respond best to an emotional presentation? A small, local development program often has the advantage here because it knows its donors so well. As a communications firm, we start to define the unique style of the organization when we are interviewing its leadership and gathering information to write the case. Because we have writers with different styles, we can select the person who best speaks to each audience."

Steege outlines the steps for writing the case in the action plan, below. The classic structure is as follows, she says.

- *Introduction:* "A brief compelling summary of your strengths, the reasons your organization is important to society, your needs, and the role of philanthropy in meeting these needs. Usually this takes one to one-and-a-half pages."

- *Your Organization:* "Focus on your strengths, how you're unique, your importance to society, your capacity."

- *Vision:* "What do you want to change and how will society benefit? This should be powerful, but can be as brief as a single paragraph."

- *Needs:* "Define the specific ways—programs, facilities, equipment, endowment— you'll achieve your vision. What does each cost?"

- *An Invitation to Give:* "In the planning study, ask for reactions to your plans. In the campaign, restate your vision and request the reader's involvement and support."

"Your case statement may contain quotes from your leadership and/or the people you serve, statistics that reinforce the urgency to take action, as well as photos and architect's sketches of the project. It should be easy to read, build awareness, and help inspire the reader to action," she concludes.

Case Statement
Action Plan

- Review background material on the organization and the project or need (including annual reports, strategic plan, etc.).

- Arrange and complete key interviews with people who can speak knowledgeably about your organization, project, and fundraising (president, board and fundraising leadership, managers/directors of project area(s) to be funded with gifts).

- Develop clear themes and messages.

- Create an outline of the case statement (optional).

- Prepare a draft of the case statement, circulate it to key leaders, and revise as needed.

- Finalize the case statement and incorporate it into your communications plan.

2. Named Facilities, Programs & Plaques

As you identify your fundraising priorities, look for "naming opportunities"; that is, the facilities, projects, or programs that can be dedicated in the name of an individual or family. Naming opportunities include:

- *Building:* Toll Pavilion *or* Seisel Library

- *School:* Dixon School of Nursing *or* Harvard University

- *Endowment:* Seidman Endowment Fund for the Advancement of Nursing

- *Fellowship:* Pew Fellows

- *Scholarship:* Carole and Richard L. Jones Jr. Presidential Endowed Scholarship

- *Center:* Muller Center

- *Award:* Nobel Peace Prize

- Or other major initiative.

New or Renovated Facility

A new or renovated facility is ideal for naming opportunities, as the building and major areas within it can be dedicated in honor of contributors. Creating naming opportunities for a facility is a three-step process; for more information, see the "Creating Naming Opportunities" sidebar on pages 134–35.

For the Topeka Civic Theatre and Academy, for example, the theater's campaign committee created a donor recognition committee. Working with staff, the recognition committee identified the most prominent areas available for naming (step one), then matched each naming opportunity with a gift required on its table of gifts (steps two and three). The most visible areas in its newly renovated building are the main theater and the children's theater, which commanded the largest gifts. The next most desirable space is the main lobby. The sidebar lists the donor recognition opportunities that appeared in the theater's campaign brochure. Not included on this list is the gift required to name the building, $2.5 million, as well as a gift that named the road leading to the theater.

It's to your advantage whenever possible to have extra naming opportunities. This gives you added flexibility should you have a greater response than you anticipate. To validate and perhaps stimulate interest among board members, have your board endorse your naming opportunities before offering them to potential donors.

Naming opportunities may be commemorated with signs (for a building or major area), with a single display, or, as in the case of Topeka Civic Theatre and Academy, with individual plaques honoring each donor and noting the area dedicated. Materials vary from metal to marble, and what was once simply a plaque now encompasses designs as widespread as engraved pillars, etched glass, mosaics, tiles, quilts, and brick pavers. In some cases, names have been engraved directly into the façade of a building, lobby, or other prominent location. Sample recognition displays for individual contributors and for giving levels are presented in chapter 12, in the sidebar "Recognizing Dream Builders."

The size of each plaque may be standardized, or scaled to the amount of the gift (i.e., the larger the gift, the bigger the plaque). When plaque sizes vary, typically your charity will select two or more minimum amounts from your gift table ($1 million, $500,000, $250,000, $100,000, $50,000, etc.) and establish a plaque size for each amount or gift range (e.g., the largest plaque for $1 million or more; the second largest plaque for $500,000—$999,999; the next largest for $100,000—$499,999; etc.).

You or your board may decide to centralize the plaques in one highly visible location, such as the lobby or courtyard of a new building. Another approach is to display each plaque at the entrance of its respective area. During the campaign, a simple sketch of the plaque or display—with a key indicating the size of the plaques and gift amount required—can be developed to help potential donors visualize how their names will appear. It's best to standardize the format of the wording on each plaque and have examples printed to give each donor. One popular format is:

Name of area

Optional   in honor of [name selected by donor]

given by [donor's name]

This format translates to:

Main Lobby

In honor of Twink Lynch

Given by Mr. & Mrs. Nick G. Costa

Finally, if your display has a modular design with individual plaques, you'll be able to continue adding plaques for new donors. It's not unusual to attract additional gifts after your plaque display is unveiled, an added reason for locating it in a well-trafficked area.

Recognition
Action Plan

- Prepare two columns. In the right column, list programs/facilities available for naming, with the largest and most visible area appearing first.

- Place a gift amount to the left of each program/facility. Start with the highest amount on your table, then select one or more programs/areas (based on prominence and visibility, as well as the potential of your donors).

- Obtain sketches of your proposed recognition. Test your recognition opportunities with key individuals whose opinions you trust.

- Refine your list and display. Establish a donor recognition committee and ask the committee to review your recommendations (or present to a development council for approval).

- Seek board approval for your donor recognition opportunities.

- Prepare a communications plan and/or materials to support your solicitations.

- Solicit gifts involving top volunteers.

- Dedicate your recognition display/plaques and, if agreeable to donors, publicize.

Creating Naming Opportunities

When planning new construction or renovations, it's easy to find ways to recognize your top gift donors. Just follow these three steps.

1. Identify the Largest and Most Visible Areas

It's best to work from final architectural drawings to get a clear view of the prominence and size of each area. Here's a view of the Topeka Civic Theatre and Academy.

Areas Available for Naming

Main Theatre

Children's Theatre

Main Lobby

Board Room

Rehearsal Hall

Main Theatre Stage

Main Theatre Stage Balcony

West Entrance Patio

Main Theatre Stage Drape

Orchestra Pit

Scene Shop

Costume Shop

Green Room

Elevator

Box Office

Control Booth

Staff Offices

Dressing Rooms

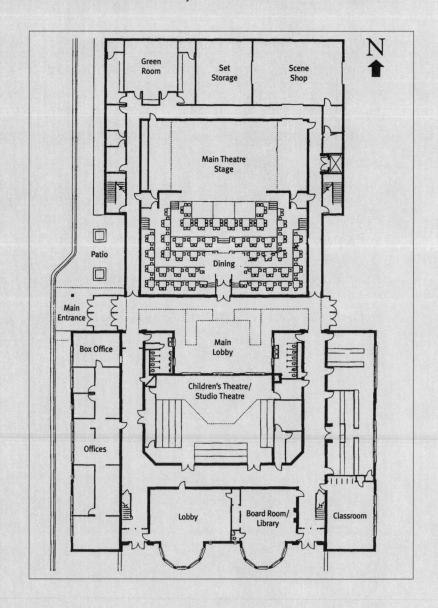

2. Develop a Table of Gifts (see chapter 9, "Goals")

Topeka Civic Theatre & Academy
Table of Gifts

#	Level	Total
1	$1,000,000	$1,000,000
1	$500,000	$1,500,000
4	$250,000	$2,500,000
7	$100,000	$3,200,000
10	$50,000	$3,700,000
18	$25,000	$4,150,000
30	$10,000	$4,450,000
50	$5,000	$4,700,000
350	<$5,000	$5,000,000

3. Match Each Area with a Specific Gift Level on the Table of Gifts

When possible, identify at least as many areas as the number of gifts you need for each amount (e.g., four gifts of $250,000 are called for on this table, so seek four or more areas for naming to meet that need).

DONOR RECOGNITION

Gifts at these levels will be recognized with engraved plaques located throughout the new Topeka Civic Theatre and Academy building.

$2,500,000	The building
$1,000,000	Main Theatre, Children's Theatre
$500,000	Main lobby
$250,000	Board room, rehearsal hall, Main Theatre stage, Main Theatre stage balcony, west entrance patio
$100,000	Main Theatre stage drape, orchestra pit, scene shop, costume shop, green room
$50,000	Elevator, box office, landscaping
$25,000	Control booth, staff offices, dressing rooms
$10,000	Large wall plaque in lobby
$5,000	Small wall plaque in lobby
$2,500	Tables on main floor
$1,500	Tables in balcony
$1,000	Chairs in Main Theatre

3. Make It Meaningful

The recognition program described previously is designed to help make a significant gift more meaningful by associating it with a specific element of the project. This approach can be expanded to encompass more donors by focusing on the next, lower levels of your gift table. Here's how. After completing your roster of naming opportunities, price out other elements of the project that may not have "naming potential," but that may give donors the feeling of accomplishment. In the example above, the Topeka Civic Theatre and Academy offered tables on the main floor at twenty-five hundred dollars each (for dinner theater), tables in the balcony for fifteen hundred dollars each, and chairs in the main theater for one thousand dollars each.

The theater didn't stop there, however. In addition to pricing out these more modest needs, TCT also included programs and projects that had yet to be funded. A "wish list" was printed in the grand opening booklet for the new Sheffel Theatre (see the sidebar "I Helped Make it Possible!" below).

Other charities have published gift catalogs with specific items and gift amounts suggested. Heifer International, which provides farm animals and supplies to struggling families internationally, asks individuals to consider a major gift in the form of an Ark of Animals ($5,000), both on its Web site *(catalog.heifer.org/index.cfm)* and in printed materials. Smaller gifts are also sought. Under the theme of "The Most Important Gift Catalog in the World," you are encouraged to make "a honey of a gift" (honeybees) or a "kids love kids" gift (a goat), or a gift of the organization's namesake, a heifer.

One word of caution. Don't overwhelm your potential donors with too many choices. Heifer International solves this challenge by keeping its materials simple and by offering a box to check for a "general gift. . . . We will use your donation where it's needed most." Other charities state that they reserve the right to substitute another item should too many contributors select the same item.

Make It Meaningful
Action Plan

- Identify needs that may not have naming potential, but that offer donors a feeling of accomplishment. Match the best projects or items to amounts listed on your gift table.

- Prepare a brief description of each need and suggested gift amount. Test these opportunities with key donors whose opinions you trust and who are comfortable giving you feedback.

- Refine your plan and present it to your recognition committee or development council for approval.

- Prepare a communications plan and/or materials to support your solicitations.

- Solicit gifts involving top volunteers.

- With consent of donor(s), publicize success.

I Helped Make it Possible!

Enable potential donors to visualize what can be accomplished by matching specific needs with gift amounts. Here's how Topeka Civic Theatre and Academy presented its needs during a campaign celebration.

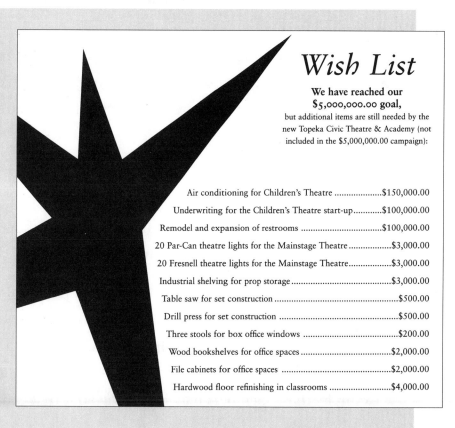

Wish List

We have reached our $5,000,000.00 goal, but additional items are still needed by the new Topeka Civic Theatre & Academy (not included in the $5,000,000.00 campaign):

Air conditioning for Children's Theatre $150,000.00
Underwriting for the Children's Theatre start-up $100,000.00
Remodel and expansion of restrooms $100,000.00
20 Par-Can theatre lights for the Mainstage Theatre $3,000.00
20 Fresnell theatre lights for the Mainstage Theatre $3,000.00
Industrial shelving for prop storage $3,000.00
Table saw for set construction $500.00
Drill press for set construction $500.00
Three stools for box office windows $200.00
Wood bookshelves for office spaces $2,000.00
File cabinets for office spaces $2,000.00
Hardwood floor refinishing in classrooms $4,000.00

4. Membership/Recognition Levels

Reward donors by creating a membership program, perhaps coupled with recognition levels, to promote specific ways of giving or gift amounts you want them to consider. Membership programs have been used effectively to secure planned gifts, increase annual gift amounts, elevate giving to major campaigns, and encourage ongoing support by recognizing donors at higher levels for total or cumulative giving.

You also can create recognition levels *without* having a membership program, but many organizations believe that membership is a way to bring donors closer to your organization.

You may develop a separate membership program for each of the specific types of gifts you want to encourage (e.g., annual giving, planned gifts, or campaign donations) or extend the benefits to more than one type of donor (e.g., anyone who makes a gift over ten thousand dollars to any program this year). Membership programs may have a charter enrollment period (see #5) and offer benefits, such as invitations to events, listing the names of members in a major publication and/or on plaques, etc. Listing donors'/members' names is a common benefit, often with a recognition display at your facility. For sample displays, see the chapter 12 sidebar "Recognizing Dream Builders."

One advantage of a membership program—or the name of a recognition level—for larger gifts is that volunteer solicitors often find it easier to say, "We're hoping you'll consider joining the Conductor's Circle," rather than asking for "an annual gift of twenty-five thousand dollars or more."

Here are several programs to consider.

Annual Giving

There are at least three ways that an annual giving membership program can increase your success in TOP GIFTS™ fundraising:

- A membership program can create a pool of potential major gift donors for the future. Your membership program enables you to capture their interest at more modest levels, then approach them in the future for a major gift for a special project or campaign. If you create a ten-thousand-dollar annual giving club, for example, these members may be among your best candidates for gifts of one hundred thousand dollars, five hundred thousand dollars, or more (paid over five years) to a major initiative or campaign. This is ideal if you can introduce your membership program at least a year or two before starting your campaign. In some development programs, the highest membership level (say, ten thousand dollars per year) is either the entry level for your major gifts program or a visible sign that these are major gifts prospects.

- An annual giving membership program with several levels ($1,000, $2,500, $5,000, $10,000) raises donors' sights, may encourage donors to move from one level to the next, and offers opportunities for building relationships. Donors not only become more knowledgeable about your organization, but also, equally important, you get to know more about the specific programs or services they'd like to support.

- Finally, membership benefits may be part of your recognition plans for major and planned giving donors. You can extend membership benefits to all of your major donors and, at a membership event, also present a special award to recognize the pacesetting donor whose gift has made a new program, facility, or service possible. To create a membership program for annual giving, you need to determine its name, the number of giving levels (one or more), and the benefits you will offer.

You can name your membership group and/or recognition levels after a prominent individual associated with your organization, a founder (such as the Ben Franklin Society), the year your organization was created or the tenure of your organization (Second Century Association, etc.), leadership qualities (the Chairman's Forum, the Dean's Circle, the Chancellor's Club, etc.), terms that add stature (Visionaries, Benefactors, Associates, Century Members, etc.) or terms that have special meaning to your organization (e.g., for Pepperdine University, Pepperdine Associate). Names have featured precious metals (such as Gold, Silver, Bronze Members, etc.). The levels can also be tied to the type of organization. For example, a membership group for a sailing club might start with a Crew Member ($500), then rise to First Mate ($1,000), Captain's Club ($5,000), Admiral's Club ($10,000), and Commander's Circle ($25,000 or more).

You can also carve out a separate membership program for a group that offers great potential for top gifts. The Boston Symphony Orchestra, for example, focuses on corporate gifts with six membership levels ranging from a member ($2,000) to three levels over ten thousand dollars (Principal Player at $10,000; Concertmaster at $15,000; and Conductor's Circle at $25,000). Among the benefits are invitations to one or more events (two geared specifically to companies), recognition in the program book, and a "meet and greet" with the conductor or guest artist (for more details, see *www.bso.org*).

For donor recognition reports, members' names appear alphabetically within each category with the highest recognition level appearing first. Some people only want to be seen in the top category, so set giving levels low enough to be attainable, but high enough to be challenging. Typically, members' names are published annually and/or displayed on plaques in a highly visible location at the organization. Omit the names of donors who ask that their gifts be anonymous.

Determine membership levels and benefits by the interests of your potential donors (see workbook at the end of this chapter). Among benefits frequently offered are: membership cards; lectures, concerts (for arts organizations), and events; free parking or admission; guest passes; annual dinner for the highest membership levels; and other perks. You may develop a logo that gives a distinctive image to your membership/recognition program (for information about logos, see the workbook in chapter 5).

For examples of recognition in a campaign, gala preview, and charter membership, see the sidebar on the Kimmel Center, "A Landmark of Our Time."

Planned Giving

If you're reluctant to launch a planned giving program due to lack of time, budget, or knowledge of the many ways to give, a membership program may be just the answer. With a modest investment in its planned giving society (about one thousand dollars in printing and mailing costs plus the cost of pins), the Florida Orchestra identified more than five million dollars in planned gifts from forty-nine individuals during a brief, four-month charter enrollment period. C. Edwin Davis, CFRE, director of development for the orchestra, explains the process.

"First, find out to what extent your organization has been the beneficiary of planned gifts. Keep in mind these donors may be living or deceased. Find out everything you can about these individuals, their families, and their connections with your organization," Davis advises. The reason?

"You want to identify an individual or family after whom you can name your planned giving membership society. For the Florida Orchestra, it was Mary Elizabeth Mitchell, a trustee and patron who loved the orchestra and supported it generously. She had funded a trust before her death at age eighty-four that today benefits the orchestra." Davis encourages you to link the name of your society with a person or family of significance to your organization. Another approach is to use an historical tie, such as Princeton's 1746 Society, which commemorates the year the university was founded.

Davis then defines the society's benefits, which include a charter membership certificate (laser printed by the development staff on an attractive form), subscriptions to the orchestra's quarterly newsletter *Noteworthy* and monthly concert programs, the member's name listed in its newsletter, and a custom-designed gold pin of a hand holding a baton. "The pin was our major expense," he says. "But it's a good investment. We wanted to give the orchestra good visibility in the community."

Among the candidates for membership whom Davis identified were:

- Long-term donors (ten or more years), or those who practiced above-average giving (in Davis's case, cumulative gifts of over twenty-five thousand dollars);

- Anyone giving over one thousand dollars in a single year;

- Current and former board members;

- Individuals inquiring about planned giving;

- Those over sixty-five; and

- Individuals who notified the orchestra that they had included it in their estate plans.

Each candidate received a membership recruitment packet consisting of a cover letter, details about the newly formed Mary Elizabeth Mitchell Society, and a response form and reply envelope. "The confidential enrollment form indicates 'Charter Membership Enrollment' available through December 31. This provided the sense of urgency that's always needed when you ask for something," Davis says.

"Many individuals gave us some specifics as to the percentage of their estate, amount of a bequest, or value of a trust. This is in excess of five million dollars. Yet at least one-third of the members gave us no figures. Our best guess is that this represents at least another two million dollars," says Davis. And the society continues to welcomed new members.

"Mitchell Society members are our gold nuggets," Davis says. "A membership society can succeed in a very small department or even a one-person operation. To this date we do not have a wills brochure, nor do we have a planned giving brochure. Instead, we include brief reference to wills and the Mitchell Society on response envelopes, and include information about wealth management, estate planning, and planned giving in our newsletter and concert programs. We continue to receive inquiries about the Mitchell Society. With a little effort and imagination, you, too, can find your fortune."

Mary Elizabeth Mitchell Society
THE FLORIDA ORCHESTRA, TAMPA, FLA.

The Florida Orchestra promotes its planned giving membership society in its newsletter, Noteworthy, *and with a membership recruitment packet mailed to carefully selected candidates. Members receive a certificate, their names listed in publications, a membership pin, a subscription to the orchestra's newsletter and concert programs, and invitations to concert events.*

The Florida Orchestra
The Musical Heartbeat of Tampa Bay

Inspires... Thrills and Entertains!

FLORIDA ORCHESTRA
Jahja Ling
Music Director

May 2002

Mary Elizabeth Mitchell Society

Many of them love music. Some never willingly miss a concert. And all of them believe The Florida Orchestra is a valued part of Tampa Bay's cultural landscape. They are members of the Orchestra's Mary Elizabeth Mitchell Society.

As of mid-April, fifty-five of these individuals and/or couples had notified the Orchestra that they had included it in their estate plans. By doing so they are helping assure the Orchestra's future while they enjoy significant benefits thanks to wise estate planning. We invite you to consider joining these visionary members of the Mitchell Society. For more information please contact Ed Davis, Director of Development, at (813) 286-1170, extension 322.

Board of Trustees

Mary Elizabeth Mitchell Society Is Established

Mary Elizabeth Mitchell with Jahja Ling

The Mary Elizabeth Mitchell Society commemorates the life of its namesake. A resident of Belleair Shores until her death in 1999 at age 84, Mrs. Mitchell loved the Orchestra and supported it generously. She served as a Trustee of its Board and enjoyed attending concerts at Ruth Eckerd Hall in Clearwater.

Organized in 2001, the Society recognizes those individuals who notify the Orchestra that they have included it in their estate plan. Mrs. Mitchell was exemplary in this regard, having contributed more than $800,000 during her lifetime and having established a trust that, subsequent to her death, funded the William A. and Mary Elizabeth Mitchell Foundation. The Florida Orchestra is a designated beneficiary of the foundation.

Your benefits as a member include distinguished recognition, invitation to luncheons and seminars, and the Orchestra's "Wise Wealth Management" newsletter.

Perhaps the *greatest* benefit is the satisfaction of knowing that *your* Orchestra will continue providing wonderful music for future generations.

You qualify for membership irrespective of the amount of your proposed estate gift or whether it is revocable or irrevocable. Indeed, there are many creative ways to benefit the Orchestra after you have provided for yourself and your loved ones. Examples include bequests, charitable trusts or gift annuities, retained life estates, life insurance, IRAs and pooled income funds.

The Orchestra extends a warm welcome to these CHARTER MEMBERS of the Mary Elizabeth Mitchell Society

If you have included The Florida Orchestra in your estate plan, please notify Ed Davis, Director of Development, at (813) 286-1170, extension 322 by December 31, 2001 and you will qualify for charter membership.

It is important to seek the advice of an attorney, accountant or your tax advisor to assist you in developing a giving plan that best meets your needs and desires.

MORT AND ELAINE STUPP
Create a Legacy for Tomorrow's Music Lovers

"We believe that music brings a cultural wellness to a community and that the Bay area is extremely fortunate to have The Florida Orchestra serving its residents," commented Mort Stupp, long-time Florida Orchestra subscriber and volunteer. His wife, Elaine, a former schoolteacher, President of the Tampa Guild from 1995-96 and Co-chairman of the Orchestra Young Artists Competition, commented further why they particularly wanted to support the Orchestra's education program.

"I started playing the piano at age six and even had the unique opportunity of attending rehearsals of the Metropolitan Opera Chorus," stated Elaine. "Later, as a teacher, I saw how much the children enjoyed music classes. That's why we decided to combine our love for music and for children, and set up an endowment for music education under the auspices of **The Florida Orchestra's Mary Elizabeth Mitchell Society** as part of our estate planning."

"To keep The Florida Orchestra as a fine jewel in the area requires careful planning. Please join us in our quest to keep the music alive and healthy in the Tampa Bay Area."

MORT AND ELAINE STUPP

FLORIDA ORCHESTRA
Jahja Ling
Music Director

Leonard David Stone
Executive Director

Thomas Wilkins
Resident Conductor

The Mary Elizabeth Mitchell Society of The Florida Orchestra

The *MARY ELIZABETH MITCHELL SOCIETY* commemorates the life of its namesake. A resident of Belleair Shores until her death in 1999 at age 84, Mrs. Mitchell loved the Orchestra and supported it generously. She served as a trustee of its Board and enjoyed attending concerts at Ruth Eckerd Hall in Clearwater.

Organized in 2001, the Society recognizes those individuals who notify The Florida Orchestra that they have included it in their estate plan. Mrs. Mitchell was exemplary in this regard, having contributed more than $800,000 during her lifetime and having established a trust that, subsequent to her death, funded the William A. and Mary Elizabeth Mitchell Foundation. The Florida Orchestra is a designated beneficiary of the Foundation.

The greatest benefit of membership is the satisfaction of knowing you have helped assure that <u>your</u> Orchestra will continue providing wonderful music for future generations. Other benefits include distinguished recognition, invitation to luncheons and seminars, and receipt of the Orchestra's "Wise Wealth Management" newsletter. New members are welcome at any time.

You qualify for membership irrespective of the amount of your proposed estate gift or whether it is revocable or irrevocable. Indeed, there are many creative ways to benefit the Orchestra after you have provided for yourself and your loved ones. Examples include bequests, charitable trusts or gift annuities, retained life estates, life insurance, IRAs and pooled income funds.

If you have made provision for The Florida Orchestra in your estate plan or would like information on ways to do so, please notify Ed Davis, Director of Development, at (813) 286-1170, extension 322.

The Kimmel Center: "A Landmark of Our Time"

Few organizations have taken recognition to such heights as the Regional Performing Arts Center (Philadelphia, Pa.), which is responsible for building, endowing, and funding operation of the $265 million Kimmel Center. Recognition levels were incorporated into:

- the campaign itself, with giving levels ranging from the *Take a Seat* recognition program ($15,000—$25,000), to *Principal Founders* who make multi-million-dollar gifts;

- the Gala Preview, a premium event (see #7), to support operations, with *Benefactors* packages ranging from five thousand dollars per person to seventy-five thousand dollars for a table of ten;

- a "charter membership" mailing for gifts from one hundred to fifteen thousand dollars.

The results are impressive. In addition to raising more than $250 million to build the facility, according to the Kimmel Center's leadership, "An initial ten-million-dollar endowment goal has been reached, making RPAC the nation's first major arts center to open with endowment funds in hand and plans in place." When combined with its building campaign, "This heartening major gifts success has provided tremendous momentum with more than forty leadership commitments of one million dollars or more, and other giving levels providing several hundred contributions between twenty-five thousand dollars and the million-dollar level."

Here are materials from three of its recognition programs.

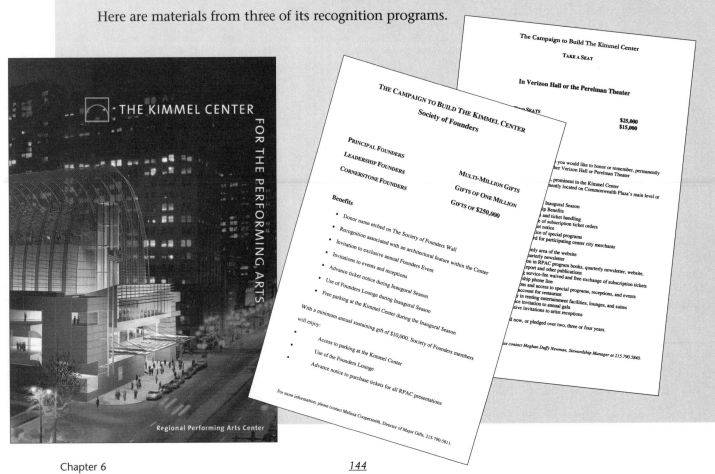

THE KIMMEL CENTER
FOR THE PERFORMING ARTS

EXPERIENCE HISTORY IN THE MAKING
AS YOU JOIN US FOR A
SPECTACULAR WEEKEND CELEBRATION...

GALA PREVIEW OF

THE KIMMEL CENTER
FOR THE PERFORMING ARTS

GALA PREVIEW OF

THE KIMMEL CENTER FOR THE PERFORMING ARTS

PRINT NAME AND/OR COMPANY ABOVE as it will appear in the
Commemorative Program and permanently in The Kimmel Center.

☐ PREMIUM BENEFACTOR PACKAGE at $75,000 ☐ BENEFACTOR PACKAGE at $50,000
☐ INDIVIDUAL BENEFACTOR PACKAGES at $5,000 X _____ # of people

YOUR NAME

TITLE

COMPANY NAME

ADDRESS

CITY / STATE / ZIP _____ FAX

PHONE

...to the Regional Performing Arts Center.
Preview, please call 215.790.5855.

PREMIUM BENEFACTOR PACKAGE (ten tickets for each evening) at $75,000 ($68,000 tax-
deductible) Includes both Friday, December 14, 2001 and Saturday, December 15, 2001:

- Cocktail Reception
- ...te luncheon December 14.
- ...to be invited
- ...m Box and First Tier seating for ten
- ...erformance dinners and dancing for ten
- ...nt recognition in The Kimmel Center

- Recognition in Commemo...
  Program Book
- Special Recognition in Op...
- Charter Membership for t...
  of The Kimmel Center, Jan...
  (details available by reques...

...OR PACKAGE (ten tickets for each evening) at $50,000 ($43,000 tax...
...n Friday, December 14, 2001 and Saturday, December 15, 2001:

- ...il Reception
- ...estra seating for ten
- ...hance dinners and dancing for ten
- ...recognition in The Kimmel Center

- Recognition in Commemorative Opening
  Program Book
- Recognition in Opening publicity
- Charter Membership for the Inaugural Season
  of The Kimmel Center, January–June, 2002
  (details available by request)

INDIVIDUAL BENEFACTOR PACKAGES at $5,000/person ($4,300 tax-deductible)
Includes both Friday, December 14, 2001 and Saturday, December 15, 2001:

- Gala Cocktail Reception
- Prime Orchestra seating
- Post-performance dinners and dancing
- Parking
- Permanent recognition in The Kimmel Center

- Recognition in Commemorative Opening
  Program Book
- Charter Membership for the Inaugural Season
  of The Kimmel Center, January–June, 2002
  (details available by request)

Seating for both evenings will be allocated on a first-come, first-served basis.

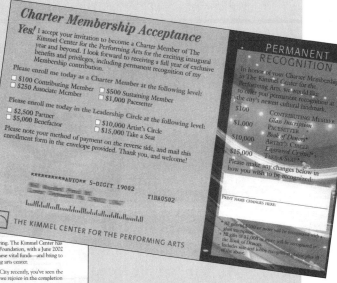

As a Charter Member of the new Kimmel Center for the Performing Arts, you'll
enjoy a full year of benefits and privileges. Each of these special rewards is

For Charter Members Only

designed to enhance your experiences at The Kimmel Center and to honor your
generous participation as a patron of the performing arts in Philadelphia.

$100 CONTRIBUTING MEMBER
- Advance notice and opportunity to purchase tickets, ahead of the
  general public, for many *Kimmel Center Presents* performances.
- Personalized Members-only discount card for participating merchants,
  including restaurants, hotels, and boutiques
- Invitation to Members-only Open House featuring a special tour of
  The Kimmel Center
- Special 10% discount at Intermission, with superb shops located at
  The Kimmel Center and in Chestnut Hill
- The Kimmel Center's quarterly newsletter
- Exclusive access to Member-only areas of The Kimmel Center
  Web site showing availability of tickets to *Kimmel Center Presents*
  performances and special offers from discount card merchants

$250 ASSOCIATE MEMBER
All Contributing Member benefits plus
- Invitations to special lectures
  and education programs
  (up to four per year)
- Opportunity to receive a
  limited-edition book
  commemorating the opening
  of The Kimmel Center for
  the Performing Arts

$500 SUSTAINING MEMBER
All Associate Member benefits plus
- Invitations to special
  receptions and events

$1,000 PACESETTER
All Sustaining Member benefits plus
- Priority seating when
  purchasing subscriptions

Charter Membership Acceptance

Yes! I accept your invitation to become a Charter Member of The
Kimmel Center for the Performing Arts for the exciting inaugural
year and beyond. I look forward to receiving a full year of exclusive
benefits and privileges, including permanent recognition of my
Membership contribution.

Please enroll me today as a Charter Member at the following level:
☐ $100 Contributing Member   ☐ $500 Sustaining Member
☐ $250 Associate Member   ☐ $1,000 Pacesetter

Please enroll me today in the Leadership Circle at the following level:
☐ $2,500 Partner   ☐ $10,000 Artist's Circle
☐ $5,000 Benefactor   ☐ $15,000 Take a Seat

Please note your method of payment on the reverse side, and mail this
enrollment form in the envelope provided. Thank you, and welcome!

**********AUTO** 5-DIGIT 19002

                                                    T1BA0502

THE KIMMEL CENTER FOR THE PERFORMING ARTS

PERMANENT RECOGNITION

In honor of your Charter Membership
in The Kimmel Center for the
Performing Arts, we would like
to offer you permanent recognition at
the city's newest cultural landmark.

$100	CONTRIBUTING MEMBER *Glass Inscription*
$1,000	PACESETTER *Book of Donors* ARTIST'S CIRCLE *Engraved Crystal*
$10,000	
$15,000	TAKE A SEAT

Please make any changes below in
how you wish to be recognized.

PRINT NAME CHANGES HERE:

THE KIMMEL CENTER FOR THE PER...

Dear Arts Patron,

It is with great pleasure that I invite you to become a Ch...
for the Performing Arts.

We in Philadelphia had long dreamed of a major arts c...
talented local artists and attract performers from around the wor...
is now a reality as we celebrate the Kimmel Center's inaugural...

This is a once-in-a-lifetime opportunity to add your n...
icon for our city. As a Charter Member, you will take part i...
and you will receive permanent recognition at the Center to...
describe in a moment).

In addition, your generosity will have an added impact this spring. The Kimmel Center has
been working to meet a $2 million Challenge Grant from the Kresge Foundation, with a June 2002
deadline. Your membership contribution will be used to help secure these vital funds—and bring to a
successful close our campaign for this new, state-of-the-art performing arts center.

If you attended our Inaugural Festival or have been in Center City recently, you've seen the
dynamic change to the Avenue of the Arts. History is being made as we rejoice in the completion
of this major project for our city.

Designed by renowned architect Rafael Viñoly, The Kimmel Center is a truly magnificent arts
facility—the crown jewel of our city's cultural renaissance. Under The Kimmel Center's soaring roof,
the arts will flourish as never before.

- The 2,500-seat Verizon Hall, with its visually stunning design and world-class acoustics, now
  serves as home to the beloved Philadelphia Orchestra.
- The 650-seat Perelman Theater—a Philadelphia first with its turntable stage—transforms
  from a recital hall to a proscenium theater, uniquely accommodating performances by our
  resident companies, as well as touring artists and community productions.

These two impressive venues are joined by the Merck Arts Education Center, The
Dorrance H. Hamilton Garden, Cadence restaurant, and multi-use spaces in a spectacular
vaulted, glass-roofed plaza.

Mirroring the legacy of the 19th-century Academy of Music, The Kimmel Center for the
Performing Arts is Philadelphia's newest cultural landmark. As a Charter Member, you have the
chance of a lifetime to make history with us as we celebrate this world-class home for the performing arts.

(over, please)

ADMINISTRATIVE OFFICES
260 South Broad Street
Suite 901
Philadelphia, PA 19102
215-790-5800
Fax: 215-790-5801
www.kimmelcenter.org

Membership
Action Plan

- Determine the type of gifts you would like to encourage (annual, cumulative, planned gifts, etc.).

- Create a name for your program. If seeking gifts of increasing amounts, distinguish each category or level with a distinctive name.

- Develop a list of membership benefits and policies. Test these ideas and the level of interest with your potential donors.

- Seek approval for your membership program (name, benefits, and policies) from your development council or board.

- Identify constituencies who may be good candidates, then prepare a list of these individuals.

- Create a communications plan to market the program and support your recruitment.

- Enlist members.

- Build on your success by publicizing your program.

5. Charter Period

Establish a deadline for action to create urgency and encourage action. When tied to recognition or membership, charter enrollment can build response even more. For the Mary Elizabeth Mitchell Society (described in #4), for example, candidates receiving an invitation to join had four months to respond in order to qualify as "Charter Members" (members are listed as "Sustaining" if enrolled after the charter membership deadline). Charter membership benefits may include being listed in this special category in your recognition publication and receiving a certificate or plaque. Deadlines for charter recognition may be incorporated into communications materials promoting annual, major, planned, and endowment gifts.

Charter Period
Action Plan

- Design your fundraising program (e.g., major gifts membership society, etc.), including the recognition/benefits you will offer.

- Determine how much time you will give people to respond for charter recognition.

- Incorporate the words "Charter" or "Charter Membership Enrollment" with your deadline in your promotional material.

Follow these steps from your *Membership Action Plan*:

- Develop a list of benefits and policies. Test these ideas and level of interest with your potential donors.

- Seek approval for your program (name, benefits, and policies) from your development council or board.

- Identify constituencies who may be good candidates, then prepare a list of these individuals.

- Create a communications plan to market the program and support your recruitment.

- Enlist members.

- Build on your success by publicizing your program.

6. Campaign Giving Policies

How your organization credits or counts gifts to your campaign or major gifts program can impact the amount your donors are prepared to give. For example, your campaign may be structured as one or more of the four types of campaigns listed below. Will gifts be recognized for:

- capital (for construction, renovation, equipment);

- endowment (often a planned gift);

- programs; or

- comprehensive (for major needs including capital, endowment, and key programs)?

Your giving policy defines what is included or counted in your campaign.

With increasingly larger goals, many development programs are asking their board(s) to designate all unrestricted gifts received (such as bequests, unrestricted annual gifts, etc.) to the specific program or campaign. This helps build momentum, directs funds to the institution's highest priorities, and answers questions about who may be recognized.

Here's an example of a concise policy from *The Anniversary Campaign for Princeton*. The policy was not only used internally, but also provided to volunteers and incorporated into training materials.

Campaign Policies

The Anniversary Campaign for Princeton seeks to raise $750 million* over a five-year period, including $125 million through Annual Giving. All gifts, pledges and realized bequests received from individuals, corporations and foundations for Campaign purposes will count towards the overall goal. As always, gifts to Annual Giving must be unrestricted and for current use. Gifts for endowment or other designated Campaign purposes may not be credited additionally to Annual Giving. A life income gift made during the Campaign will receive full Campaign credit if the youngest beneficiary is 55 years or older. Bequest intentions cannot receive Campaign credit. Campaign pledges may be paid on a schedule established by the donor, preferably within a maximum of five years.

*Author's note: Campaign goal later increased to $900 million

---

7. Premium Event That Raises Sights

Remember Leslie Wexner, who challenged the Ohio Center for Science and Industry to create a vision for a new century (chapter 5)? In the 1980s, according to *The Chronicle of Philanthropy*, he organized a black-tie dinner at his home for donors who gave five thousand dollars or more to the United Way—an amount that, at the time, was considered a high-level annual gift. Wexner arranged for Diahann Carroll and Andy Williams to provide entertainment, then allowed the United Way to promote the event as part of its solicitations. The event became a "must attend" for Columbus socialites. In one year, the number of donors giving five thousand dollars or more, more than doubled (from 95 people giving $597,000 to 229 donors contributing $1.3 million).

Events that encourage high levels of giving have been used successfully by many organizations. After raising approximately $250 million for a new performing arts center and an endowment, the new Kimmel Center in Philadelphia, Pennsylvania raised two million dollars for its first year's operating expenses with several premium events during its opening weekend. The event showcased the world-class facility and was televised, giving viewers an intimate look at the impressive glass-enclosed concert hall as well an introduction to Sidney Kimmel, the pacesetting donor after whom the center is named.

Major events for top donors can be effective for most charities, large and small. Events can be as varied as "Opening Night" for a new facility and a special event in a private home. If hosted in a private home, take a lesson from Wexner and ask permission to promote the event in your solicitation materials. Match the giving level to your audience's potential, your goal, and the type of event. Here are two examples of recognition events within the reach of smaller organizations:

- A wine tasting for trustees or another select group, each of whom contributes twenty-five hundred dollars or more to an annual appeal. Ask those putting on the event to help keep costs down by donating the use of the home or estate hosting the event, the sommelier making the presentation, and wine and catering expenses.

- A dinner in a private, upscale home for ten-thousand-dollar annual contributors to a membership group. Homes and other private locations should be selected for their uniqueness: country retreats (complete with a pond and ducks), antique furnishings, gardens, or other features. Each year, introduce and extend a warm welcome to new members. One organization profiled in *Dream Builders* saw membership grow from 30 to 120 members with such a program.

Finally, to demonstrate the power of this technique, I offer this story. Walter Annenberg, publishing magnate and philanthropist, opened his home to donors who gave twenty-five thousand dollars or more to the annual campaign of the his local Jewish Federation. With its great success, he agreed to repeat the event the following year. According to one donor, "During the second year, there were so many people who wanted to attend that his home could no longer accommodate the group! The recognition dinner had to be moved to a local hotel."

Events That Raise Sights
Action Plan

- Select your event and determine how to make it truly special.

- Determine your audience. Match the giving level to your audience's potential, your goal, and the type of event.

- If the event is in a private home, ask permission to promote the event in your solicitation materials.

- Seek approval from your development council or board.

- Prepare a communications plan and/or materials to support your solicitations.

- Ask top volunteers to solicit participants.

- With consent of host, publicize your success.

8. Sponsors & Underwriters Elevate Special Events

Get the most from the special events you offer by creating one or more sponsorship opportunities to recognize major contributors. One option is to enlist an underwriter who contributes sufficient funds to cover all or a majority of your event's expenses, allowing you to retain proceeds from ticket sales.

Sponsorships are also valuable. A gala that nets fifty thousand dollars a year, for example, could offer a "lead sponsorship" opportunity at five or ten thousand dollars, or more. The underwriter's name or logo would be printed below the name of the event on all printed materials and publicity (invitations, program book, etc.). Two or more "associate sponsorships" also could be offered at three thousand dollars each, with the company's names listed in smaller type below the lead sponsor. With these three gifts alone, you have increased revenue by more than 20 percent, with little additional expense. There are many variations on this theme. A popular running event, for example, offers each participant a T-shirt with the names of lead and associate sponsors printed on the front; twenty or more co-sponsors' names are printed on the back for twenty-five hundred dollars each. Consider where sponsorship messages should appear, as well as amounts and sponsorship levels for each of your events.

Sponsorship
Action Plan

- Identify one or more sponsorship or underwriting opportunities to recognize major contributors.

- Determine suggested amount for each sponsorship or underwriting opportunity, as well as benefits you will provide.

- Seek approval from your development council or board.

- Prepare a list of potential sponsors or underwriters.

- Prepare communications plan, including printed materials describing program and benefits.

- Enlist top volunteers to assist you in solicitations.

- Solicit and recognize sponsors or underwriters.

9. Special Attention

A second opportunity to increase proceeds from events is by adding value for participants. If your event is often oversubscribed, you could offer a reception or preview party for those who contribute a larger donation. The reception may be offered just before the event, or on another evening. For example, one charity features a celebrity at a dinner for donors of one thousand dollars or more, but offers a private reception before the dinner for contributors giving over five thousand dollars.

Another organization provides a dinner and a less congested view of its flower show for several hundred dollars a couple. This compares to the much lower entry price of about twenty dollars for general admission.

Recognition levels often are established for gifts made above the usual charge. For an event that normally charges $175 per couple, you could offer a chance to become a *Benefactor* at $500 per couple, a *Patron* at $350, or a *Sponsor* at $250. Send an early mailing to encourage donors to commit to the event and subscribe at the higher amounts. Then list the names of donors who give at the Benefactor, Patron, and Sponsor levels under their respective categories in future mailings and/or the program distributed at the event.

The names of the recognition levels can be customized to your charity and/or function. For example, if a museum hosts an event to benefit its building program, for which the entry charge is typically $75, a contributor might be listed as a *Museum Pillar* at $500 per person, a *Museum Baluster* at $250 per person, or a *Museum Brick* at $100 per person.

Similar to recognition is advertising in a program book, which charges extra for prime placement (back cover, inside front and back covers), silver or gold pages (named for the background ink colors) or other special visibility. These advertising promotions can be bundled with attendance at the event (e.g., a gold page and table of ten offered at seventy-five hundred dollars) as yet another way to increase proceeds. You'll need to consider the approaches and amounts that work best for your organization.

Special Attention
Action Plan

- Determine the added value you will provide to participants and the incremental gift amount(s) required.

- Create names and suggested gift amounts for recognition levels (if offered).

- Prepare a list of potential contributors. Test program ideas with selected members.

- Seek approval from your development council or board.

- Prepare communications plan including printed materials describing program and benefits.

- Enlist top volunteers to assist you in solicitations.

- Solicit and recognize.

10. Challenge Gifts

Challenge gifts, sometimes called *challenge grants* or *matching gifts*, can be structured to meet nearly any goal. A challenge gift is essentially a partnership with a donor who agrees to give you a certain amount if you meet the terms of the challenge. Depending on your relationship with the donor funding the challenge, you may be able to negotiate or even set the terms.

Here are several examples.

- You have a donor who will give you twenty-five thousand dollars if you are able to raise fifty thousand from new or increased gifts. There's a caveat, though. You will only receive the match if you raise *all* fifty thousand dollars. (In other words, the match is *"all or nothing"* and depends on raising the *full* amount).

- One of your trustees is disappointed that 100 percent of your board members are not giving and that the gifts received are (in his view) relatively modest. He offers a one-hundred-thousand-dollar challenge gift that matches, dollar for dollar, all new or increased gifts up to the one-hundred-thousand-dollar challenge. If trustees don't raise the full amount, he agrees to match what is given in new/increased gifts (a *partial payout*, which is preferred to the "all or nothing" approach outlined above).

How have challenge gifts been used by specific charities? Here are several historic examples:

- The United Way of Southeastern Pennsylvania made history during the 1980s when, of fifty-six major cities in the U.S., it moved from last to first place in the number of dollars raised and the number of members of the Alexis de Toqueville Society. (The society honors contributors who give ten thousand dollars annually.) The phenomenal growth from 124 to more than 300 members began with two challenge gifts of one million dollars each that were designed to stimulate interest and match giving.

- Author James Michener helped a museum bearing his name with a challenge gift to build the museum's collection of works by artists from the region. He provided funds for the museum's endowment for every qualified gift of art donated. Michener went so far as to collaborate with museum staff on a process for evaluating the artwork and a schedule for partial payments when acquisition milestones were met.

- The last example is considered to be one of the first challenge gifts in the United States. Benjamin Franklin asked the colonial government to fund part of the construction of a hospital in Philadelphia if he could raise the rest. The legislature, thinking Franklin would not be successful, agreed. Franklin met his goal, and the country's first hospital was built.

Some challengers will assist you by signing a letter that describes the terms of the challenge and why it's being made. This letter can be included with your solicitations (letters, proposals, solicitation packets), lending credibility to the offer and encouraging others to give. Finally, the formula for the match can vary. For example, your challenger could offer two or three dollars for every dollar you raise. Or the formula may require that you raise more for each dollar than your challenger provides. The Kresge Foundation, one of the largest sponsors of challenge gifts, requires that as much as three or more dollars be raised for every dollar it gives in matching support.

Challenge Gift
Action Plan

- Prepare a list of your best potential sponsors of a challenge gift.

- Research each source and, if it is a corporation or foundation, obtain giving guidelines. Determine if your use for the challenge matches the interests of the potential challenger.

- Plan your solicitation of your best candidate for the challenge. Complete the solicitation.

- If successful, confirm the terms of the challenge in writing. When possible, enlist the involvement of the challenger in publicizing the opportunity.

- Create a communications plan that increases awareness of the challenge and supports your solicitations.

- Promote the challenge and solicit.

- Keep your challenger informed of your progress. Celebrate and publicize your success.

11. Make It Easy to Give

By making it easy for people to give and take advantage of financial and tax incentives, you can raise more top gifts. Here are a few ways to structure gifts.

Stock Gifts & Mutual Fund Shares

For most Americans, a charitable gift of appreciated stock or shares in a mutual fund owned for more than a year offers two tax benefits: a charitable deduction for the value of the stock and avoidance of capital gain tax on its increased value. A stock purchased for one thousand dollars that is today worth five thousand dollars is an ideal gift to your charity. That's because most donors receive a five-thousand-dollar charitable deduction, and the capital gains tax on the four-thousand-dollar increase ($5,000 value minus the $1,000 purchase amount) can be totally avoided. In order to accept these gifts, your organization must establish an account with a brokerage firm (or some firms have a generic "charitable account" from which stock gifts to all charities are sold). Most firms require that your board pass a resolution that indicates who is authorized to sell the stock. Many firms, *when asked*, will discount their commissions for charities and, for extremely large gifts, give even deeper discounts on the sale. In rare instances, if your organization or one of your trustees has a large account with the firm, it may waive the fee on your trades completely. You can also have the donors' brokers wire stock into your account, then sell these securities online for minimal fees. To learn more about accepting stock gifts and shares in mutual funds, ask your attorney, broker, and/or a planned giving officer at another charity about establishing a program.

Gifts by Credit Card

With some credit card companies offering frequent flier miles and even "cash back" incentives, some donors prefer to use credit cards to give. Credit card gifts are also growing in popularity as giving over the Internet increases. If you only have a small number of transactions, however, credit card fees can be high.

Online Giving/Electronic Funds Transfer

Technology can make it easier to give, through the Internet (online giving) or with automatic debits from the donor's credit card or checking account (electronic funds transfers). Although relatively new to many donors and organizations, these techniques are growing in popularity.

Pledges

Giving donors the opportunity to extend payments over time (such as for two, three, or five years) inspires the largest gifts possible. That's why, for most campaigns and a number of major gifts, multiyear pledges are so popular. For donors reluctant to sign a pledge card, ask the donor to consider signing a letter of intent. It can be a simple note which indicates, "If I am able, it is my intention to give [name of your organization] $10,000 [or another amount] a year during the next five years."

Payment schedules also can be tailor-made to the donor. I've developed *balloon pledge payment schedules* for top execs who wanted to increase their payments as their incomes presumably rose. Payments on a fifty-thousand-dollar pledge over five years might be structured as follows: Year 1: $7,000; Year 2: $8,000; Year 3: $10,000; Year 4: $12,000; and Year 7: $13,000.

A great discussion is ongoing over whether a pledge is legally binding and what action, if any, a charity should take if the donor defaults. I've had donors who have had business reversals and, as friends of the organization, approached me or my staff, asking if the pledge could be written off. I've cancelled the pledge and added, "I know someday your business will be back and you'll be financially stronger than ever. Perhaps, then you'll consider making a gift again." Treating all donors as our friends has paid off. One new gift of fifty thousand dollars was made by the very same couple who just a few years earlier had asked to be relieved of a previous, smaller pledge obligation. Your organization may need to consider how it will address these situations.

Finally, some of your most committed supporters may be comfortable making an ongoing or open-ended pledge. The Salvation Army, for example, encourages individuals to pledge a monthly amount through a membership program called the Bed and Bread Club™, which enrolled 300 members its first year and grew to 3,700 participants in six years. This approach has increased the total amount given annually by many donors and provides a steady stream of income each month for feeding, clothing, and sheltering the homeless.

Make It Easy to Give
Action Plan

- Select the program or service you will offer.

- Determine the resources required (e.g., staff, legal counsel, budget). Make necessary commitments.

- Create an implementation and evaluation schedule. Include a communications plan, if required by your program.

- Seek development council or board approvals, as needed.

- Implement your new program.

- Evaluate.

12. Planned Gifts

Organizations that achieve success in planned giving often have active marketing programs that let constituents know they are interested in receiving these gifts and educate potential donors and their advisors about the benefits of planned gifts. Here are specific ways that your donors can make planned gifts.

Bequests

Bequests are one of the easiest forms of gifts to promote and a source of some of the largest gifts for many charities. Essentially, the donor instructs his or her attorney to name your organization in his or her will. The donor has many options; charitable bequests can be an exact amount, a percentage of the estate, or all or part of what remains of the estate after other distributions have been made (the *residue* or *residuary*). The bequest may be either restricted to a specific purpose or unrestricted.

There are several easy ways to promote bequests, including membership societies, brochures, and ads in your organization's publications. A simple brochure can be mailed with thank you letters for annual donations, placed in membership packets, or distributed at financial or planned giving educational programs. Your brochure may be entitled "Continue Your Interest in [name of your organization]." As a service to the donor's attorney, your bequest brochure could include sample language for making a bequest to your charity.

If your organization has a publication, promote bequests by developing ads or articles that feature individuals who have included your organization in their wills, and their comments on what motivated them to do so and the satisfaction it gives them. To create such an ad, simply identify the groups who are good candidates for bequests (current and former trustees, employees, volunteers, etc.), ask several of the most influential to consider including your organization in their estate plans, and then request that they allow you to interview and photograph them for your publication. Finally, a special mailing promoting bequests can be sent to older constituents (ages fifty or sixty-five and above) involved with your organization.

The San Diego Zoo promotes bequests and other kinds of planned gifts in its brochure "Sharing the Vision . . . Sharing the Commitment," which is mailed with membership cards. The piece makes it easy for the recipient to ask for other brochures on a number of ways to give, ranging from life insurance to bequests and life income gifts.

Life Income Gifts & Trusts

Have you ever heard, "I'd like to make a large gift to your organization, but I need the income?" You'll have the perfect response if you establish a life income program. Life income gifts to your organization pay the donor(s)—or other individuals specified by the donor(s)—income for life or for a term of years. Some life income gifts, such as *charitable gift annuities*, make relatively high payments, a definite advantage to people who are looking to supplement their income. Other types of life income gifts include the pooled income fund (which operates like a charitable mutual fund) and charitable trusts that can be customized to meet each donor's unique needs. For many charities, establishing a trust typically requires a gift of one hundred thousand dollars or more.

In addition to increasing his or her income, the donor may receive favorable tax benefits. For example, when a donor gives appreciated stock owned for more than a year, he or she can minimize or avoid capital gains taxes on the appreciation and receive an income tax charitable deduction for a portion of the gift, based on IRS calculations. Naturally, it's wise for contributors to consult with their advisors to determine how a gift may best be structured to meet their financial and tax goals.

To establish a life income program, look for an attorney familiar with state and federal laws regulating charitable gifts. Some states have registration, licensing, and investment regulations that need to be followed. Talk with planned giving officers in your area to learn more about their life income programs and receive recommendations for the attorneys and banks in which they have the most confidence.

An alternative to setting up your own program is to work with local and national community foundations and professional organizations that allow charities to pool and invest their life income gifts. For a charitable trust, the donor may work with you to establish the trust or create one independently, using his own advisors.

Continued on page 164

Planned Giving Marketing
Princeton University, Princeton, N.J.

Having an effective marketing plan is essential to success in planned giving. Among the ways Princeton University markets planned gifts are with a newsletter, a column in its alumni publication, brochures describing ways of giving, and its annual Unitholders' Meeting.

Invest in Princeton and help ensure your future.

POOLED INCOME FUNDS: A GIFT THAT GIVES BACK

One of the easiest ways to provide for Princeton's future as well as your own — while saving taxes and receiving regular payments for life — is to support the University through one of its three pooled funds.

A gift to one of these funds allows you to support Princeton and:

- provide life income to yourself and/or another beneficiary
- benefit from a charitable income tax deduction
- donate your highly appreciated securities without incurring capital gains tax
- take advantage of investment knowledge that makes Princeton's endowment so strong
- reduce eventual estate taxes

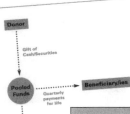

YES! I'd like to receive information on:

☐ Sample wording for a bequest to Princeton

☐ Gifts to Princeton that pay lifetime income (birthdate(s) of beneficiary/ies _____)

☐ Reducing gift and estate taxes on my large estate

☐ A gift of real estate

You are entitled to membership in THE 1746 SOCIETY if you support Princeton through a bequest, trust, or life income gift, or have named the University as beneficiary of an IRA, pension plan distribution, or life insurance policy.

☐ I have named Princeton in my estate plans. Please enroll me in The 1746 Society.

Name _____ Class _____ Day Phone (___) _____

Address _____ Evening Phone (___) _____

City _____ State _____ Zip Code _____ A good time to call: _____

Jac Weller '36
Remembering a Tiger Football Legend

Member of the College Football Hall of Fame, and named as a starter on the "All Century Team" by the Princeton Football Association, Jac Weller '36 has made an indelible mark on Tiger Football. He was called by his Head Coach, Hall of Famer, Herbert O. "Fritz" Crisler, "a remarkable combination of size, quickness and smartness" and by his Line Coach, Elton E. "Tad" Wieman, "the greatest lineman I ever coached."

Weller played offensive guard and defensive lineman for the Tigers from 1933 to 1935, and was a major factor in the team's two undefeated seasons during his tenure.

An Electrical Engineering major at Princeton, Weller went on to a successful career at General Motors Corporation where, during World War II, he was involved in manufacturing aircrafts for the United States Navy. Later in his career, he joined G.R. Murray, Inc., an insurance and investment company, where he went on to become President.

Weller was also a military historian and an expert on firearms, who wrote nine books and more than 250 articles on these subjects. He was selected to be an Honorary Curator of the U.S. Military Academy Museum at West Point and of the British Army School of Infantry Museum at Warminster.

Jac Weller left another personal legacy at the University: a significant gift from his estate helped construct the new Princeton Stadium.

For information on how a bequest can help you leave a legacy at Princeton, please contact the Planned Giving Office at:

Office of Planned Giving
Princeton University
330 Alexander Street
Princeton, NJ 08540
(609) 258-6318

Director
Ron Brown '72
Associate Directors
Sue Hartshorn
Susan C. Robichaud

or visit our website at:
www.princeton.edu/pg

The Princeton University
Planned Giving Office
invites you to a

UNITHOLDERS' MEETING

Thursday, May 3, 2001
11:30 a.m. – 2:00 p.m.

at the Nassau Club
6 Mercer Street
Princeton, New Jersey

Speakers:

Michael William Cadden, Ph.D.
Director, Program in Theatre and Dance
Princeton University

Christopher McCrudden, M.P.A.
University Treasurer
Princeton University

Please RSVP by April 27, 2001

Financial Report: 11:30 – 12:00

Reception: 12:00 – 12:30

Lunch and Keynote Speaker: 12:30 – 2:00

This meeting is held annually for all participants in Princeton University's Planned Giving program.

Keynote speaker will be Michael William Cadden, Ph.D., Director of the Program in Theatre and Dance at Princeton. Dr. Cadden has taught courses in Modern and Contemporary Drama, Irish Drama, Shakespeare, and Performance History and Criticism at Princeton for the past eight years. In 1993, he was the recipient of the University's President's Award for Distinguished Teaching.

Christopher McCrudden, M.P.A., University Treasurer, will report on investment strategies for Princeton's charitable trusts and pooled funds from 11:30 a.m. until noon. Questions and discussion will follow this presentation.

Spouses and guests are welcome.

Host: The Planned Giving Staff

Limited parking is available at the Nassau Club.

Planned Giving Marketing
Abington Memorial Hospital, Abington, Pa.

Abington Hospital promotes planned gifts with ads in its publications as well as with seminars for the public and financial advisors. These sample materials illustrate the different messages that can be used. Both Princeton and Abington highlight useful tax information. Princeton also shows the benefits of a bequest and ways to give. Abington features testimonials, as well as humor (illustration courtesy of Henry Martin). Abington's seminars often incorporate planned giving into a larger topic, such as retirement planning, ways to increase your income, or tax law changes.

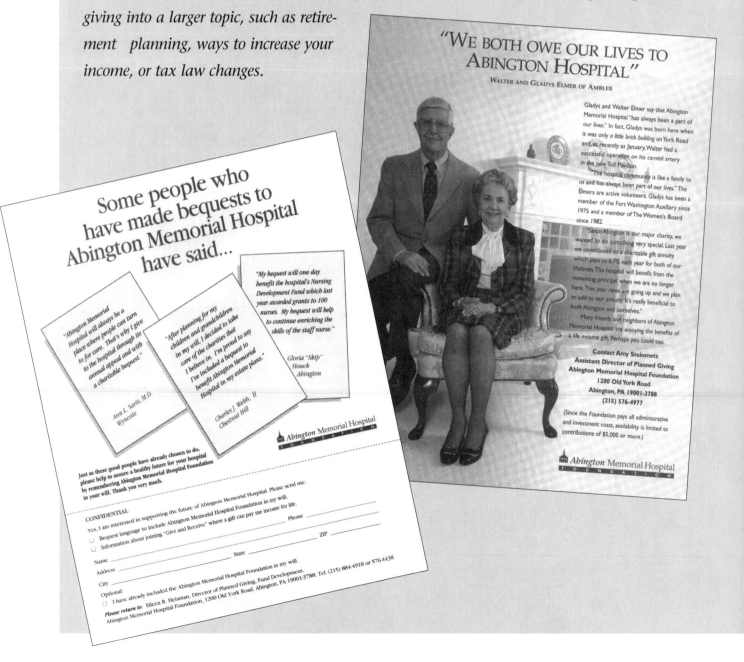

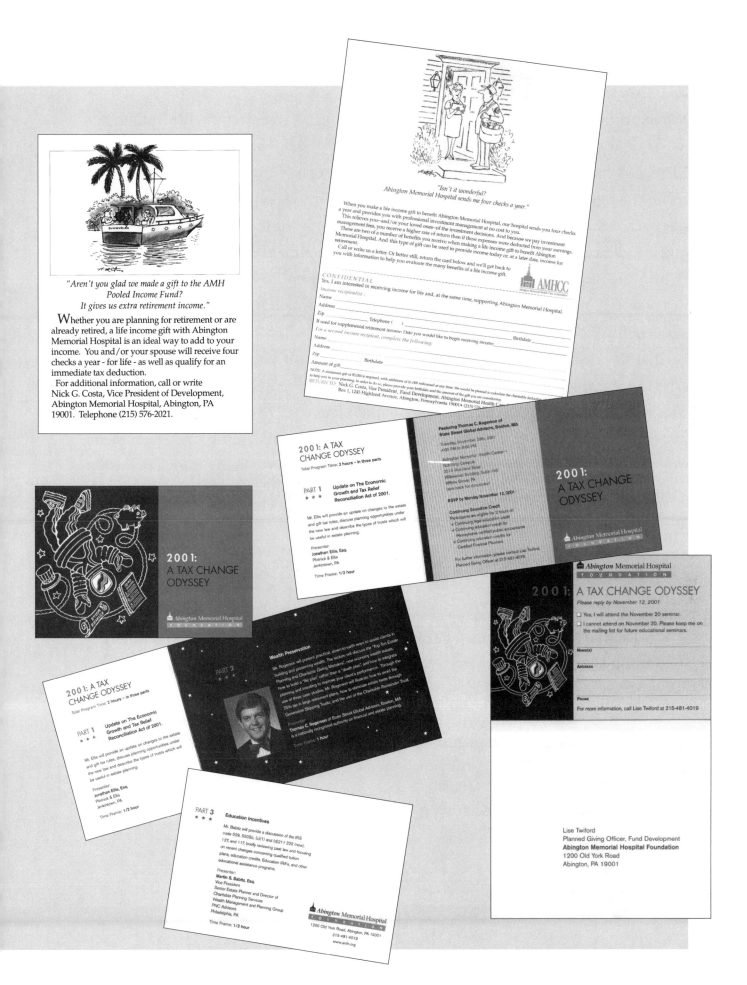

"Aren't you glad we made a gift to the AMH
Pooled Income Fund?
It gives us extra retirement income."

Whether you are planning for retirement or are
already retired, a life income gift with Abington
Memorial Hospital is an ideal way to add to your
income. You and/or your spouse will receive four
checks a year - for life - as well as qualify for an
immediate tax deduction.

For additional information, call or write
Nick G. Costa, Vice President of Development,
Abington Memorial Hospital, Abington, PA
19001. Telephone (215) 576-2021.

Real Estate

While planned gifts may be funded with a wide range of assets (stock, life insurance, art, antiques, etc.), gifts of real estate are often overlooked. There are many ways these gifts can be made. The donor may deed the property to your organization, but retain the right to use it during his or her lifetime. Or the donor may make the gift now; sell it to you at a discount (called a *bargain sale*); contribute it to fund a life income gift; or use a combination of strategies. Environmental groups may not need to own the property, but could instead may ask the donor to limit its use for the public good (e.g., no development of ocean frontage) for which he or she could receive tax benefits.

Charities need to carefully evaluate real estate gifts. If you plan to sell the property, for example, how quickly can it be sold and what costs will you incur (realtor's commissions, legal expenses, taxes, condo fees, etc.)? Will an environmental assessment study for toxic materials be required? Are there zoning or development limitations? After collecting information about the property being offered, consult with knowledgeable real estate brokers and attorneys to determine if this is a good gift to accept.

Planned Giving
Action Plan

- Select the type(s) of planned gift you will market (e.g., bequests, charitable gift annuities, etc.).

- Determine the resources required (e.g., staff, legal counsel, etc.).

- Create an implementation and evaluation schedule. Include a communications plan.

- Seek development council or board approvals, as needed.

- Implement.

- Evaluate.

A Bonus: The Very Best Way to Say "Thanks"?

Many of your TOP GIFTS™ donors are accustomed to receiving prompt and personalized service from their attorneys, CPAs, and trust departments. Distinguish your charity by extending the same level of attention. Smile when you meet them; take an interest in what they do. Be available to educate them about your organization's plans and, should they have a question or problem with your organization, be responsive to their needs. Educate them about ways of giving and any recognition you provide.

Through your service, practice philanthropy. The word philanthropy comes from the Greek words *phil*, meaning love, and *anthropos*, meaning man. In 1628, *philanthropie* first surfaced in the English language, but it can be traced back to the Romans, Egyptians, Hebrews, Greeks, and Chinese. In the words of William Wordsworth, "The best portions of a good man's life [are] his little, nameless, unremembered acts of kindness and love." Yet that selfless spirit, extended throughout your fundraising, often will be remembered and rewarded in your TOP GIFTS™ program.

TOP GIFTS™ WORKBOOK
Interest Survey for a New TOP GIFTS™ Program

What would motivate your very best prospects to make a major gift each year? What size gift do they consider "major"? Is a major gift ten thousand dollars a year, twenty-five thousand dollars annually, or only one thousand? When they give at this level, how would they like you to thank them? What have other charities done to recognize their major gifts and, among the actions taken (recognition dinners, plaques, etc.), which do they value the most? Are they happy with your organization and, if not, what steps would they like you to take to improve your performance?

Wouldn't it be great to have the answers to these and other questions? While working to develop a major gifts program at one organization, these are the questions with which I continually struggled. Maybe you have, too.

To really zero in on the answers, complete this *Interest Survey for a New Top Gifts Program*. It takes you step by step through the survey process, from identifying your best candidates for top gifts to the questions to include in your survey.

Based on the responses you receive, you'll be able to tailor a new leadership giving program or club to recognize donors of annual top gifts. You'll be able to develop membership materials, recognition programs, and other incentives and know exactly what benefits to offer—i.e., the benefits your best prospects say they are most likely to respond to.

TOP GIFTS™ WORKBOOK
Interest Survey for a New TOP GIFTS™ Program

1. Profile Your TOP GIFTS™ Prospects
What are the qualities of your best TOP GIFTS™ prospects? Can you identify qualities they share? Are they current or former board members? Long-term donors? Donors of the largest gifts? Etc. Create specific criteria of those individuals and groups most likely to make a leadership gift.

2. Identifying Your Best 10 to 25 Prospects
From your profiles, prepare a list of individuals matching any of the criteria above. Then select the top 10 to 25 individuals, companies, and foundations from which you will be seeking TOP GIFTS™ support in the future (save all other names for marketing your programs in the future). List your top prospects below.

1.	6.
2.	7.
3.	8.
4.	9.
5.	10.

3. Arrange the Interview
Depending on your relationship with each, call or write asking to "meet with you to get your reactions to a new program I'm considering for my organization. I value your opinion and would like to incorporate your ideas into shaping this program." You may need only 20 to 30 minutes with each individual. Be flexible. Be available to meet early morning, late afternoon, for lunch—whenever it is convenient for the individual. Visit them in their homes or offices. Thank them for any help they can provide; they are doing you a favor. If you'd like, bring a small thank you gift (optional) from your organization.

4. Suggested Questions to Ask
Begin by thanking the individual for his or her time and interest. To establish a relaxed tone for the meeting, present the small thank you gift and/or discuss a topic that you think is of interest (involvement with organization, known hobbies or interests, etc.). Then state that you are seeking to establish a new program—aimed at increasing support to your organization—and his or her thoughts would be helpful. Ask the following questions. If it would help the individual visualize each program, share sample materials from *Dream Builders* or from other organizations. If you have a name for your program or would like to evaluate specific concepts, add questions about them to this list.

A. If you were to evaluate our services, how would you rate them?

☐ Poor ☐ Fair ☐ Good ☐ Very Good ☐ Excellent

If "Fair" or "Poor," ask, "How could we improve our services?"

Answer: _____

TOP GIFTS™ WORKBOOK
Interest Survey for a New TOP GIFTS™ Program

B. Do you think we are an organization that could attract major gift support?
   ☐ Yes   ☐ No   If not, what changes should we make to earn that support?
   Answer: _____

C. When you think of a major gift on an annual basis, what amount comes to mind? $ _____
   When you think of our organization, what amount do you think of for a major gift? $_____

D. If we were to start a major gifts program, who do you think we should recruit to lead it?
   Do you know this individual well? Who else should be involved?
   Name(s): _____

E. When you make a major gift to another charity, what benefits do you receive? Which benefits do you value most? What specific benefits do you think we should offer?
   List suggested benefits:_____

F. Are there specific services or programs that we offer that you would be interested in supporting [if yes, list below]? Or do you prefer to allow our organization to direct your gift where it's needed most?
   Answer: _____

G. (Optional) Some of our donors have suggested that we allow individuals to make gifts of stock or by credit card. Is this something that would interest you? (Note: You may substitute other program ideas you are considering, such as life income gifts, online contributions, etc.)   ☐ Yes   ☐ No

4. Thank
Ask any remaining questions you may have, then thank the individual for his or her ideas. Later, send a note or card expressing your appreciation for the visit.

5. Tabulating the Results
From your interviews, determine which benefits were mentioned most frequently, those with the greatest interest. Use the chart below.

6. Benefits (List below)	Least Interest			Most Interest		
A.						
B.						
C.						
D.						
E.						

7. Program Design
If your responses demonstrate sufficient interest in a major or TOP GIFTS™ program, begin to design it based on your survey results. Then present your findings for review by your development council or campaign committee; seek board approval.

Attract leaders. Identify the people and organizations that can make top gifts, whose actions will serve as a model for others to follow . . . people who will help you cultivate and solicit others. Understand and respond to their best aspirations.

"Inspirational Leaders define and then champion a Cause—a magnetic vision so powerful that it draws people and their passion to it from afar."

Lance Secretan
Inspirational Leadership

"A passion for excellence means thinking big and starting small . . . excellence is achieved by people who muster up the nerve (and passion) to step out . . . They may step out for love, because of a burning desire to be the best, to make a difference."

Tom Peters & Nancy Austin
A Passion for Excellence

The best leaders often serve in two roles. As

- *Volunteers*, those dedicated, charismatic, and influential people who serve on your board and committees, and share your vision of the future; and as

- *Leadership donors*, the small percentage of your donors who make the top gifts that comprise 80 to 95 percent of your goal.

When you have leaders who embrace and embody both roles, there's a synergy that's virtually unstoppable!

Aim for Involvement

The importance of involving top leaders is repeatedly validated in many major gifts campaigns and in the fundraising literature. In his book *Mega Gifts*, Jerold Panas points out that of the thirty donors he surveyed who make gifts of one million dollars or more, twenty held leadership roles as members of the boards of the organizations they supported (see "What Motivates Million-Dollar Gifts?" and "Million-Dollar Gift Strategies"). Findings from *The Seven Faces of Philanthropy* reinforce the value of board participation in at least three ways. *When leaders are involved, the researchers say, it not only raises their commitment to the organization, but also increases the size of their gifts, and can produce a multiplier effect: leaders become more willing to recommend the organization to their friends.*

These findings are confirmed by the staffs of nearly all the Visionary Organizations profiled in *Dream Builders*; they recruited top leaders to their boards (or other major committees), involved them in meaningful decisions, and then solicited them for progressively larger gifts. The organizations were frequently able to tap into the social and business networks of board members, to enlist other leaders to make top gifts. Often, the newly recruited leader is invited to sit alongside his or her friend on the same board, committee, or panel, enriching the friendship and the relationship with the organization.

What Motivates Million-Dollar Gifts?

When was the last time you made a significant gift to a charity before you were asked? Most people answer, "Never." That answer is confirmed by research findings reported in a Gallup survey: "The reason people do not give is because they are not asked."

Yet experienced fundraisers also know that the largest gifts are received when "the ask" is made in person, by the "right person"—someone who knows the donor, who commands his or her attention.

These and other factors that influence why people give were researched by Jerold Panas and reported in his book *Mega Gifts*. To qualify as a Mega Gift, a contribution needed to be for one million dollars or more. But, in approximately twenty-five years in development, I've seen donors of *all* size gifts give for many of the same reasons.

In great detail, Panas ranks thirty reasons why people make large gifts. For our purposes, I've grouped the top ten reasons into four broad categories (the rank for each reason also is listed), then briefly highlighted strategies for integrating the benefits of these findings into your TOP GIFTS™ fundraising plan. These strategies are integrated into specific chapters of *Dream Builders*.

Interest in the organization and/or project

Belief in institution (1)

Great interest in project (2)

Respeect for institution (5)

Involvement

Serves on a board or committee (3)

Involved in the campaign (4)

Adult history of involvement with the institution (7)

Leadership

Influence of the solicitor (6)

High regard for volunteer leadership (9)

Recognition/other benefits

Memorial opportunity (8)

Tax benefits (10)

Million-Dollar Gift Strategies

Among the lessons you can take from MegaGifts are:

Interest in the organization and/or project. Prepare a list of those closest to your organization—those who endorse your mission, who have spoken favorably about the work you do, and who take pride in your organization's mission and accomplishments. List individuals and groups who may have an interest in projects for which you would like to raise funds. If you have yet to plan your fundraising project, involve in the planning process those with the greatest interest in your organization and the ability to make a large gift.

Select several of your best projects to attract interest from the largest number of top gift donors. Research individuals, businesses, foundations, government agencies, and others whose interests may match yours and/or who have a history of supporting projects similar to yours.

Increase your organization's stature and respect by differentiating or "branding" it. Are you the oldest, largest, most effective in your community or in the country? Communicate your strengths.

Involvement. Recruit top leadership on your board, committees, and campaigns. You want people who are able to give generously and who command the respect of your best potential donors. Some board members who are uncertain about fundraising may say, "We don't recruit people just for their ability to give money." I agree, but often people who can give money are also astute business leaders who have great analytical skills, communicate clearly, and make good decisions. With so much to offer, your organization needs their talents now more than ever.

Study lists of current and former board members. List those with the potential to make top gifts. Also, prepare a list of other individuals who should be recruited as board candidates in the future. It is not a coincidence that organizations with successful fundraising programs also have top-notch board recruitment and development efforts. In some instances, their past and current board members have given 25 percent, 50 percent, or more of their campaign goals.

Study lists of current and former contributors, active and past volunteers, committee members, alums, and other groups who are likely supporters. Depending on your organization's services and culture, find ways to involve people who can make a difference (as tour leaders, guest lecturers, award recipients, etc.).

Leadership. In addition to your board members, recruit the best solicitors. The higher the stature of these volunteers, the greater their potential impact. Their influence will open doors for you, attract attention to your campaign, and elevate your organization in the minds of potential donors. Take a lesson from fundraising consultants: Leadership is so important to the success of most major campaigns that questions about leadership are always asked of potential donors as part of the planning or feasibility study. "Who do you believe has the best leadership qualities to ensure the success of this campaign?" Or, "If you were asked to make a leadership gift, who would be most effective in making this request?" The names mentioned most often are the people you want on your team.

The involvement of top leaders has two levels of positive influence: both on the person being asked and on the person making the request. You'll be building commitment among your volunteers by involving them in planning and conducting your fundraising. In meetings, presentations, and with their personal gifts, you'll be educating them about the importance of your project and fundraising campaign.

Recognition/other benefits. Integrate recognition opportunities, including memorial tributes, into your campaign planning. To maximize effectiveness, match recognition opportunities with the gifts required on your table of gifts (covered in chapter 9, "Goals"). If your organization is able to integrate planned giving vehicles into your fundraising, you'll be able to provide the tax benefits many contributors are seeking.

Mega Gifts by Jerold Panas, © 1984 Bonus Books

Top Volunteers Bring Leverage, Influence & Counsel

Top leaders, whether serving as board members or solicitors—or leveraging their effectiveness in both roles—add credibility, prestige, and, in some cases, celebrity status to your organization and campaign. "If *they're* involved," many potential donors believe, "this must be a project of importance. It's worthy of taking the time to learn more about it, consider it . . . maybe even support it." The stature of these leaders will open doors for you, helping you obtain appointments where it would otherwise be difficult or impossible. Their involvement has an added bonus as well: often, by working on committees, attending board meetings, and learning about your organization's problems and potential, they serve as advisors in strategic decisions. Through the experience, you are educating them about those critical needs or giving them opportunities to make top gifts.

The best leaders elevate your organization's stature and draw attention to the work you do. Your organization and community have countless business leaders, financial advisors, judges, educators, and others who are held in high esteem and who can influence their friends, colleagues, and neighbors to support your organization. National organizations often have a network of contacts throughout the country. Look within and outside your organization to recruit people who would attract favorable attention to your fundraising, people who may be interested in your cause and who, after developing an awareness of and appreciation for the opportunities you face, may be willing to support it generously.

Don't overlook spouses of local, regional, and even national leaders; they can be highly effective spokespersons and fundraisers. Barbara Bush, for example, is as well known and well respected as her husband, George. In her lectures, television appearances, and interviews, Barbara frequently advances the cause of literacy. Madeline Abramson, treated suc-

People I

cessfully for cancer, effectively championed the need for a cancer research center, which resulted in a one-hundred-million-dollar gift from her husband, Leonard, founder of U.S. Healthcare. Leadership traits very often run in families.

Four Ways to Identify Top Leaders

You'll want to find ways to involve leaders with your organization, on your board(s) and on your planning committee and development council. Assess the strengths and weaknesses of each of your leadership groups. If you do not have a committee, council, or board focused solely on fundraising, consider establishing one.

There are at least four models for identifying top volunteers to help build an existing group or establish a new one.

- One technique is to look for people you believe are able to make leadership gifts, who are already in leadership roles, and who, perhaps, could be convinced to help your organization (see chapter 8 for a useful screening tool). If your top candidate already serves on your organization's board or is a former board member, you're in an ideal situation. This individual is already well versed about your organization. If you need to look outside your organization, network with individuals or groups with whom you have a relationship. For example, a local food bank may want to consider an owner or executive of a supermarket with whom it already has a relationship; a hospice program may want to approach the influential spouse of a current or former patient who has stature in the community; etc.

- A second approach is to be alert for people with leadership qualities. Take time to study how people react when presentations are made at board meetings and community events. Has this ever happened to you? You're at a meeting and six people give reports. Of these, five presentations are rote; the presenter shows little enthusiasm and conveys little confidence. The sixth presenter is different. He or she knows the subject. Delivers it with conviction. Maybe introduces some humor. Piques your interest. You're interested in what this person has to say. These are the qualities you want in *your* top volunteer.

- The third approach begins by developing a profile of the leadership qualities you are seeking, and sharing it with influential people such as your board members. Then, ask them to suggest names of individuals who best match the qualities you desire. Essentially, you are tapping into their social, business, and peer networks; you want to involve them in recruiting the people they nominate. For a capital campaign, most fundraising consultants will ask board members, "Who in this community do you see as having the qualities needed to successfully lead this campaign?" In other words, who has the prestige, ability, charisma, and leadership skills to serve as chair, vice chair, or in other top volunteer campaign positions? You can adapt this technique for identifying your development council chair by conducting your own survey.

- Finally, if you completed the TOP GIFTS™ workbook in chapter 6, you have a fourth approach that may be among the most effective. One product of your interest survey is a ready-made list of people who your best potential donors believe have strong leadership qualities. These are the leaders to whom they are most likely to respond favorably when they are solicited for a top gift. Increase your effectiveness by enlisting one or more of these contacts.

Regardless of the approach you use, you'll personally want to review this list for the person most qualified to serve as chair of your development council and others to serve as members of this fundraising team. Share your selections with your president or CEO, both to refine and improve the list, and to obtain administrative approval for organizing your development council. Seek board approval as well and, if needed, modify your bylaws to allow for naming this committee, to define its role, and to have its chair serve as a member of your board.

Finally, be sure you can work successfully with the volunteer you select. If your styles and expectations are radically different, it's best to keep looking. Chemistry is important.

How Important Is Your Development or Campaign Chair . . .
And the Size of His or Her Gift?

How important is leadership to the success of your fundraising?

The late Harold "Si" Seymour, the father of American fundraising, professed that leadership is "rare, beyond price, and always the nucleus of significant achievement . . . you need [leaders] more than money."

Yet your top leader, your chair, *does* need to give—and at the right level—if you are to be successful. The "right level" does not need to be the largest gift; what's important is that this gift be perceived as significant, as a "stretch gift" given the leader's finances. Is it a gift that will inspire others? Generally, at a minimum, this gift should be one of the higher amounts on the table of gifts in your fundraising campaign.

One professional I approached to lead a campaign, Ed, shared with me the size of the gift he was considering. "Is this enough?" he asked, genuinely concerned that his gift be large enough to compel others to give at high levels. "Yes, Ed, that's really quite generous," I responded. But he wasn't convinced. "Why don't you call a few trustees and tell them I asked you to call? Indicate that I'm being considered as a possible chair for the campaign and that I'm prepared to give this amount. Then, ask them if it's enough for me to chair the campaign. Let me know what they say." Fortunately for me, the response to the phone survey was *extremely* favorable. One donor had the best answer: "If Ed gives that amount," he chuckled, "I'm going to have to increase my gift." Clearly, Ed was the person we needed. You should strive for that kind of impact.

How to Recruit A TOP GIFTS™ Chair

Ideally, the best candidate to chair your campaign or TOP GIFTS™ program is someone who has these qualities:

- A close affiliation with your organization;

- An awareness and understanding of your organization's needs and opportunities;

- A strong commitment to your organization;

- A personal or family tradition of philanthropy.

If these qualities are present, you may want to consider making a *double ask*. That is: first, seeking leadership in service; second, asking for a leadership gift. If your candidate has a close bond with your organization, both tasks can be accomplished in one meeting.

If the candidate's relationship with your organization is not close, you may need to stagger these two requests. First, ask the individual to serve in a key role or on an important committee; then, later, ask the individual to consider making a leadership gift. Take time to evaluate your situation.

The Double Ask

Here's one approach to recruiting a key leader using the double ask.

Begin by preparing a description for the position, which defines the two responsibilities just described:

- The leadership role and related tasks; and

- The leadership gift to your program or campaign.

When you meet, present the candidate with a copy of the job description and ask him or her to consider serving as chair. You'll appear well organized, and the position description will put the gift discussion on the agenda. Your position description needn't be complicated. Here are some responsibilities you might want to include:

- With the consent of the vice president of fund development and approval of the board of trustees, recruit members of the development council and conduct up to four meetings per year to encourage leadership gifts to our organization;

- Make a leadership gift commensurate with your ability;

- Serve as a trustee of our organization and make regular reports on the council's progress to the board;

- Recommend policies that enhance the effectiveness of the fundraising campaign;

- Working with council members and staff, identify and cultivate individuals, business leaders, and foundations able to make leadership gifts;

- Assist in developing programs and strategies to attract and recognize these gifts; and

- Participate in asking for key gifts from five to ten key individuals.

When candidates review the position description, I find that the discussion often will focus first on the administrative responsibilities. Then the candidate may ask, "What did you have in mind with 'Make a leadership gift commensurate with your ability'?" Here's where your table of gifts has particular value (we'll create one together in chapter 9). Share the table of gifts with the candidate and wait for a response. If the candidate says he or she is not able to give at any of these levels, emphasize the importance of the chair setting an example, inspiring others to follow. Point out that the campaign will not succeed without these gifts. Perhaps, through a gift of stock or a payment over several years, this gift would be possible.

If the individual is unable to make a leadership gift, ask if more time would help. If not, emphasize the importance of the individual's involvement in the campaign in some way. Perhaps he or she can suggest others who would be able to serve as chair. Thank the individual for his or her ideas and time. Stress how much you value this input.

Who Should Be Involved in Recruiting the Chair?

Ideally, you want two people: someone who knows the candidate well and a top-level person from your organization. Whenever possible, I'm a strong believer in the "buddy system" for solicitations (i.e., two people), both for when you're seeking volunteers and for when you're asking for top gifts. The person who knows the candidate sets up the appointment, perhaps in the candidate's office or home. This can be done by phone or a simple letter, asking for time "to discuss a project that may interest you at XYZ organization. I'd like to bring [name of top-level person] who is [title] of XYZ to explain it in more detail." Keep the topic general . . . *the goal is to get the appointment, not to make the request*.

When you do meet, allow time for relationship building. The person who knows the candidate may ask about the candidate's health, family members, hobbies, business, vacation, or other topics. This discussion is important both for displaying a genuine interest in the individual and for helping set a relaxed tone for the meeting. If the candidate has had a direct involvement with your organization, so much the better. You can briefly talk about his or her contributions to its success and its current status.

Then present your case: explain what you're seeking from the individual, the importance of the task, and why you hope the candidate will agree. If it's to organize and serve as chair of your new development council, the conversation might go as follows: "When we asked board members to suggest the names of individuals who could lead our new fundraising program, your name was mentioned most often. They said such things as, 'There's really only one person for the job and that's Janice. . . . If you can get Janice involved, I'd be willing to help. Also, when Janice was involved, we got a lot done and she made it look easy. We had a lot of fun working with her.' You can see why we're here today. We hope you'll consider serving as chair of our new development council. We'd be happy to work with you in selecting members. To help you evaluate the position, we've prepared this position description for you to review."

When to Accept "No" . . . And When Failure Isn't an Option

What if the person says, "No, I don't want to chair or serve on your development council or campaign"? What's next?

The answer can be found in your response to this question: how important is this person to the success of your fundraising?

For one organization, I was convinced that there was only one person who could do the job. Several trustees confirmed that belief. I used the buddy system (a highly regarded trustee joined me) in approaching the candidate, yet, the first time, he turned us down. "I'm really too busy. I'm involved in a campaign for my college," he replied. We thanked him for his time and asked him to suggest others to serve. As he named others who might be candidates, we discussed the merits and weaknesses of each person. No one seemed "just right." We agreed to meet in a week.

At our next meeting, I had the president of my organization join us. We again reviewed the names of others who might serve in this role. We were stymied. "What can I do to help you say 'Yes'?" I asked. "My time is really limited," he said. "I'd like to say yes, but I'm under a lot of pressure."

I suggested some ways it *might* work. "We'll keep it to four meetings a year, recruit a strong chair for each of the subcommittees where most of the work will be done . . . You can pick your own committee members and I'll even help you recruit them." He said he would think about it.

At our third meeting, the president, the trustee, and I waited silently for his response. He began by defining a way that it might work. "If there's a problem or decision to be made, before calling me, clearly define the problem, develop possible responses, and select the one that you think will be most effective. Then call me and briefly present the problem and solution. If I need the other options, we can review them. I really don't have the time to put into researching solutions." We agreed to his conditions. "Okay," he said finally. "I'll do it." We had our campaign chair. And we were right. He was the best volunteer leader I had worked with; he worked joyfully, focusing on results and inspiring us to raise nearly twice our original goal.

What Does the Chair Expect of Staff?

What your chair and development council members are really looking for is assurance that *they will be successful* and you'll be there with them, helping them succeed.

The specific working style and level of support required varies with each volunteer. Most chairs will expect you to host meetings, send out notices, and take minutes. The minutes can be as simple as recording the name of the committee; date, time and location of the meeting; who attended; and what assignments and progress were made. A few of the volunteers I've worked with have offered the services of their secretaries.

Avoid "high maintenance" volunteers. Often these individuals get so hung up on the details, they lose sight of your goal . . . which is raising funds to strengthen your organization.

Board Recruitment

The same approach can be used to recruit board members. Start by drafting the position description, then personally meet with each candidate to make the request. Use the buddy system and ask a trustee or another person of importance to join you. Be persistent to secure the best candidates. Remember, your board sets the direction of your organization, and the quality of your board members contributes to whether you receive top-level gifts.

In most fundraising campaigns, the board gives 10, 20, or 30 percent or more of the campaign goal, and a positive board experience can be a great way to cultivate and inspire leadership gifts. It's the role of your nominating committee or board development committee to recruit the very best leaders and to engage them in the work you do.

The Honorary Chair

In addition to appointing a chair for a major gifts campaign, many organizations name one or more honorary chairs. Most often, these individuals have made the highest-level gifts, and are deserving of recognition. In one building campaign, for example, the couple who made the top gift were listed as honorary chairs along with another couple who had consistently been among the organization's top five donors for every major campaign. Also, consider this recognition if you believe the names of your honorary chairs will add prestige to your efforts and they have—or are likely to—support your fundraising with a major gift.

Leadership Staff

In many organizations, fundraising staff make as many—or more—requests for major gifts as top volunteers. With a shortage of fundraising professionals, it's not surprising that organizations have had to become creative in finding qualified and talented individuals to staff, lead, and manage their fundraising programs.

One approach I'm seeing increasingly often is for people to be hired who have a well-established network of contacts and/or are who already well known and respected among key constituents. But, for every success story, there is also the possibility of failure. For the right individual, the rewards can far exceed the risks. Here are several examples to guide you if you are considering adding "celebrity" staff.

Failures

After launching a successful fundraising program, a friend of mine, Sally, decided to accept a position with another organization. She was asked to suggest candidates for the director of development position, and she identified three people with considerable depth in fundraising. Instead, the organization hired an individual "who worked in the mayor's office. He really will be great. Tom has a lot of contacts and can build the program you started," Sally was told. Not long after, the chair of the organization's development council, who could easily give ten thousand dollars or more a year, called Sally to say, "Tom is replacing your annual fund with a raffle. Each ticket is one hundred dollars. What do you think?"

"Sam," she said, "Do you plan to continue to give ten thousand dollars this year?"

"No, I probably will just buy a couple of tickets," he replied.

Sally called Tom and informed him that Sam was "willing and able to write a check for ten thousand dollars. All you have to do is ask him."

Tom replied, "But, Sally, this will be fun." Sally later learned that, within two years, Tom was no longer with her former employer. Clearly, Tom didn't understand the role of TOP GIFTS™ fundraising.

Successes

A religious university is experiencing unprecedented growth, both in adding new buildings and programs, and in fundraising. One online fundraising journal believes that a major factor is the new development director, a well-liked retired football coach with a record number of winning seasons. When it comes to asking for major gifts, the former coach confides, he knows the "players." Plus, when the college's football team is winning, the development director says, he's especially successful. People like to be associated with winners, he says.

The spouse of a leading national official was hired to solicit big gifts, preferably over one million dollars each, for a major new facility. While the local newspaper questioned the appointment, this articulate and enthusiastic fundraiser successfully solicited more than twenty million dollars during her eighteen months in fundraising. "For me, fundraising is not a big deal. I love being with people and, working in political campaigns, I'm accustomed to asking for money. This is a great cause for which I'm working, so it really feels natural for me."

TOP GIFTS™ WORKBOOK
Recruiting Top Leaders

Elevate the stature of your TOP GIFTS™ program by enlisting the very best leadership. You'll consider five approaches to identify leadership, prepare a list of candidates to chair your program, select the recruitment team, and begin assembling people to serve on your leadership committee.

1. Select the approach(es) you will use to recruit a top leader:

    ☐ Recruit people already in leadership positions and able to make lead gifts; may already be involved in your organization

    ☐ Recruit people demonstrating leadership qualities—may be involved with other organization(s)

    ☐ Develop leadership profile and network with trustees for suggested candidates

    ☐ Recruit candidates recommended during interest survey

    ☐ Other/combination of techniques

2. List your preferred candidate(s) for chair of development council or campaign. Then list the people whom you believe would be most effective in recruiting each individual.

    Candidate(s) for Development Council Chair   *Recruitment Team*

    1. _____   _____

                                                 _____

                                                 _____

    2. _____   _____

                                                 _____

                                                 _____

    3. _____   _____

                                                 _____

                                                 _____

3. List groups you plan to solicit. Then, for each group, list the person you believe would be most successful in representing that group's interest on your development council and effective in helping you solicit its members:

    Group   *Top Volunteer*

    Trustees

    Administrators   _____

    _____   _____

    _____   _____

    _____   _____

TOP GIFTS™ WORKBOOK
Recruiting Top Leaders

---

4. Prepare position description for chair, development council including description of:

   ☐ the leadership or management tasks

   ☐ a leadership gift to your program or campaign

   Complete your list of Opportunities (see chapter 5). In chapter 9, we'll learn how to create a table of gifts for each Opportunity you select for fundraising

---

5. Meet with your president/CEO to determine what, if any, approvals are needed to name your development council. Ask him or her to review your list and make suggestions for additions/deletions. Prioritize your candidates for chair (first, second, third choices), as well as council members.

   ☐ Administrative approval (pres./CEO)   ☐ Board vote/approval

   ☐ Board chair approval   ☐ Change in bylaws

   Ask your president/CEO to review, refine, and approve your list of fundraising opportunities.

---

6. Enlist recruitment team members. Determine who on the team will set up the meeting(s), discuss and role-play how you plan to present your request. Determine if it would be helpful to describe Opportunities for fundraising.

   For each candidate:

   Candidate's Name   *Daytime Phone*

   _____   _____

   Recruitment Team Member   *Daytime Phone*

   1. _____   _____

   2. _____   _____

   Strategy

---

7. Meet with candidate and make request. Present position description. If possible, lock in commitment for service, possible members, process for recruiting council.

   If candidate needs time to consider, set date for follow-up meeting.   Date _____

---

8. Regardless of outcome, send candidate note thanking him or her for considering your request.

---

9. If necessary, re-strategize or go to second candidate on your list.

A ttract leaders. Identify the people and organizations that can make top gifts, whose actions will serve as a model for others to follow . . . people who will help you cultivate and solicit others. Understand and respond to their best aspirations.

"Attempt the impossible in order to improve your work."

Bette Davis

"Building self-confidence in others is a huge part of leadership. It comes from providing opportunities and challenges for people to do things they never imagined they could do— rewarding them after each success in every way possible."

Jack Welch (former CEO of General Electric) with John A. Byrne

Jack: Straight from the Gut

Congratulations! By now, you've identified several Opportunities for fundraising and recruited the People (your development council or board) who will assist you in reaching your goals. These are the foundation on which you'll build. In this chapter, we'll identify the people who can make top gifts and evaluate their potential.

Who are they? Where do you find your best sources of leadership gifts? Historically, fundraisers have first appealed to those closest to the organization, then worked their way out to the uninitiated. There's a lot of history to that approach (see "'Poor Richard' Was Rich in Fundraising Wisdom," below).

"Poor Richard" Was Rich in Fundraising Wisdom

To many, Benjamin Franklin is also known as "Poor Richard," author of the *Farmers' Almanack*.

In 1751, Franklin launched a campaign to build the first hospital in the United States. Describing his journey, he said, "My practice is to go first to those who may be counted upon to be favorable, who know the cause and believe in it, and ask them to give as generously as possible. When they have done so, I go next to those who may be presumed to have a favorable opinion and to be disposed to listening, and I secure their adherence.

"Lastly, I go to those who know little of the matter or have no known predilection for it and influence them by presentation of the names of those who have already given."

Franklin's methodology is classic fundraising: Start with the institutional family and prior contributors (those "who know the cause and believe in it"). Next, contact the people you serve and/or who have an interest in your work ("those who may be presumed to have a favorable opinion and to be disposed to listening"); and finally, go to those who respond to leadership and influence ("those who know little of the matter . . . [I] influence them by presentation of the names of those who have already given.").

Creating Your TOP GIFTS™ Lists

Your best candidates for major and planned gifts are likely to be found in the following groups.

Prior Contributors

Start with two lists:

- *Largest Gifts:* Prepare this first list by printing the names, addresses, and gift amounts of your largest contributors in descending order (largest gifts appearing first).

- *Loyal Donors*: Your second list consists of your most loyal donors. It should follow the same format, and indicate those individuals who give consistently, year after year.

If you're organizing a new development program and do not have the data to develop "largest gifts" and "loyal donors" lists, you may find that your organization has had campaigns for special projects during its history. If so, ask your treasurer's office or finance department for records of past gifts. Don't be surprised if you are told, "Sorry, we didn't keep records of our past campaigns." Check your institution for plaques with the names of families closely allied to your values and purposes. Recruit a volunteer to transcribe the names of contributors from the plaques along with the plaque size (or gift amount, if you have a key that correlates the two). Then, using a telephone book, alumni directory, online searches, or other references, create a list of names, addresses, and telephone numbers of your past donors. Continue to explore with your finance department if there are ledgers of gift records in storage. Often, with some prodding, these records can be found. Organizations without a history of campaigns will want to explore other options listed below.

Your "Institutional Family"

List your trustees, former trustees, highly paid staff (administrators, faculty, deans, coaches, doctors . . . the top earners in your organization), members of your leadership committees, and your most loyal volunteers who may have the ability to make major gifts. If they commit to a leadership gift and allow you to publicize it during your campaign, you'll have a ringing endorsement, which often inspires others to give. Focus on those who are able to give most generously.

New Potential Donors

There are many ways to add to your list. The real challenge is zeroing in on the names with the best potential. Here are some sources I've used effectively:

- *Recommendations from Board Members and Fundraising Volunteers:* In most capital campaigns, consultants look for two types of names. The first is leadership volunteers; the second is leadership donors. Ask board members, other leaders of the organization, and financial advisors (bankers, CPAs, investment brokers, etc.) to provide the names of people of stature and wealth who should be involved in your program. These are the people who can make big gifts and/or encourage others to do so. Individuals whose names are indicated most frequently are the people you want to find ways to interest and involve.

- *People You Serve or Benefit:* Whom do you serve? Students, parents, and alumni? Doctors, patients, parents and family? Who are the people who cheer most enthusiastically when you succeed or are saddened by your setbacks or defeats?

- *Recognition Reports, Directories, and News Stories:* Often, people who give generously support many nonprofits. By reviewing recognition reports from other organizations, you can assess the giving capacity of some of your prospects and identify other individuals to add to your lists. I have several volunteers who regularly send me donor reports from the United Way, colleges, leading arts organizations, and other groups.

Recognition reports can also demonstrate the potential of current donors. Here's an example:

One of my most loyal fundraising volunteers shared with me that "I love volunteering here. You are my favorite organization." Each year, she donated one thousand dollars, sometimes before we even asked. When I received a donor report from her college, her name was listed under the *ten-thousand-dollar* category. "Clearly, I'm confused," I told her one day. "You indicated that *we're your favorite charity*. We're grateful for your support. But why are you giving ten thousand dollars to your college each year and only one thousand dollars to us?" She looked at me and smiled. "Oh that's easy. You never asked!" That's a problem we overcame. As a result of this simple inquiry, this donor started writing *two* checks for ten thousand dollars each year: one to her college and one to us.

But the story is not over. We asked her, "Would you help us encourage some of your friends to make a leadership gift to us as well?"

"Absolutely," she said. Later, she made good on her commitment. She asked one individual to give twenty-five thousand dollars. He did. Then she asked him again a year later. He repeated his gift.

This is not an isolated story. A local couple, Steve and Linda, were personally solicited for an annual gift of ten thousand dollars—which, at the time, seemed like a real stretch. We thanked them repeatedly. Less than a month later, a news story honored this couple for making a one-hundred-thousand-dollar gift to another organization. Since they were not as involved with our organization, I decided that, if there was ever an opportunity, I'd invite one of them to serve. Later, after Linda joined our planning committee, she was excited by the progress we were making. With her influence, a local foundation directed a grant to us and she personally contributed one hundred thousand dollars to our program.

Directories and membership listings also can be useful. One membership directory useful for recruiting new board members and donors, for example, features young business owners who have achieved great financial success. I've also obtained directories of residents of more affluent retirement communities; some of these residents later make large gifts after being contacted by letter or by a volunteer.

A word of caution: Some organizations and communities prohibit outside use of their directories, so use good judgment. Even if there are no known restrictions, you'll want to keep the sources of your data confidential.

Take time to network with your volunteers to learn what directories and recognition reports are available, and consider securing those that would be most helpful.

Businesses, Foundations, and Government Programs

There are several ways to identify businesses that may be good candidates for gifts:

- Review a list of those companies from which you purchase goods and services;

- Review business directories, journals, news stories, and other public sources for the names of companies, foundations, and government programs with a potential interest in your needs, and with which you could establish a relationship. The Internet can be a helpful source. Prospect researcher Jan Grieff shares some leads (see "Top Prospect Research Internet Sites"). Later in the chapter, research scientist David Newburg, Ph.D., adds his own tips for successfully competing for grants.

- Ask your volunteers to indicate which businesses they could assist you in approaching. Some companies only support charities in which one of their executives or other employees is involved. If appropriate, consider nominating its president or other member of its executive staff to your board or another major committee.

Finally, you can also consider renting lists of names. One firm specializing in list rentals recommends they you first develop a profile of the characteristics of your top donors, then match lists to this profile. For example, if your best donors typically were gardeners who read *U.S. News and World Report*, the company would rent you a list of people with these two interests.

Top Prospect Research Internet Sites

By Jan Grieff, jgrieff@jgresearch.com

Addresses

Many address and phone sites are available; *www.theultimates.com* provides access to a wide variety of them. One in particular is:

- **Infospace:** *www.infospace.com/info/wp/index.htm*
- **Infospace Reverse:** Also at this site, you can look up people in reverse—find them by entering only an address or a phone number. *www.infospace.com/info/wp/reverse.htm*

Biographic Information

Biographic information is best accessed through profession-specific sites, although some information may be available through newspapers and periodicals accessed via search engines or specific newspaper sites. In addition, for an individual who is a director of a public company or among its the five highest-paid officers, biographical information can be found on proxy statements, 10-Ks, and other SEC documents. Many company Web sites also list profiles of employees—even those companies that are not public and those individuals who are not among the highest-paid officers or directors.

PROFESSION-SPECIFIC SITES

- **Lawyers—Martindale and Hubbel:** *lawyers.martindale.com/xp/Martindale/home.xml*
  Search by individual or firm; good biographical information.

- **Physicians—American Medical Association:** *www.ama-assn.org*
  Search by name or specialty; limited biographical information.

- **Stockbrokers:** *www.nasdr.com/2000.htm*
  Search by broker or company; very specific; limited biographical information.

ACCESSING BIOGRAPHIC INFORMATION THROUGH NEWSPAPERS AND MAGAZINES

The most comprehensive link to newspaper and magazines may be found at Library Spot:

- **Newspapers:** *libraryspot.com/newspapers.htm*

- **Magazines:** *libraryspot.com/magazines.htm*

ACCESSING BIOGRAPHIC INFORMATION THROUGH CORPORATE INFORMATION

- **Hoovers:** *www.hoovers.com*
  Provides links to biographic information on top corporate officers. Once at the company's profile page, you can access other biographic information available about the management team.

Top Prospect Research Internet Sites

By Jan Grieff, jgrieff@jgresearch.com

- **10k Wizard:** *www.10kwizard.com*

  Provides access to proxy statements and other government-mandated public company information.

- **Dun and Bradstreet:** *www.dnb.com*

  Provides limited biographic information about officers/owners of private companies. It is an expensive way to obtain biographic information, but, in some cases, the only alternative.

Wealth Information

Wealth information on the Internet focuses primarily on earnings found by reviewing salary and stock-holdings. Salaries are available for individuals who are among the five highest-paid officers of a public company. In addition, newspaper and magazine articles frequently discuss salaries of the highest-paid CEOs, and regional business journals will sometimes publish lists of the highest paid CEOs in their area (often compiled from government [SEC] information). Job-type salary information can be obtained through various profession-specific or salary survey sites.

SALARY INFORMATION FOR OFFICERS OF PUBLIC COMPANIES

- **Yahoo:** *finance.yahoo.com*

  Provides salary information about top executives. This information is condensed and simplified from government documents such as proxy statements.

- **10k Wizard:** *www.10Kwizard.com*

  Provides access to SEC documents.

PROFESSION-SPECIFIC SALARY INFORMATION

- **Architects:** *www.e-architect.com*

- **Lawyers:** *www.lawjobs.com*

- **Physicians:** *www.physicianssearch.com/physician/salary.html*

- **Veterinarians:** *www.AVMA.org/cim/vstat3.htm*

SALARY SURVEY SITE

The very best salary survey site is *jobstar.org*. Also see *www.salary.com*.

STOCKHOLDINGS

SEC regulations require that certain individuals declare their holdings in a public company when a trade occurs, or that the company publish a list of certain individuals once a year as part of the proxy statement. Directors of public companies, anyone who owns more than 5 percent of the outstanding shares of a public company, and the five highest-paid officers of a public company are required to disclose their holdings annually or when a trade is made.

- **Proxy Statement Information:** *10kwizard.com*
  Allows searching by an individual's name.

- **Stock Transaction Information:** *finance.yahoo.com*
  Provides a year's worth of transactions searchable by individual's name.

REAL ESTATE

The University of Virginia *(indorgs.virginia.edu/portico/home.html)* has compiled the most comprehensive set of "free" real estate sites on the Web. These sites are organized by geographic region and provide good access to tax assessor databases throughout the country.

- **Yahoo:** *realestate.yahoo.com/realestate/homevalues/*

- **Domania:** *domania.com/index.jsp*
  Provides comparable real estate sales in a given neighborhood.

- **Assessment Ratios:** *pubweb.nwu.edu/~cap440/assess.html*
  Provides the ratio of assessed value to market value.

News

- **Newslink and Newspapers.com:** *www.newslink.org or www.newspapers.com*
  Provide links to newspapers and magazines throughout the U.S.

- **Google:** *www.google.com*

Qualifying Individuals on Your Lists

As you review names from these and other sources, your list of potential TOP GIFTS™ donors will grow to where you need to prioritize. How do you know which individuals are the most likely to make large gifts, the best people to personally contact?

To qualify individuals, use the simple "four Cs" screening method. These four criteria create a snapshot of giving potential; they are indicators of wealth, interest in and involvement with your organization, influential relationships, and charitable inclination. The four Cs stand for:

CAPACITY, CONNECTIVITY, CONTACT AND CHARITY

By answering the following questions and using information sources suggested, you can develop a charitable interest profile for each individual, helping you further refine and narrow your list.

Four Cs Screening Method		
Indicators	*Questions to Ask. Does this individual . . .*	*Data Sources*
Capacity	Have the ability to make a top gift?	Internet/published information Prospect/ family/friends Applied research
Connectivity	Believe in what you do? Have a sense of belonging to (or identifying with) your organization?	Organization/donor files Prospect/family/friends Internet/published information
Contact	Have contact or a connection with your organization and/or its top leadership (trustees, staff, others)? If so, with whom?	Organization/donor files Prospect/family/friends Internet/published information
Charity	Have a history of charitable giving? What is the amount of his/her largest gift?	Donor files Prospect/family/friends Internet/published information

CAPACITY

Does this individual have the ability to make a large gift? Finding the answer is not an exact science.

"It's impossible to get a precise or complete measure of an individual's wealth from public sources, even with the full resources of the best libraries or the Internet," says Jan Grieff, a professional prospect researcher. "An *exact* measure of wealth involves subtracting liabilities from assets. This information is just not publicly available, nor is it necessary to be an effective fundraiser. Instead, look for *indicators of wealth* that help you assess the level or capacity to give. Three wealth indicators are: earnings and assets; recent inheritance; and marriage."

Earnings include salary and bonuses; income from investments, royalties, and other sources of income. *Assets* include stock holdings, real estate, and art and collectibles, Grieff says. *Inherited wealth* can be identified from a recent will. If an individual has died during the past five or ten years, this information may be meaningful. Wills that are probated are public information; there usually is an estate settlement report, and this information typically is available at your local or county courthouse. Another approach is to research family information such as social registers or biographical information on parents, Grieff advises.

If the potential donor has acquired wealth through *marriage*, research the spouse's earnings and assets. "It's critical to find out who has the earnings and assets, and incorporate this into your plans. I find a spouse is less likely to give away the partner's earnings or assets. You need to involve the *right* person or include both in your cultivation strategies," Grieff says.

When there are several sources from which gifts can be drawn (business, foundation, inheritance), this increases the individual's capacity rating.

Someone earning $250,000 per year may have the capacity to make a ten-thousand-dollar annual gift (see "Capacity and Giving" table, below). A gift of one hundred thousand dollars or more annually, however, would be difficult for this individual unless there are assets to draw on, several funding sources (such as personal/family wealth, business, or foundation), and/or a payment schedule of five or more years. This gift also could be made if the individual recently had a financial windfall (such as the sale of a business, stock, or home). Factors such as these (large asset holdings, several sources to fund a gift, financial windfall) can improve your chances of a major gift commitment.

Don't overlook published sources for ratings of wealth and gifts to other organizations. One of our donors recently sold his business for $150 million; the buyout consisted of seventy-five million dollars in cash and seventy-five million in stock. The business is less than five years old. How did I learn this? I read a news article appearing in the business section of my daily newspaper. The news article also appeared on this paper's homepage.

Grieff has compiled several lists of the most useful Internet sites for fundraisers (see "Top Prospect Research Internet Sites"; see also appendix D, "Top Listservs for Development Professionals"). Yet, even with these resources, she says, often the most timely, accurate, and useful information comes from the individual, family members, and business and social contacts. I agree.

"Start with your high-level volunteers," she says. "Meet one-on-one; ask them to identify those individuals who would be best able to help your organization. Through this informal review process, they may also share information about their capacity, whether they have charitable intent, how closely they feel affiliated with your organization, and who is the right contact. Anecdotal information can be better than what you find on the Internet or in a directory. It's more timely, useful, and can result in a referral."

Here's an example. From a volunteer, I learned that a donor giving one thousand dollars annually had just sold her vacation home for one million dollars. She was interested in learning how to offset some of the gain with a charitable deduction. Would I give her a call? A fifty-thousand-dollar gift resulted. Another donor, a trustee, was helping me identify potential donors to our campaign. He suggested a young businessman who "bought my land for five million dollars." This comment gave me insights into both the trustee's wealth and that of the person being suggested.

Planned gifts, such as bequests and life income gifts, can be significantly higher than the guidelines provided in the table "Capacity and Giving: What You Should Ask for Based on Salary." This is because these gifts are from assets, and there are likely to be other planning considerations (e.g., the donor is determining the disposition of his or her estate; he or she may want the additional income that a life income gift could provide; etc.). In the case of a bequest, a donor may leave you 20 percent of his or her estate—or all of it.

For public corporations and large foundations, "It's much easier to do research," Grieff says. "Everything is out there for you on the Internet. Most public corporations and many of the larger foundations put as much information as possible on the Web to minimize phone calls requesting basic information and to encourage better-directed proposals. With a privately held company, it's different; the gift is coming out of the owner's pocket. The key to success in such cases is to build a relationship with the owner.

"Cultivate small foundations as you would an individual. Determine what their interests are and speak to those interests."

Grieff says that government agencies have "very specific interests and guidelines which must be met. Larger organizations, such as colleges and universities, find that having a lobbyist can help. But even smaller nonprofits can establish connections with their political leaders, which may be helpful."

Capacity & Giving
What You Should Ask for Based on Salary

For annual giving programs, a common practice is to ask individuals to consider a gift for an amount that is equal to 1 to 3 percent of their annual earnings; some organizations may be more ambitious in their requests. Some colleges and universities suggest amounts averaging 2 to 5 percent of net annual earnings, while religious organizations may ask for 5 to 10 percent of salary. Major gifts and campaign contributions may be in the 5 to 10 percent range, paid over a number of years.

If I make . . . (annual earnings)	Ask me to consider a gift of . . . 1% annually	5%	10%	5 yr. pledge*
$50,000	$500	$2,500	$5,000	$7,500 to $12,500
$100,000	$1,000	$5,000	$10,000	$15,000 to $25,000
$250,000	$2,500	$12,500	$25,000	$37,500 to $60,000
$1,000,000	$10,000	$50,000	$100,000	$150,000 to $250,000

* Five-year pledge based on 3% to 5% of annual salary. May be a higher percentage.

People II: Leadership Donors

CONNECTIVITY

The best candidates for top gifts are those who believe in your mission and the project for which you are seeking funds. Assess the level of knowledge and involvement the individual has with your organization and/or the individual's commitment to the work you do. Are they "connected"? Remember: the greater the involvement, the larger the commitment and potential gift that results.

Records of involvement include your organization's board membership lists, course attendance rosters, donor records, favorable letters, and survey responses. Don't overlook comments from the individual, family and friends, or published news stories, which may indicate high levels of satisfaction or an interest in a particular program or service that you provide.

If the individual is unaware of your organization, a major or top gift is unlikely. Creating a connection can occur through a friend or business associate, or through a natural interest in the project or program you seek to fund. Robert Mondavi, as you might suspect, has a passion for excellence in food and wine. It's not surprising, then, that he is at the vanguard of several major projects advancing food and wine education, including a gift of twenty-five million dollars to the University of California at Davis for the Robert Mondavi Institute for Wine and Science. Ed Piszek has an interest in advancing Polish causes. He both applauded and supported Little League Baseball's plans to build Little League facilities in Poland.

"It's all about being donor-driven," Jan Grieff says. "You want to identify those needs and opportunities that match your donors' interests. Look for connections to the potential donor's interests, and relationships with people who know the potential donor well and are loyal to your organization."

CONTACT

Research confirms that peer groups have a powerful influence; relationships with and endorsements from family, friends, and the groups to which individuals belong influence their attitudes and behavior. These contacts often are with your president, a board member, or other leader within your institution. As indicated previously, in the $7.9 million campaign for Arcadia University (Glenside, Pa.), a donor stepped forward and contributed an additional one million dollars—bringing her total campaign giving to $2.5 million—to name the library after a close friend, the college's president, Bette Landman.

Volunteer-training materials for *The Anniversary Campaign for Princeton* identified signs of or opportunities for large corporate gifts as follows:

> Volunteers in companies that are prospering in areas related to Campaign priorities, such as finance, biotechnology and material science, can provide valuable leads to new corporate donors. Volunteers can also help to secure gifts honoring top executives who retire during the next five years. Retirements offer special opportunities: companies that might not ordinarily consider a gift to endowment may well make one to honor company leaders who are Princeton alumni.

If you cannot find contacts and connections, look for clues. Jan Grieff believes strongly in asking your insiders (board members, alumni, financial advisors who will assist you, etc.) to review your lists and indicate people who could be good prospects. "I like to meet one-on-one with people, but many colleges have screening sessions in which each person in a group is asked to privately scan a list. In both cases, you can quickly find out who knows who," she says.

Alumni and membership directories allow you to determine college affiliations and groups to which individuals belong. I've also met some individuals in social settings and casually asked who they know who is closely involved with my organization. Usually, there's at least one person whom they'll talk about with enthusiasm.

Where there is no known relationship, seek ways to create one. Among the most frequently used are:

- *Networking:* One executive or celebrity helps you recruit another one. Look for individuals who serve on other boards together, play golf, are business partners/associates, or whose children attend the same schools or are on sports teams together.

- *Volunteering:* Colleges and universities ask professionals and celebrities to teach courses, not only to benefit students, but also to build interest in, awareness of, and a relationship with the organization. Top leaders may serve on a presidential advisory committee (formed by your president to give him or her feedback on key issues) or on your investment or planning committee, or contribute their expertise in other ways. Retired professionals may assist as volunteers (tracking budgets, maintaining computer databases, etc.) in your finance or development office, or in other areas.

- *Small Favors:* An art museum may ask a key individual for the loan of a painting or other collectible for a special exhibit, or a realtor may be asked to provide pro bono advice on property your organization seeks to acquire.

- *Awards:* Present an honorary degree or award; or induct the individual into a Hall of Fame.

- *Cultivation:* If the person you want to involve makes a gift to your organization, however modest, call to personally extend your thanks. If he or she calls to ask for assistance (e.g., enrolling in one of your programs), provide exceptional service.

CHARITY

Knowing if an individual is philanthropic—and the extent of his or her giving—can be especially helpful in projecting both the amount of the gift request and your likelihood of success. Unless the individual prefers to remain anonymous, gift information may appear in donor recognition listings and news stories, appear on an organization's homepage, and be known to close friends.

Don't be too quick to draw conclusions if there's a lack of public information about charitable giving, Grieff warns. "Some religions believe that true charity is an anonymous act. Other reasons include a concern that a large gift will encourage more requests than the donor can handle, or concerns over security."

Giving is an acquired skill and, like many new experiences in life, most people take to it gradually, increasing the amounts of their gifts over time. Sadly, some people never learn how to give and do not want to be taught. If that's the case, look for other individuals with a more positive view on life, who can appreciate the remarkable work your organization is accomplishing, and would welcome becoming a part of it through their gifts.

What is Your Goal: Top Gifts for a Campaign or Annual Giving?

After compiling these names, you'll want to continue your screening to assess each individual based on the type of TOP GIFTS™ program you are considering: a special project or major campaign; or a major gifts program as part of your annual fundraising.

Special Project or Campaign

If you are screening names for a special project or major campaign, you'll be seeking large gifts of varying amounts. If your campaign has a goal of one million dollars, for example, you might target as few as twenty-six gifts—requiring individual contributions of $10,000 to $250,000—to reach your goal:

Table of Gifts One-Million-Dollar Goal		
# of gifts required	*Gift level*	*Cumulative total*
1	$250,000	$250,000
2	$100,000	$450,000
5	$50,000	$700,000
8	$25,000	$900,000
10	$10,000	$1,000,000

By screening your lists, you can assess who are the most likely donors to give $250,000, $100,000, $50,000, and other levels on the gift table.

Major Gifts Club

The second approach is to screen your names for potential donors of large gifts to establish a major gifts club for your annual giving program. While the funds raised may not be as large as for a campaign, this approach has the advantage of raising sights for gift amounts and creating a cadre of loyal supporters on which a future campaign may be based. Consider it a valuable building block.

If you conducted an interest survey (see chapter 6) and most individuals responded by saying that a major gift for them is ten thousand dollars (or fifty thousand dollars or more; the amount will vary by organization), your screening will be focused primarily on identifying individuals who can give the minimum amount of your new major gifts club level. For this example, based on our chart "Capacity and Giving," most of these individuals will have annual incomes of three hundred thousand dollars or more (at a giving level of roughly 3 percent of salary).

Identifying Your Best Potential Donors

You can refine your lists and identify your best potential donors by meeting with volunteers one-on-one or conducting a group screening session. Jan Grieff, who has worked with colleges, hospitals, and social service agencies, uses the following steps:

1. Organize names into groups with which your volunteers are likely to have some knowledge and affiliation. A college or university may group names by graduating class, area of the country, and/or major; community groups by profession (doctors, business leaders, etc.) or neighborhood; a national organization by chapter location and Zip Code ranges; etc. Invite volunteers who are affiliated with each group to meet with you individually or as part of a small committee to confidentially review your lists.

2. To prepare for the meeting(s), print the names of your potential donors in a column on the left side of the page, with names double-spaced for easy reading. Grieff says that for each name listed she is looking for the answers to these four questions, which coincide well with the four Cs screening method described in this chapter:
   - At what level is he or she able to give?
   - Does he or she have an interest in our charity and/or a project for which we are seeking funds?
   - Who is the best person to request the gift, and is this person willing to make the request?
   - Is he or she charitable?

For ease in rating names and recording information, create column headings for Capacity, Connectivity, Contact, and Charity to the right of your names.

3. Ask your volunteer(s) to scan the list, page by page. For a major gifts club, ask volunteer(s) to look at each page and indicate those who have the capacity to make a minimum gift for membership. For each name that qualifies by Capacity, ask your volunteers to provide information about Connectivity, Contact, and Charity, if known. Collect the information, then move on to the next name that qualifies, proceeding through the list.

4. If screening for a campaign, determine the minimum level on your table of gifts. For the one-million-dollar campaign described earlier, you would need twenty-six gifts of ten thousand dollars or more. Your volunteer(s), then, would scan each page looking for individuals capable of giving ten thousand dollars or more. A suggested gift amount would also be elicited from your volunteer(s). Information about each of the other factors, if known, would be added for each name with gift potential. Some fundraisers like to see three to four names for each gift on the table (or seventy-eight names for our twenty-eight gifts). Yet, depending on the level of involvement, contact with your organization, and experience with philanthropy, you may need fewer names.

Securing Grants from Corporations, Foundations & Government Agencies

David S. Newburg, Ph.D., is a scientist and program director at the Shriver Center of the University of Massachusetts Medical School (Waltham, Mass.). He funds his research projects with government, foundation, and corporate grants. Dr. Newburg follows this seven-step process for securing and administering grants:

1. Identify potential funders.

2. Develop "elevator pitch."

3. Make initial contact to qualify level of interest in program.

4. Follow up, as needed, to clarify request, build relationship, and complete and submit proposal.

5. Meet with program officer.

6. Grant awarded; continue contact with program officer.

7. Final report.

Identification of Potential Funders

Dr. Newburg uses four ways to identify institutional funding: networking with colleagues; notices appearing in professional journals; participation at conferences; and searches on the Internet.

"Corporations, foundations, and government agencies interested in the sciences will identify the types of projects they want to address," he explains. "Often they will use professional journals, conferences, and meetings to attract the best people in the field and promising young scientists to work in areas that advance their priorities. Often, I'll hear about these funding opportunities through a colleague, or the foundation may place a notice or ad in a journal, or help sponsor a meeting or conference in the field in which it has an interest. Government agencies may actually host their own conferences to draw attention to the research and availability of funds."

Organizations not involved in research may also network with colleagues and scan professional journals, such as the *Chronicle of Philanthropy* or the *Chronicle of Higher Education*, to learn about corporations, foundations, and government organizations that are currently making—or have previously made—grants to programs for which they seek funding.

Dr. Newburg believes that differentiating your organization's unique role and impact are positive assets for securing grants. "In research, it often is to your advantage to publish your findings and present papers at conferences so that you and your organization are recognized as having expertise in a specific field. A foundation, government agency, or corporation may actually approach you."

The Internet and online directories are useful tools as well. "By searching keywords, I often can identify a new funding source. My research is on human milk and its health benefits. My keyword search might include 'pediatrics,' 'infant formula,' and 'nutrition.' From the hits, I pull up Web sites of organizations that are likely to have funding potential. Usually, information on a foundation, corporate, or government Web site is explicit (such as, 'We do not support meetings or equipment purchases'). This information helps determine which organizations I'll contact," he says.

The "Elevator Pitch"

Based on the goals and funding priorities, Dr. Newburg develops an "elevator pitch," a brief summary of his project and its impact for each foundation, corporation, or government agency he will approach. "This term is used by venture capitalists, who want to know—within the first few minutes—what you plan to do and its impact. When I am researching a foundation's or government agency's funding priorities, for example, I pay close attention to its phraseology. How closely does my research meet its goals? If there's a match, I want my elevator pitch to emphasize that what I am proposing is a good match for what the organization wants to achieve."

Initial Contact

The initial contact with an organization is usually by phone and "qualifies the level of interest. Start with your elevator pitch. If there's interest, the program officer will give you more time and explain the process. It may be as simple as, 'Send us your proposal and we'll evaluate it.' Other funding organizations have their own forms, meetings, and deadlines. If this is the case, filling out the application may be as simple as taking the information you already have and reconfiguring it onto the forms they provide."

What if you've missed a deadline? "There are likely to be other funding cycles and you may be able to submit your project for the next cycle. Or, if the foundation or corporation has a great interest in your project, it may offer you some flexibility to apply in the current cycle. Also some program officers will tell you informally what type of decision to expect. While this information can be helpful, it's nonbinding, of course."

What if the program officer has no interest in your project? "It can still be a productive call. I might ask 'Do you have any ideas of who else might be interested in supporting this project?' Often, I'll receive a lead for another foundation or government agency that is a better fit with my research goals."

Shape & Submit Proposal; Meet with Program Officer

Follow up, as needed, with the program officer to clarify your funding request. You'll be not only honing your proposal, but also building a relationship.

"The program officer may bring you in to make a presentation about your project. Often, it's as much to get to know about you and your organization as it is to learn more about the project. Often, there's a desire to create a comfort level; by making things less formal, you'll be willing to talk about both your progress and your problems.

Dr. Newburg says that the conversations and meetings "can create a sense of community or shared goals. Both the funding organization and researcher are part of an important activity. Together, we're discovering answers to questions that might otherwise not be asked."

Grant Awarded & Final Report

When the grant is awarded, the exchange of information continues. "Once approved, there usually is an onsite visit and the funding organization is interested in seeing the data as it develops. You want to complete your project as defined in your proposal. If something adversely affects your project, I find that telling the truth is easiest and best. For example, if the electricity goes off and our cells die because there's no air conditioning, inform the program officer who represents the organization funding your research. At worse, it may push back your timeline, but they'll know that you're doing everything possible to bring in your project successfully."

Corporations & Government Agencies

Dr. Newburg has found that "as you might suspect, large corporations are more businesslike in their approach. They look at 'What makes sense for the company to support?' Or, 'How does this research or project fit in with our products or priorities?' A shift in the leadership of a large corporation can produce an abrupt change in what they are funding in research and other forms of grant-making."

Large government agencies tend to be "more formal with more paperwork. You're judged by the quality of paper that you put in (i.e. your application or proposal). In many programs, there is a peer review process. But even with peer review, it's good to first contact the program officer who can tell you if there's likely to be interest in supporting your project. If you have a project that impresses the reviewers, congratulations. But as many as 10 to 20 percent of applications are in the 'gray zone,' that is, they have merit and are determined to be in the 'fundable range' by the peer reviewer. It's here that the program officer can have some discretion. If you have had contact with the program officer, you have created awareness for your project and the importance of your goals."

TOP GIFTS™ WORKBOOK
Screening for TOP GIFTS™ Donors

1. Use the four Cs (Capacity, Connectivity, Contact, and Charity) as a tool to identify and evaluate individuals who could make top gifts. On a separate page, list and screen organizations (foundations, government agencies, etc.) based on how well your needs match their funding guidelines and the interest level demonstrated by program officers.

2. From your best sources, list those individuals who have the Capacity to make a minimum gift for your major gifts club or campaign.

For your annual major gifts club, use the "Capacity and Giving" chart to assess the minimum income level to qualify. Select the individuals that you believe qualify by income and/or assets (mark with a √). Then rate Connectivity, Contact, Charity on a 0–5 scale, with 5 being the highest rating. Focus first on those people marked with a √ and ratings of 3 or more in each of the other categories.

For your campaign, establish the minimum gift you are seeking. Select those names which you believe qualify by income and/or assets (mark with a √). Then rate Connectivity, Contact, Charity on a 0–5 score, with 5 being the highest rating. Ask your volunteer(s) the amount of the gift that is possible (add to list under "Suggested Gift"). Focus first on those people with high gift potential (a √) and ratings of 3 or more in each of the other categories.

Names	Capacity	Connectivity	Contact	Charity	Suggested Gift
1.					
2.					
3					
4.					
5.					
6.					
7.					
8.					
9.					
10.					
11.					
12.					
13.					
14.					
15.					
16.					
17.					
18.					

Copy page to list additional names

Establish challenging goals. Test their viability by constructing a table of gifts and matching the people and organizations to the gifts required.

"Make no little plans. They have no magic to stir men's blood. . . . Make big plans; aim high in hope and work, remembering that a noble logical diagram will never die. . . . Let your watchword be order and your beacon beauty. Think big."

Daniel Burnham

"A goal is nothing more than a dream with a time limit."

Joe Griffith

M anagement guru Zig Ziegler perhaps said it best. *"If it's not written, it's not a goal. It's a wish."* In this chapter, I'll share with you a technique to convert your wishes into goals, a technique to hardwire your pathway to success with a *table of gifts*. Your gift table defines each step of the way by indicating the number and levels of gifts needed to ensure success. With a table of gifts to guide you, you'll be able to focus your attention on cultivating and securing the high-level commitments required.

Your table of gifts also can raise the sights of your volunteers and serve as an easy-to-use scorecard to track progress during your campaign or major gifts solicitation period. You'll develop momentum, fuel your performance, and, with a sufficient number of qualified people (identified in the workbook in the last chapter), accelerate well beyond your goal.

The Traditional Gift Table

For many years, fundraisers have relied on a model for creating a table of gifts described as the Rule of Thirds. This model was popularized by Harold Seymour in his classic book *Designs for Fundraising*. Seymour divides the campaign into three segments—leadership gifts, major gifts, and special gifts—proceeds from each of which account for one-third of the campaign's dollar goal. Seymour then presents two campaigns to demonstrate the model's effectiveness. The tables work well, but it's clear that you need to be flexible; in both campaigns, one segment targeted for "about a third" of the goal came in with slightly less (28 percent), which was covered by gifts in other categories that exceeded their projections.

This model, presented below, has been a standard for creating gift tables. Because of its longstanding reliability, I've labeled it the *traditional* table of gifts. Since the 1960s when Seymour's book was published, however, more aggressive tables have developed in which fewer gifts are required to reach the goal. Today, there are at least three successful models—traditional, moderate, and aggressive. We'll look at the traditional table as a baseline, then explore the other two.

To better understand the traditional process, let's create a Table of Gifts for a five-million-dollar major gifts program.

Pacesetting Gift

Although Seymour's model does not specifically discuss the importance of the top gift—known as the *pacesetting gift*—numerous campaigns over the years have demonstrated that this gift should equal a minimum of 10 percent of the goal. This threshold is further confirmed by recent gift tables on file in the resource centers at the Association of Fundraising Professionals and the Association for Healthcare Philanthropy. The top gift is called the pacesetting gift because it sets the standard by which other gifts are calculated and often inspires others to give at high levels. It's not uncommon for the pacesetting gift to be 10 to 15 percent or more of your goal. At 10 percent, for our five-million-dollar goal, one $500,000 gift is indicated.

For the largest campaigns (i.e., one hundred million to one billion dollars or more), more than one gift may be required to provide the 10 percent suggested for the pacesetting gift. Larger organizations with campaigns of this size, such as colleges and universities, may be consolidating several gift tables and/or have a larger number of potential donors for major or top gifts. A separate gift table may be created for each school or division (with a pacesetting gift of each of at least 10 percent of that school's goal); then the tables (and their totals) are combined into one overall campaign goal.

For *The Anniversary Campaign for Princeton*, which raised more than $1.14 billion, separate goals and gift tables were established for individual capital gifts ($500 million) and for annual giving ($150 million). Goals were projected for other gift sources as well (e.g., corporations: $60 million; foundations: $100 million; etc.). The campaign was launched with a one-hundred-million-dollar gift, representing both 20 percent of the final goal in the individual capital gifts division and, equally impressive, more than 11 percent of the total campaign goal, clearly qualifying it as a pacesetting gift.

Returning to building *our* table, however, in addition to listing a pacesetting gift of 10 percent of the goal ($500,000), let's list individuals and groups who could be prospects for this gift. You'll want to do the same when you create your own campaign table.

Table of Gifts $5 Million Goal			
# of gifts required	*Gift level*	*Cumulative total*	*Prospect(s)* *(all names fictitious)*
Pacesetting Gift: 1	$500,000	$500,000	Nancy Costa Sandra Star

Leadership Gifts

The top eight to ten gifts, including the pacesetting gift, should total approximately one-third of your goal (on our table the total is roughly $1.75 million, slightly above the one-third line).

Generally, the second-highest gift is one-half the amount of the pacesetting gift, and there are twice as many gifts (or more) at this level. Each level that follows uses the same formulas (twice as many gifts as at the preceding level, at roughly half the dollar amount). You are allowed and encouraged to adjust figures on your table to:

- Match the gift potentials of your best prospects and/or present gift amounts that are more meaningful to donors (e.g., you learn that many corporations and foundations frequently give $100,000 to endowed scholarship funds, a component in your campaign. Your table calls for three gifts of $125,000, but instead, to better respond to the preferences of your audience, you substitute four or five gifts of $100,000 each.);

- Account for any extraordinary gifts (e.g., you have a trustee who has suggested that he or she would give $350,000 to this campaign. One gift of this amount would be entered on the table between the $500,000 gift and the $250,000 level).

In developing our table, we are not aware of any extraordinary gifts and list three gifts of $250,000 and five gifts of $100,000 to meet our standard (about ten gifts equaling approximately one-third of the goal).

To test the viability of the gift amounts on our table, I'll continue to list the names of potential donors. Here is our table through the leadership giving levels:

Table of Gifts
$5 Million Goal

# of gifts required	Gift level	Cumulative total	Prospect(s) (all names fictitious)
Leadership Gifts			
Pacesetting Gift: 1	$500,000	$500,000	Nancy Costa Sandra Star
3	$250,000	$1,250,000	Willis Gates Fdn. Tommy Jones Ginger Bush Dick O. Reedock Sally Simpson
5	$100,000	$1,750,000	Price Depot Sylvia Glen Perkins Cove M. Rich (To be determined)

Major Gifts

The next third of our goal is represented by as many as one hundred gifts. Some fundraisers refer to these as the campaign's *major gifts*. We'll follow similar formulas for each lower level—an increase in the number of gifts, at roughly half the dollar amount of the next highest level. The number of gifts may be a progression (e.g., 20, 30, 40) or multiples (10, 20, 40), based on the number of potential donors.

Adjustments should be made to the number of gifts listed to more accurately match your potential (e.g., your progression may be changed to 10, 25, 50). Continue to fill in all known prospects. Many consultants use a general rule that, for the highest gift amounts, you should have as many as three to four prospects for each gift. Instead, I suggest that you take time to assess the commitment and capacity of your key prospect(s): what is their level of interest and involvement; do they have the ability to make the desired gift; how close is your organization's connection or contact with the individual; are they known to be philanthropic? Depending on the quality of the relationship, you may find that you may need only one, or at most two, potential donor(s) for each gift.

This early in your planning, it's unlikely that you will have identified a prospect for every gift indicated. Your development council and/or board should be able to assist you in completing the prospect pool for your table of gifts.

# of gifts required	Gift level	Cumulative total	Prospect(s) (all names fictitious)
Table of Gifts _$5 Million Goal_			
Leadership Gifts			
Pacesetting Gift: 1	$500,000	$500,000	Nancy Costa Sandra Star
3	$250,000	$1,250,000	Willis Gates Fdn. Tommy Jones Ginger Bush Dick O. Reedock Sally Simpson
5	$100,000	$1,750,000	Price Depot Sylvia Glen Perkins Cove M. Rich (To be determined)
Major Gifts			
10	$50,000	$2,250,000	Thomas Sylvan Jeremy Tyrone Samuel Tool Tobias Anderson
20	$25,000	$2,750,000	John Spirits Andrew Tony Albert Talent Walter Terrence
30	$15,000	$3,200,000	Percy Canter Rob Dalton Tim Fager Ursula Don
40	$10,000	$3,600,000	Andy Tinder Bob Crater Victor Tundra Art Garcia

Special Gifts

The next 25 percent to one-third of your goal is often called *special gifts*. In our example, we are seeking to encourage each member of an annual giving club to make a three-year commitment that is at least five times their annual gift. By studying the group's annual membership lists, we project that at least 40 percent of these members will respond favorably. The balance of gifts required to complete the goal is listed as "Many," which reflects the large number of smaller gifts we anticipate receiving.

Here is our complete table with our early attempts to identify potential donors.

<table>
<tr><th colspan="5" align="center">Table of Gifts
$5 Million Goal</th></tr>
<tr><th colspan="2"># of gifts required</th><th>Gift level</th><th>Cumulative total</th><th>Prospect(s)
(all names fictitious)</th></tr>
<tr><td colspan="5">Leadership Gifts</td></tr>
<tr><td>Pacesetting Gift:</td><td>1</td><td>$500,000</td><td>$500,000</td><td>Nancy Costa, Sandra Star</td></tr>
<tr><td></td><td>3</td><td>$250,000</td><td>$1,250,000</td><td>Willis Gates Fdn.
Tommy Jones, Ginger Bush
Dick O. Reedock, Sally Simpson</td></tr>
<tr><td></td><td>5</td><td>$100,000</td><td>$1,750,000</td><td>Price Depot, Sylvia Glen
Perkins Cove, M. Rich
(To be determined)</td></tr>
<tr><td colspan="5">Major Gifts</td></tr>
<tr><td></td><td>10</td><td>$50,000</td><td>$2,250,000</td><td>Thomas Sylvan, Jeremy Tyrone
Samuel Tool, Tobias Anderson</td></tr>
<tr><td></td><td>20</td><td>$25,000</td><td>$2,750,000</td><td>John Spirits, Andrew Tony
Albert Talent, Walter Terrence</td></tr>
<tr><td></td><td>30</td><td>$15,000</td><td>$3,200,000</td><td>Percy Canter, Rob Dalton
Tim Fager, Ursula Don</td></tr>
<tr><td></td><td>40</td><td>$10,000</td><td>$3,600,000</td><td>Andy Tinder, Bob Crater
Victor Tundra, Art Garcia</td></tr>
<tr><td colspan="5">Special Gifts</td></tr>
<tr><td></td><td>80</td><td>$5,000</td><td>$4,000,000</td><td rowspan="5">Projection:

>40% response rate
from current
members</td></tr>
<tr><td></td><td>120</td><td>$2,500</td><td>$4,300,000</td></tr>
<tr><td></td><td>300</td><td>$1,000</td><td>$4,600,000</td></tr>
<tr><td></td><td>500</td><td>$500</td><td>$4,850,000</td></tr>
<tr><td></td><td>Many</td><td><$500</td><td>$5,000,000</td></tr>
<tr><td colspan="2">Totals: 1,109+</td><td></td><td>$5,000,000</td><td></td></tr>
</table>

Smaller Can Be Better: Moderate and Aggressive Gift Tables

As indicated above, an even smaller number of gifts can propel your TOP GIFTS™ program. By increasing the amount of your pacesetting gift, you can decrease the total number of gifts required.

When the pacesetting gift represents 20 to 39 percent of the goal, your table of gifts is known as a *moderate* gift table. When the pacesetting gift is 40 percent or more of the goal, it is an *aggressive* table.

How do the moderate and aggressive tables compare to the one we just created for our five-million-dollar campaign? Instead of the over 1,109 gifts required in the traditional table, as few as eighty-five gifts are called for in a moderate table of gifts, and only eight in a truly aggressive table. Let's take a closer look.

Table of Gifts
$5 Million Goal

Moderate				Aggressive			
	# gifts	Level	Cumulative total		# gifts	Level	Cumulative total
Pacesetting (20% to 39%)	1	$1,000,000	$1,000,000	Pacesetting (40%+)	1	$2,000,000	$2,000,000
Leadership	2	$500,00	$2,000,000	Leadership	1	$1,000,000	$3,000,000
	4	$250,000	$3,000,000		2	$500,000	$4,000,000
Major	8	$100,000	$3,800,000		4	$250,000	$5,000,000
	10	$50,000	$4,300,000				
	15	$25,000	$4,675,000				
	20	$10,000	$4,875,000				
	25	$5,000	$5,000,000				
Totals	85		$5,000,000	Totals	8		$5,000,000

A Pivotal Role

In assessing the goal for your campaign, *you'll want the largest gift on your table—the pacesetting gift—to be as high a percentage of your goal as possible.* But your table of gifts must be tailored to the giving potential of your donors. Assess your goal by the quality and dedication of your leadership, the ability of your vision to inspire the largest gifts, and the preparedness of your potential supporters to make the top gifts required to realize your dream.

Raising Sights with High Expectations

A mentor early in my career once told me, "People only reach as high as you raise the bar." This advice generally is true, whether you are managing people or asking for top gifts. So set a high goal and giving standards. Although it can happen, donors rarely make gifts *larger* than what you request.

How do you identify the key people who can make the pacesetting gift? What are the factors that increase—or decrease—the chances of this gift being made?

Start with the people you identified in your TOP GIFTS™ workbook in chapter 7. Pay special attention to those with high four-C scores and with the five factors listed below, which offer an increased chance of securing a pacesetting gift:

1. Leadership position with your organization;

2. History of giving;

3. Commitment to project or field;

4. Recent financial windfall; and

5. Several sources from which to fund the gift (personal, family, company, foundation, etc.).

There also are factors which can *decrease* the chances of a gift being made. These are:

1. Financial loss: recent loss of job, divorce, death of income earner, etc.;

2. For community or regional organizations: moved outside your service area; or

3. Problem or issue with your organization: listen, apologize, and address the issue. Restore and rebuild the relationship.

Building the Total

By identifying your largest potential gift, you are starting to "build the total." This is a common practice in major gift campaigns. During the planning or *feasibility* study, consultants often create a table of gifts for the desired goal, then test to see if many of the top gifts are available, meaning the campaign is *feasible*. This is accomplished either by asking potential donors to indicate where they see themselves on the gift table or by totaling the ten highest gifts suggested by survey participants and projecting the overall goal. If a sufficient number of the gifts can be identified, the consultant can "build" the table or total and validate the goal. If the gifts cannot be found, the goal may be reduced.

With an established development program, you can build your total for your annual fund (by assessing those major gifts that will be repeated or increased and projecting new major gifts) or for your major and planned gifts campaign (by projecting the largest gifts from those who are most able and involved).

Recognition Opportunities & the Gift Table

Several studies point to the motivational value of donor recognition. What better way to use recognition than to link specific naming opportunities to the top gifts identified on your table?

For Abington Memorial Hospital's campaign *Protect the Future of Nursing*, for example, the hospital named its school of nursing for the donor of its pacesetting gift of five million dollars. For a gift of one million dollars or more, a donor could have the day care center named in his or her honor or have a named endowment fund. Donors of one hundred thousand dollars or more were offered a (named) Presidential Endowed Scholarship, and, for fifty thousand, a (named) Founders Award. Plaques commemorate all gifts of twenty-five thousand dollars or more. Recognition was extended to donors of gifts over one thousand dollars through the hospital's membership programs.

Working with the table of gifts we just developed, here's a sample recognition plan for a five-million-dollar science center, museum, or education center:

	# gifts	Level	Total	Prospects	Recognition
Table of Gifts & Recognition Plan **$5 Million Science Center**					
Pacesetting (20% to 40%)	1	$1,000,000	$1,000,000	Nancy Costa Sandra Star	Building or named endowment
Leadership	2	$500,000	$2,000,000	Ginger Bush Dick O. Reedock Sally Simpson Robert Thomas Sondra Brinks	Main lobby Conference center
	4	$250,000	$3,000,000	Price Depot Sylvia Glen Perkins Cove M. Rich	Auditorium Dining area Library Reception desk Main garden
Major	8	$100,000	$3,800,000	Thomas Sylvan Jeremy Tyrone Samuel Tool Tobias Anderson	(10) Exhibit areas Administrative area
	10	$50,000	$4,300,000	John Spirits Andrew Tony Albert Talent Walter Terrence	(12) Offices
	15	$25,000	$ 4,675,000	Percy Canter Rob Dalton Tim Fager Ursula Don	(12) Research cubicles w/ Internet Access (6) Archive/display construction areas
	20	$10,000	$4,875,000		(35) Named rows in auditorium
	25	$5,000	$5,000,000		(125) Individual plaques (for all gifts of $5,000+)
Totals	85		$5,000,000		

Setting a TARGETed™ Goal

While conducting research for the Association for Healthcare Philanthropy, I discovered that many of their most successful members adopted fundraising goals with similar characteristics. Often, these goals were reflected in reports that served as planning, management, and evaluation tools for communicating the status of their fundraising, alerting these executives to weaknesses and trends, and improving their overall effectiveness. When volunteers were involved in goal-setting, interest in—and the potential success of—their fundraising improved. Allen Stern, CAHP, then managing director of York Central Hospital Foundation in Ontario, Canada, revealed that, when "each chairman is involved in goal-setting, it creates an ownership for his or her program that goes beyond what you might believe. It's a powerful incentive for each person to achieve his goal." The involvement built pride and a sense of ownership in what can be accomplished.

Other fundraising executives had similar success stories to tell. From their insights, I developed an acronym, TARGETed™ goals, which represents six essential elements from the most dynamic and successful programs. These elements are:

TARGETED to specific programs for impact.
ACHIEVABLE, given the history of your program and/or the potential of your people.
RESULTS- or numbers-oriented.
GROUP consensus; having the commitment of your top volunteers.
EXECUTIVE approval.
TIMETABLE or deadline for completion.

After you have built your table of gifts, evaluate your goal according to the TARGETed™ criteria.

Three Ways to Increase Your Potential

Enhance your chances of success by:

- Remaining focused on identifying qualified prospects for top gifts;

- Matching opportunities for recognizing contributors with the gifts indicated on your table; and

- Determining if your goals match criteria for TARGETed™ goals.

A simple way to focus attention on top gifts is to present a report to staff and volunteers that tracks efforts and movement in identifying and securing leadership/major/special gift prospects. Help motivate your volunteers by incorporating this chart into regular meetings:

Campaign Progress			
Campaign Goal $5,000,000		**Since Last Meeting:**	
Number of Gifts Required: 85			
Number of Prospects: 100 (Note: general rule is 3 prospects for 1 gift)		New Prospects 2	
Number of Gift Commitments: 52		New Gift Commitments 12	
New Gifts & Pledges			
Gift Commitments	$3,291,100		
Verbal Commitments	$70,000		
Total Cash Available	$1,591,100		
Pledge Balance	$1,700,000		
Total Raised (incl. verbals)	$3,361,101		

How to Raise $490,000 to $1.14 Billion

What is your goal? From these successful campaigns, find the gift table that comes closest to your goal, then study the number and amounts of gifts received. Do you have anyone involved with your organization who could match the amount of the pacesetting gift? If not, what is the amount of your largest potential gift? Does it meet the standard percentages of the goal: 10 percent for traditional; 20 percent for moderate; or 40 percent or more for aggressive?

$490,000 Campaign
($267,000 goal; 379 gifts)

New Ocean View Library Campaign, Friends and Foundation of the San Francisco Public Library, San Francisco, California

Pacesetting Gift:	$125,000 or 47% of goal
Top 10 gifts:	$420,000 or 157% of goal
Top 60 gifts:	$485,500 or 99% of *campaign*

Table of Gifts			Gifts Received		
#	*Level*		#	*Level Total*	*Cum. Total*
	$100,000		2	$225,000	$225,000
	$50,000		1	$50,000	$275,000
Not Available	$25,000		3	$85,000	$360,000
	$10,000		6	$80,000	$440,000
	$5,000		3	$15,000	$455,000
	$1,000		20	$20,000	$475,000
	$250		25	$10,500	$485,500
	<$250		319	$4,500	$490,000

$5.2 Million Campaign
($5 million goal; 1,100 gifts)

A Proud Heritage, A Future Full of Promise, Topeka Community Theatre and
Academy, Topeka, Kansas

Pacesetting Gift:	$1 million or 20% of goal
Top 10 gifts:	$2.3 million or 46% of goal
Top 25 gifts:	$3.24 million or 65% of goal
Top 158 gifts:	$4.45 million or 89% of goal

Table of Gifts			Gifts Received		
#	*Level*	*Total*	#	*Level Total*	*Cum. Total*
1	$1,000,000	$1,000,000	1	$1,000,000	$1,000,000
1	$500,000	$1,500,000	1	$500,000	$1,500,000
4	$250,000	$2,500,000	0	0	$1,500,000
7	$100,000	$3,200,000	11	$1,100,000	$2,600,000
10	$50,000	$3,700,000	8	$410,000	$3,010,000
18	$25,000	$4,150,000	19	$500,000	$3,510,000
30	$10,000	$4,450,000	51	$600,000	$4,110,000
50	$5,000	$4,700,000	67	$335,000	$4,445,000
350	<$5,000	$5,000,000	942	$755,000	$5,200,000

$6.3 Million Campaign
($6 million goal; 65 gifts)

New Hope Initiative, Samaritan Inns, Washington, D.C.

Pacesetting Gift:	$2 million or 33% of goal
Top 10 gifts:	$4.6 million or 77% of goal
Top 25 gifts:	$5.8 million or 97% of goal
Top 30 gifts:	$6+ million or >100% of goal

Table of Gifts				Gifts Received		
#	*Level*	*Total*		#	*Level Total*	*Cum. Total*
1	$1,000,000	$1,000,000		1	$2,000,000	$2,000,000
3	$500,000	$2,500,000		3	$1,500,000	$3,500,000
4	$250,000	$3,500,000		3	$785,000	$4,285,000
8	$100,000	$4,300,000		9	$1,050,000	$5,335,000
12	$50,000	$4,900,000		9	$454,000	$5,789,000
20	$25,000	$5,400,000		7	$219,000	$6,008,000
25	$10,000	$5,650,000		17	$231,000	$6,239,000
30	$5,000	$5,800,000		9	$54,000	$6,293,000
50	<$5,000	$6,000,000		7	$13,000	$6,306,000
	In-kind			36	$350,000+ (Est.)	$6,656,000

$10.2 Million Campaign
($10 million goal; 4,000+ gifts)

Protecting the Future of Nursing, Abington Memorial Hospital, Abington, Pennsylvania

Pacesetting Gift:	$3 million or 30% of goal
Top 10 gifts:	$7.5 million or 75% of goal
Top 25 gifts:	$9 million or 90% of goal
Top 63 gifts:	$10 million or 100% of goal

Table of Gifts			Gifts Received		
#	*Level*	*Total*	#	*Level Total*	*Cum. Total*
1	$3,000,000	$3,000,000	1	$3,061,000	$3,061,000
2	$1,000,000	$5,000,000	2	$2,616,000	$5,677,000
3	$500,000	$6,500,000	1	$600,000	$6,277,000
4	$250,000	$7,500,000	3	$880,000	$7,157,000
12	$100,000	$8,700,000	16	$1,750,000	$8,907,000
14	$50,000	$9,400,000	6	$300,000	$9,207,000
20	$25,000	$9,900,000	15	$417,000	$9,624,000
Many	<$25,000	$10,000,000	4,000+	$589,000	$10,213,000

And $15 Million More . . .

After meeting its initial goal of ten million dollars, Abington Hospital raised its sights by seeking an *additional* ten million. The new, aggressive gift table started with a five-million-dollar pacesetting gift and six more gifts. With less than three top gifts, it surpassed the new goal.

Table of Gifts			Gifts Received		
#	*Level*	*Total*	#	*Level Total*	*Cum. Total*
1	$5,000,000	$5,000,000	2	$10,000,000	$10,000,000
1	$2,500,000	$7,500,000			
1	$1,000,000	$8,500,000	2	$2,150,000	$12,150,000
2	$500,000	$9,500,000	2	$1,190,000	$13,340,000
2	$250,000	$10,000,000	3	$800,000	$14,140,000
–	$100,000	–	5	$500,000	$14,640,000
–	$50,000	–	3	$150,000	$14,790,000
–	<$50,000	–	1,000+	$214,000	$15,004,000

$353 Million Campaign
($300 million goal; 30,128 donors)

Challenged to Lead, Pepperdine University, Malibu, California

    Pacesetting Gift: $50 million or 17% of goal
    Top 10 gifts: $167.8 million or 56% of goal
    Top 25 gifts: $221.3 million or 74% of goal
    Top 100 gifts: $298.75 million or 99.6% of goal

Table of Gifts		Gifts Received		
#	*Level*	#	*Level Total*	*Cum. Total*
1	$50,000,000	1	$51,695,000	$51,695,000
Not Available	$25,000,000	1	$34,100,000	$85,795,000
	$10,000,000	4	$48,727,000	$134,522,000
	$5,000,000*	6	$46,598,000	$181,120,000
	$2,000,000	14	$42,180,000	$223,300,000
	$1,000,000	39	$50,080,000	$273,380,000
	$100,000*	167	$52,775,000	$326,155,000
	$10,000*	515	$13,244,000	$339,399,000
	$1,000*	3,422	$9,914,000	$349,313,000
	<$1,000*	25,959	$4,015,000	$353,328,000

Giving levels are consolidated for reporting purposes.

$1.14 Billion Campaign
($900 million goal; 50,000+ donors)

With One Accord, The Anniversary Campaign, Princeton University, Princeton, New Jersey

Princeton's five-year, *comprehensive* campaign sought to expand annual giving, secure major capital gifts, and "achieve the broadest participation and highest levels of support." While individual capital giving had *always* been central to the university's campaign plans, the response far exceeded expectations. The original campaign goal of $750 million was increased to $900 million, but the campaign came roaring to a close with a record $1.14 billion, contributed by an unprecedented 78 percent of its undergraduate alumni.

Pacesetting Gift:	$100 million or 13% of initial goal/11% of revised goal
Top 11 gifts:	$321.8 million or 43% of initial goal/36% of revised goal
Top 110 gifts:	$564.1 million or 75% of initial goal/63% of revised goal
Top 803 gifts:	$703.9 million or 93.9% of initial goal/78.2% of revised goal

Here are gift tables for both goals ($750 million and $900 million), and for gifts received.

Table of Gifts			Gifts Received	
	$750 Goal	**$900 Goal**		**Total**
Annual Giving	$125	$150		$154.6
Individual Capital	$370	$500		$718.2
Amount	#	#	#	*Level Total*
$50.0	1	2	2	$153.1
$25.0	1	2	2	$59.2
$10.0	2	6	8	$109.5
$5.0	8	11	13	$76.1
$2.5	14	22	25	$80.1
$1.0	50	60	61	$86.1
$0.50	75	80	82	$52.2
$0.25	100	100	106	$34.0
$0.10	200	300	255	$37.4
$0.05		300	250	$16.2
<$0.05	Many	Many	7,928	$14.4
Bequests	$85	$85		$104.3
Corporations	$80	$60		$63.1
Foundations	$80	$100		$102.3
Other	$10	$5		$3.6

(Dollars in millions; category totals may vary due to rounding.)

TOP GIFTS™ WORKBOOK
Creating a Table of Gifts

Goals 1. From your planning, determine the amount of your project and, from that, the amount you would like to raise. Indicate these amounts in the column to the right.	Project Amount $_____	Fundraising Goal $_____	
Pacesetting Gift 2. Determine the amount of your pacesetting gift. This gift may be: Traditional: 10 to <20% of goal Moderate: 20% to <40% Aggressive: 40% or more *Aim high.* Typically, one gift at this level is needed. If you believe there is strong potential for additional gifts of this amount, adjust the number and enter the amount of your pacesetting gift. Begin to list the names of potential donors and recognition opportunities.	Number of Gifts _____	Amount $ _____	Prospects Recognition
Leadership Gifts 3. In a traditional table, about 10 gifts (8 to 10 of the largest) total approx. one-third of your goal (including the pacesetting gift). For several of the campaigns highlighted in this chapter, however, these gifts represent 75% or more of the goal. Identify the number and amounts of these gifts, modeling them after both formulas and campaigns highlighted in this chapter and what you believe is your giving potential. Then total pacesetting and leadership gifts and calculate the percentage of your total goal. Seek to have these gifts reflect as large a percentage of the goal as may be possible. Continue identifying potential donors and recognition opportunities.	Number of Gifts _____ _____ _____ _____	Amount $ _____ $ _____ $ _____ $ _____ **Pacesetting &** **Leadership Gifts** Total Amount: $ _____ Total Percentage: (% = Amount of Top 10 Gifts / Goal x 100) _____%	Prospects Recognition

TOP GIFTS™ WORKBOOK
Creating a Table of Gifts

	Number of Gifts	Amount	Prospects
Major Gifts 4. In a traditional table, the next 100 gifts represent the next third of your goal. By contrast, in a moderate or aggressive table, these gifts may reflect the balance of your campaign. Using examples cited in this chapter, indicate the number and amounts of these gifts. Calculate totals and percentages indicated. If you have additional funds to raise, complete *special gifts*, below. Continue identifying potential donors and recognition opportunities (consider existing membership programs for potential donors).	_____ _____ _____ _____ _____ _____ _____ _____	$_____ $_____ $_____ $_____ $_____ $_____ $_____ $_____	Recognition
	Major Gifts Total Amount: $ _____ Total Percentage: (% = Amount of Major Gifts / Goal x 100) _____%	**Pacesetting, Leadership & Major Gifts (PLMG)** Total Amount: $ _____ Total Percentage: (% = Amount of PLMG Gifts / Goal x 100) _____%	
Special Gifts 5. For the traditional table, indicate the remaining gifts you need. Total the amount and percentage for this category.	Number of Gifts _____ _____ _____ _____ _____ _____ _____ _____	Amount $_____ $_____ $_____ $_____ $_____ $_____ $_____ $_____	
	Special Gifts Total Amount: $ _____ Total Percentage: (% = Amount of Special Gifts / Goal x 100) _____%	**All Levels** Total Amount: $ _____ Total Percentage: (% = Amount of All Gifts / Goal x 100) _____%	

TOP GIFTS™ WORKBOOK
Creating a Table of Gifts

Prospects/Recognition

6. Review names of potential donors and recognition and membership opportunities you have listed, paying special attention to pacesetting and leadership gifts, then focusing on all remaining levels.

TARGETed™ goals

7. *Optional:* To build consensus and add effectiveness, assess your table based on criteria for TARGETed™ goals.

Yes   No

Is your table of gifts . . .

☐ ☐ **T**argeted to specific programs for impact

☐ ☐ **A**chievable given the potential of your people

☐ ☐ **R**esults or numbers, oriented

Does it have . . .

☐ ☐ **G**roup consensus/commitment of top volunteers

☐ ☐ **E**xecutive approval

☐ ☐ **T**imetable or deadline for completion

Create opportunities to involve potential donors of top gifts. Build awareness and interest; find ways to communicate the impact of each gift.

"Tell me who you hang out with
and I'll tell you who you are."

Burke Hedges

"Birds of a feather flock together."

The duchess, *Alice's Adventures in Wonderland*

W hat are the elements that contribute to a pacesetting or leadership gift? And what actually prompts these gifts to be made? Here are a few examples from which we can glean some answers:

- In one of the largest gifts to education in history, *George Soros*, the Hungarian-born international financier and philanthropist, created a $250 million endowment for Central European University (CEU), which is located in his homeland. Soros had been one of the university's founders who met in 1989, the watershed year in which historic revolutions led to the collapse of communism in Central and Eastern Europe. The founders' visionary discussions had led to the creation of the university, which educates leaders from emerging democracies throughout the world. Prior to funding the endowment, Soros's previous gifts to CEU had totaled approximately $250 million.

- *Jack Farber*, chairman of CSS Industries, the U.S.'s largest manufacturer of gift wrap, ribbons, and bows, gave Thomas Jefferson University (Philadelphia, Pa.) ten million dollars to establish the Farber Institute of Neurosciences. According to the university, "The new institute will be a multidisciplinary center initially focusing its efforts on basic and clinical research in Alzheimer's disease, Parkinson's disease, amyotrophic lateral sclerosis (ALS) and  other neurodegenerative disorders. . . . Mr. Farber and his wife Vickie have been touched personally by neurodegenerative diseases. Mrs. Farber's father died from ALS; her mother has Alzheimer's disease. Mr. and Mrs. Farber have given to Jefferson generously in the past. He established the Farber Health Professions Scholars Program in the College of Health Professions . . . and created a Geriatric Fellowship in the Department of Family Medicine." Mr. Farber was chairman of Jefferson's board of trustees from 1995 to 2000, and Mrs. Farber is active on the university hospital's women's board, as well as the board of overseers of the ALS Chapter of Greater Philadelphia.

- *Gordon Moore* is also looking to have impact. In the largest donation to an environmental cause in U.S. history, he and his wife, Betty, pledged $261 million to slow the rate of plant and animal extinction worldwide. (The gift came just six weeks after Gordon Moore, co-founder of Intel, gave another record-setting gift, three hundred million dollars, to the California Institute of Technology in Pasadena.) The Moores' gift for the environment is directed  to Conservation International (CI), which is focusing its attention on twenty-five hot spots, super-rich ecological areas that cover just 1.4 percent of the earth's land surface but support more than 60 percent of its biodiversity. The Moores' money will establish national parks in rain forests, help build scientific field stations, and provide "competitive capital," that is, seek to save forests by outbidding loggers. Gordon Moore admits that "Political lobbying is an important part of the environmental movement, but it isn't the part I'm interested in. There are a lot of things that can be done on the ground, particularly in developing countries. . . . This is an attempt to be science-based. . . . Being trained as a scientist I thought that was a good way to go." An avid fisherman, Moore has traveled extensively with Conservation International scientists in the past ten years and joined the group's board. With Harvard professor Edward O. Wilson, he co-chaired a conference, Defying Nature's End, organized by the Center for Applied Biodiversity Science at CI.

- While many students receive college scholarships, not everyone reflects on its role in changing their lives. Yet, *Gerhard R. Andlinger*, a member of the Class of 1952 at Princeton University, did. His latest gift, twenty-five million dollars, propelled Princeton's recent campaign past one billion dollars. When Andlinger arrived on campus as a student, he had a scholarship and eight dollars in his pocket. Andlinger went on to create Andlinger and Company, a private investment firm. "Princeton holds a special place in my heart," he says. "I feel privileged to be able to give back to this great university and to the country that has offered me a welcoming home and a wealth of opportunity." Andlinger says he makes a point—not a habit—of giving to Princeton. He is active with his class, serves on the advisory council for the university's Benheim Center for Finance, and established a named professorship of social sciences in 1991.

What are the common elements of these extraordinary gifts? What unites these donors in their passion for giving? Here are some traits I see:

- A great personal interest in the program or project being funded;

- A desire to make a difference, to have a significant, perhaps even historic, impact;

- Prior involvement with—and an appreciation for the work of—the organization;

- Leadership positions on boards and roles on key committees;

- A close and trusting relationship with its leadership; and

- In some cases, personal recognition.

In the very best gifts and campaigns, one frequently sees a growing, burning ember in the passion and commitment of a handful of key people, a fire that spreads to others. But that ember must start with someone.

A Two-Way Street
In most cases, the leadership of a nonprofit organization will bring its ideas and opportunities to donors of pacesetting and leadership gifts. Increasingly, however, donors have their own visions and will research and approach charities to carry their ideas forward. The basis of success in both cases is a relationship based on trust and accountability.

Relationships

No fewer than three major studies—and countless stories from successful fundraising practitioners—stress the important of establishing and cultivating relationships with individuals of "influence and affluence."

- Among the top ten reasons people made gifts of one million dollars or more, Jerold Panas reports in *Mega Gifts*, are the following two: the influence of the solicitor and a high regard for volunteer leadership. Both instill a sense of legitimacy and trust that donors of the largest gifts say they are seeking.

- According to a study by the National Committee on Planned Giving, individuals who have made charitable bequests in their wills say the relationship with a representative of a charity is among their top five motivators.

- According to research in *The Seven Faces of Philanthropy*, six out of seven types of donors of gifts of fifty thousand dollars or more say that when they're motivated to give, they are greatly influenced by others in their decision-making. Many of these donors would like to have greater involvement with the charity, to be consulted, to participate, and to have a sense of empowerment. To meet these criteria, the integrity of the charity's leadership must be strong enough to receive the endorsements of the donor, his or her family, and peers.

What methods can you use to effectively establish and nurture positive relationships with the people who are pivotal to the long-term success of your organization? The answer may be found in these four models:

1. Establishing awareness of your organization and building a personal relationship;

2. Maintaining and renewing important relationships;

3. Networking through peer relationships; and

4. Inviting the individual to serve on a leadership committee, panel, conference, or board.

Let's take a closer look.

Establishing Awareness and Building a Personal Relationship

Sometimes it's the simple things in life, the small acts of kindness, that can start and maintain the closest relationships.

Just ask Milton J. Murray, retired director of philanthropic services at the Adventist World Headquarters (Silver Spring, Md.). He says he does a number of small things for potential donors that show warmth and feeling, and have impact. "This might include sending a postcard or writing a note, making a phone call on a matter that has nothing to do with asking for money, or sending the person a book, newsletter, or clipping that might interest them." He is known to send a congratulatory note when he learns that a prospect has made a gift to another charity.

Murray establishes a personal relationship by going out of his way to show that he cares about the individual. And, because it's unexpected, Murray's actions are likely to be noticed and appreciated. His relationship-building works with donors and non-donors alike.

Like many fundraisers interested in befriending people who can transform their organizations, Murray sends birthday or anniversary cards to donors and prospects alike. Donors receive notes and reports telling them about the benefits their past gifts have made possible.

He finds future friends by asking others in his organization for names and by poring over his organization's newsletters and magazines for the names of people who have either made large gifts or, he believes, have that potential.

Building Billion-Dollar Relationships

James I. Luck is president emeritus of the Columbus Foundation (Columbus, Ohio), a community foundation serving central Ohio. He charted a billion-dollar goal for the foundation's assets in less than fifteen years, a nearly fourfold increase. But, rather than first focusing on the size of the gift from his prospects, his primary attention is on creating awareness and relationships.

"In major gifts fundraising, our goal is to get to know our donors and to discover what they would like to do with their philanthropic dollars. At the Columbus

Foundation, if we received a $250 gift from someone we've never heard of before, we'll invite the donor in for lunch to get to know the individual. We're not aggressive; our goal is find out where donors would like to invest their money in the community and then help them accomplish it. We see ourselves as a service organization. For us, development is not about asking for five-million-dollar gifts, but about going out and developing relationships, which in five to ten years will result in large gifts."

It is no accident that the number of volunteers involved in the Columbus Foundation's work has increased nearly one-hundred-fold. "When I started at the foundation, we had a seven-member board and that was about it. With our many committees and affiliates, today the foundation has more than six hundred people. It's a wonderful way to create awareness and involvement."

Recognizing that a strong link with an organization is important to giving, Luck has developed his own *pyramid of giving*, which lays the foundation by creating *awareness*, nurturing *relationships*, and instilling *knowledge* about the programs and services of the foundation. This philosophy has enabled the foundation's assets to double every five years.

First and Lasting Impressions

The value of creating a strong first impression is documented in several success stories in the development programs led by David Mitchell and James "Jim" L. Bowers, Ph.D., at Scripps Foundation (La Jolla, Calif.) During Mitchell's tenure, he instituted a program by which staff call donors of gifts of one hundred dollars or more to thank them for their support. One of those gifts came from an individual who led a foundation known for making multi-million-dollar gifts. Through the initial and future contacts, Scripps was able to forge a relationship that resulted in a one-hundred-million-dollar donation.

Bowers's efforts to create lasting impressions on which to build enduring relationships are equally important. Scripps is credited with being the first healthcare organization in the U.S. to complete a one-hundred-million-dollar campaign, a tribute to Bowers and his staff. How he and Milt Murray organized their respective programs is described next.

Nurturing Relationships

Building solid relationships takes time and organization. For each individual with whom Milt Murray would like to cultivate a relationship, he creates two files, one containing background information, the second for correspondence he sends or receives.

"Some professionals manage fifty or a hundred individuals, but I focus on the top twenty or thirty," he says.

Other major gift fundraisers use different tools, but achieve equally impressive results. Jim Bowers, engineer of Scripps' one-hundred-million-dollar campaign of the early 1990s, uses fifty three-by-five index cards for his top prospects. On each card, he lists the prospect's or donor's name, address, home and business phone numbers, name of spouse, giving history, involvement with Scripps, and other key information.

"When I was with a university, the president asked what he could do to help in fundraising," Bowers says, explaining the origins of his system. "So I gave him information about my top fifty major gift prospects, with each person detailed on a single three-by-five card. I asked him to make contact with at least one of them each day. It could be as simple as calling or visiting them, sending them a note or news item on a topic that would interest them, or building a relationship in some other way. Each day, he was to move on to someone else in his pack and eventually start over. After he did it for a while, he told me that it was the best part of his day. It made him feel good. I decided to make it part of my daily routine and I feel good doing it, too.

"I guess today most people would be managing this process with PDAs or Palm Pilots," he says. "The key to its success is not in which tool you use, but finding a way to keep in touch with your donors."

Both Murray and Bowers add or delete names from their lists, focusing on those who can have the greatest impact on their organizations.

Educate & Involve

According to Murray, many of the best donors to the Adventist World Headquarters learned to give generously "by seeing what others are doing. I invite many of my top thirty prospects to our annual dinner and look for ways to involve them in religious education. When they see what others are doing, they often feel they'd like to do the same.

"We're all social beings and need to find ways to invest ourselves in causes which are bigger than ourselves. There's a great deal of benefit in inviting a prospect to meet socially with people of similar or higher wealth. Often the prospects meets new friends and develops a bond with your organization," he says.

Qualifying Philanthropic Interest

After Murray establishes a relationship, "I ask for a gift as soon as possible. I usually will ask for an amount that is relatively modest for the individual. I'd rather ask for ten thousand or fifteen thousand dollars—even if the person is capable one day of giving ten times that—just to get the person involved." Through relationship building, he and other professionals encourage donors to move up the giving pyramid from an entry-level gift to their largest or ultimate ones, helping them realize the benefits and joys of giving.

Moves Management, a system for cultivating donors that is growing in popularity, maps out the steps for building the relationship, with each step labeled a "move." Building awareness is accomplished through your organization's usual communications (mailing publications, newsletters, etc.), as well as more personal contacts. An important part of the process, however, is learning about the individual's philanthropic nature and interests. Initial moves may start by asking the potential donor for a modest commitment, a gift that may be small in the donor's eyes (as in Murray's example), the loan of a piece of art for an exhibit (for a college or arts organization), a guest lecture, or similar commitment.

During the contacts or moves, it's important to keep the focus on learning about the individual's philanthropic interests. For example, asking questions such as, "We're seeing a high growth rate in our services and may need to expand. Do you think this would be a good decision for us?" If the individual has a positive response, you might say, "If we were to move forward with our expansion plans, we'd like to get the input of individuals who can help guide us and perhaps provide leadership support. Is this a project that might interest you?"

Moves management also seeks to identify "partners" and a "manager" for each potential donor. *Partners* include friends who can help you understand the individual's motivations and capacity, and help advance cultivation and solicitation. A *moves manager* is an individual within your organization who is assigned the responsibility for planning and tracking moves for each potential donor.

For Milt Murray, his cultivation and stewardship appear seamless; he never seems to forget to maintain the relationship. Ten years after a donor gave five thousand dollars as a challenge, which garnered twelve thousand dollars in other gifts, Murray sent the donor a news clipping announcing that the fund had recently raised more than $175,000. Attached to the clipping was a note from Murray stating, "Just look at what you started!"

"This shows good stewardship and that I have integrity as a fundraiser. The next time I ask this contributor to give, he'll know I'll take good care of his gift," Murray says.

Maintaining & Renewing Important Relationships

Regardless of the people they serve, the success of many of the Visionary Organizations is due in large part to staff and volunteer leadership who are not afraid to reach out in one of two ways:

- To stay connected with individuals who are important to their futures. These may be current and former trustees, major donors, people who have previously benefited from the organization (such as alumni of a college or university); and,

- To find new supporters. This may be through social and business networks of the charity's leadership, staff, and most loyal supporters.

Maintaining and strengthening relationships can be accomplished in a multitude of ways: through leadership groups and advisory boards (described below); tours and events; personal contacts (sending news items, birthday, anniversary, and holiday cards); calls and visits to ask for reactions to programs your organization is considering; and good acknowledgment and stewardship for gifts received.

Many colleges and universities also reconnect with alumni through reunions, with "five-year milestones" being the focus for major and planned gifts. With the advent of major campaigns, however, colleges have found other ways to "reconnect," by expanding the kinds of events to reach out to their best supporters and/or by producing materials that help rekindle college memories. During the planning for Stanford

University's campaign, for example, volunteers and staff realized that the university needed to broaden its horizons, to look beyond California, where many of its alumni donors resided, in order to attain its breathtaking goal ($1.1+ billion). A major challenge they faced, however, was, *how do you build a sense of involvement for alumni unable or unwilling to return to campus?* One answer for Stanford was the National Centennial Celebration, which brought the university to alumni in major cities across the U.S. The program included faculty presentations, student performances, and a dinner for major donors. To make the event strictly Stanford, in each city a stage set replicating the campus' inner quad was erected. The effect was dramatic. As alums entered for the celebration event, they were transported back to Stanford.

Other colleges and universities have hosted programs designed to renew college spirit and ties. With a five-year campaign, Princeton University's reunion cycles were a focal point for soliciting leadership gifts. Regional events were held as part of its 250th anniversary celebration, to bolster pride in being a Princetonian and to complement the campaign's goals. A steering committee for leadership gifts and regional campaign committees served as the backbone of the campaign, focusing on capital gifts in addition to significant annual fund gifts from "some 3,000 of Princeton's prospective donors—who are thought to be capable of leadership gifts: combined Annual and capital gifts of $100,000 or more," Princeton's volunteer orientation materials explain. With annual giving providing critical operating funds for the university, joint ask strategies were developed that included "specific requests for major reunion and off-year Annual Giving and for capital priorities."

Another university launched a Vision 2000 tour in several cities, during which the university's president shared her views of the most promising projects on the horizon.

Printed materials, CDs, and videotapes also have been used. At Princeton, small, attractive books with full-page photos of campus buildings, leading faculty members, and facts about the university's educational leadership were prepared as leave-behinds when staff, trustees, and volunteers made calls on prospective donors. Campaign newsletters showcased progress, boldly printed in orange and black, Princeton's colors.

Similarly, healthcare organizations have initiated reunions for former patients, ranging from "neonates" or premature babies who have achieved good health status to survivors of heart disease, cancer, and other illnesses. Included in many of these programs are presentations on the organization's accomplishments and plans for improving patient services.

Networking

How can volunteer and staff leadership help your organization secure top gifts?

Little League Foundation trustee Bill Piszek points out that board members of Little League Baseball and its foundation helped its campaign in three ways: opening doors for the organization's president to present its case; endorsing the campaign to potential donors behind the scenes whenever possible; and, in some cases, participating in funding requests. "I invited a close friend of mine to make a presentation at our prep school," Piszek says. "After his presentation, I walked him back to his car and started telling him about what we're trying to accomplish with Little League Baseball. It's such an important project I thought he should be aware of it. That's how it got started. We later received a six-figure gift."

Volunteers at some organizations invite their close friends to attend meetings in their homes or at the charities, and to participate in tours, lectures, and/or donor events.

Perhaps one of the greatest success stories of building on social contacts is from Pepperdine University—which, in its last campaign, received about half of its goal from individuals who had never attended the university. Pepperdine's transformation from a small college into a world-class university was championed by leaders such as Dr. Charles B. Runnels, today Pepperdine's chancellor, and Blanche Ebert Seaver, whose husband supported the college. Dr. Runnels took a company-paid leave of absence from Tenneco in the 1960s to advance Pepperdine's mission, including joining important clubs in the area and networking with business and community leaders, many of whom are today among Pepperdine's most ardent supporters.
Mrs. Seaver became the school's dream builder in several ways. She not only demonstrated her own commitment but also personally conveyed the urgency and importance of Pepperdine's mission to her many friends (see sidebar "Changing a University's Destiny,").

Changing a University's Destiny

If you've ever wondered if one person can make a difference, consider the story of Blanche Ebert Seaver. Mrs. Seaver stepped forward in a number of remarkable ways that forever changed the destiny of Pepperdine University.

"First, she was very much aware of the problems associated with our original site in Los Angeles, at Seventy-ninth and Vermont. During the late 1960s, the Watts riots were within a couple of miles of the campus and the National Guard actually used the Pepperdine campus as its staging area. Mrs. Seaver knew student safety was at risk at this location and offered the college property in Palos Verdes for a future Pepperdine campus," recalls Larry Hornbaker, Ed.D., Pepperdine's vice chancellor.

Frank and Blanche Seaver

"She was deeply involved in selecting a new campus, which included a search of over forty-four sites. Once she saw the potential of the Malibu location, she chose it over her own. She gave Pepperdine her property, which we sold to offset the expenses of the Malibu campus," he adds.

Her role in reshaping Pepperdine's future did not end there. "After the Malibu site was selected, Mrs. Seaver was asked to give eight million dollars to jumpstart our fundraising for the new campus. Based on our anticipation of her making the gift, we set the date for the announcement of our new Malibu campus. We did not get Blanche's agreement to make the commitment until ten days before the event! With her commitment, however, we got great press: Governor Reagan attended, and this magnificent gift was announced, with pictures of Pepperdine University's new Malibu campus. This was the backdrop for the unusual success achieved over the next twenty months.

"Mrs. Seaver clearly wanted the campaign to succeed. She invited many of her friends to a private lunch or dinner with her and one or two leaders from Pepperdine. We would share our vision, talk about the new campus and the buildings we planned. She was really wonderful in encouraging her friends to give. In some cases, she was so passionate about the university that she would offer to make a personal challenge gift so that friends could have their names on buildings on our new campus. Through her leadership and the help of many of her dear friends and other supporters, we secured $24.6 million in gifts."

Serving in a Leadership Role

As previously indicated, here's nothing like direct involvement in a leadership role to build awareness and educate potential donors about your organization's mission. And the opportunities for leadership involvement are many, including service on a committee, panel, leadership council or advisory board, conference, or board. While not essential for all top gift donors, it is clear that all visionary donors highlighted in this chapter assumed—and enjoyed—leadership roles with the organizations they supported:

Visionary Donor	Leadership Role
George Soros	Founding Conference
Jack Farber	University Board
Gordon Moore	CI Board, Conference Co-chair
Gerhard Andlinger	Advisory Council
Blanche Seaver	University Board

Nearly all the Visionary Organizations profiled have designed ways to successfully involve potential donors of pacesetting and leadership gifts in the important work of their organizations. At Samaritan Inns, for example, a development foundation board was established in addition to Samaritan's governing board; Pepperdine University actually tripled the size of its governing board and, for the first time in its history, invited non—church members to serve. An impressive advisory council was launched as well, offering new opportunities to share Pepperdine's vision and benefits with the most promising benefactors. Children's Hospital (Boston) increased opportunities to involve more people through a new trust board and its Philanthropic Leadership Councils, designed to bring major donors closer to research and cures. Princeton University created leadership gift committees for its campaign, which built upon a strong and responsive reunion program. Topeka Civic Theatre enlisted top-level leadership on its campaign committees. At Abington Hospital, a project-focused panel engineered solutions to a looming crisis, then set about raising funds for the panel's findings (see sidebar "Engaging Top Leaders").

Engaging Top Leaders

You can confront challenging issues with several models—by convening a blue ribbon panel, organizing a leadership council, or creating a strategic planning committee or conference. All have the same goal: to engage top minds and potential donors in addressing key problems or opportunities. At Abington Hospital in the 1980s, the panel approach worked well—raising millions of dollars in gifts—to address government funding threats to medical education. The model was repeated in 2000 when the hospital confronted a nursing shortage. Members of the development staff suggested panel members, and subcommittees were chaired by hospital leadership to lend credibility and build in accountability.

Here are five lessons to gaining maximum benefit from such a group (adapted from my article "The Nursing Imperative: Can Fundraising Help Overcome the Nursing Shortage," which appeared in the AHP Journal published by the Association of Healthcare Philanthropy).

Recruit top leadership and top gifts: The stature of the leadership of any initiative or campaign has a direct effect on its outcome. You want leaders who can set the pace, openly explore issues, invent solutions, and personally invest in their implementation. Seek the very best leadership.

Research the problem and involve panel members in finding solutions: Complex problems often require multifaceted solutions. When individuals have a role in charting solutions, they generally take on more ownership. Once you have a vision of where you're headed, consider fundraising as but one way to get there.

Create inspiring fundraising goals and strategies: Big goals are needed to inspire big gifts. Be visionary in identifying your needs and forward-thinking in developing your strategies.

Rebuild partnerships: For this issue, hospital and nursing professionals needed to make elected officials aware of the national shortage and work to restore federal funding prompted by budget cuts. Other nonprofits have taken similar action, including many colleges and universities that seek to rekindle relationships with their alums before asking for large campaign gifts.

Deal with issues openly and honestly: Donors, community leaders, board members, and administrators were partners in finding solutions to this challenging problem. In pursuing new opportunities, welcome multiple viewpoints and an honest exchange of ideas. Some leaders of your organization may find it uncomfortable to allow outsiders to view your organization's challenges or weaknesses. One way to counteract this discomfort is invite qualified staff to chair or co-chair subcommittees or task forces. Their knowledge and insights will provide the panel with real-world experiences and possible solutions. They can help guide the discussions. Often, a lack of resources is the main reason many solutions were not implemented previously.

Involvement

Membership on your board offers the potential to build awareness, involvement, and commitment. In addition, there's the prestige of being in a leadership role, a stature that studies show is highly desirable among many donors of top gifts. In meetings and presentations, and with their personal gifts, you'll be educating your leaders about the importance of your organization's mission, vision, and fundraising initiatives.

Regardless of the approach you take (board, panel, council, etc.), it's important to identify and involve volunteer leaders able to help shape your organization's future.

Tracking Progress

For organizations with a small number of donors and potential donors to track, it is easy to collect and store information on key individuals on index cards and in paper files. But when the number of potential top gift donors increases into the hundreds or even thousands, storing information and tracking progress can become more difficult.

One solution for up to four or five hundred names is to supplement your paper files with a simple database or spreadsheet, as seen in the sidebar "Tracking Top Gifts Prospects with Excel." Major advantages of this approach are that a spreadsheet is low-cost and is readily accessible to most nonprofits. A disadvantage is that the information you enter is not often stored in the individual's record. It's likely to be written over or lost when you move to a new tracking system or campaign.

Another option is to purchase specialized fundraising software to store research data and plan and track progress in cultivating and soliciting your top prospects. This may be required if you are tracking a large number of prospects or if your program is likely to grow. Having a database offers the added advantage of creating an archive of information for each individual that can be easily retrieved in the future.

Four of the most important features available in some software programs are outlined below.

Integration

Some software packages are integrated into existing fundraising accounting and management systems, while others are standalone products. With integration, you may have more seamless access to data. With standalone software, there may be more features. Evaluate your needs and working style, then determine which software best meets them.

Research

Among the options for storing information are record fields for you to indicate assets, wealth ratings, screening information, relationships, proposals, planned giving, sources of data, and stewardship. At least one system allows you to attach electronic files, such as scanned photos and news clippings, typed profiles and news releases, and other materials that are entered into your system. Another feature is that relationships may be graphically portrayed in a tree or mapped format.

Actions, Tasks, Stewardship & Reminders

The action, tasks, stewardship, and reminder features of some software packages can be powerful. For each individual, you may create an action goal, then build one or more tasks to achieve it. Let's say an individual is an ideal candidate for your board. You would enter into your system an action for "board appointment." You then may create several tasks leading up to this step. These tasks could include: invitation to your organization's annual meeting (or other event); a breakfast or luncheon meeting with a trustee or volunteer this individual knows well; and an exploratory meeting with your president to discuss possible interest in a board appointment. With the action and each of the tasks, a deadline can be set and entered into the database. You may also enter dates for reminder notices for each action and task.

This notice can prompt you if you are a user on the system or can be formatted to appear in reports. Some packages include provisions for stewardship, allowing you to indicate how often follow-up is required.

Reporting

Here's one area where specialized software can benefit you most, so carefully evaluate each product for these features. You'll want to be able to readily retrieve information in an easy-to-read format. Consider how you'll be managing your program and what reports would help you oversee the process. If you are meeting biweekly with staff, you'll likely want to generate a report for each staff member that lists the individuals for which he or she is responsible, along with associated actions, tasks, and deadlines. This report would be printed and given to the staff person prior to the meeting.

A meeting for a solicitation committee focusing on trustees may require a different report and presentation. Here, your report would include each volunteer's assignments, including the individuals he or she has agreed to contact, and information that would assist in the solicitation. This data may include the amount and date of the prospect's largest gift, its purpose, the current gift request, and any response or gift commitments received.

When selecting new software, you'll want to evaluate how effective it is in meeting reporting requirements for each of your committee or group's needs. If changes to reports are needed, ask the software vendor if these changes can be made, and find out the cost and timetable involved.

Tracking Top Gift Prospects with Excel

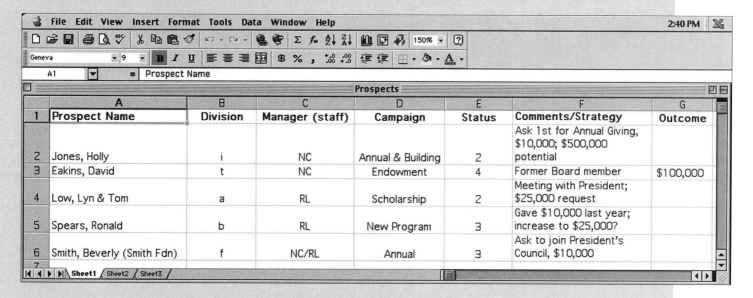

An Excel spreadsheet is a convenient way to record and monitor progress with your top gifts prospects. To construct your spreadsheet, create columns for the individual's full name (for ease in sorting, enter the last name, then the first); division (trustee, business, or other group); prospect manager (typically a staff person), partner(s) or volunteers; campaign; involvement status (identification, cultivation, solicitation, recognition, stewardship); comments or strategy; and the outcome or gift.

To compress your data to present it in a readable format, initials can be used to correspond to volunteers or staff (NC = Nick Costa, RL = Robert Lewis), and codes can be set up to facilitate entering and sorting data. For a division, your codes could include t = trustee; i = individual; b = business; a = alumni; f = foundation. Alphabetical or numeric codes could denote the status or level of cultivation, such as 1 = identification; 2 = cultivation; 3 = solicitation; 4 = recognition; and, 5 = stewardship.

Excel is a registered trademark of Microsoft.

Take time to analyze lists compiled from previous workbooks to identify the individuals you would like involve in your organization. Then, create a plan for cultivating and soliciting each individual by following the steps in this workbook.

1. From your workbooks Creating a Table of Gifts and Screening for TOP GIFTS™ Donors, zero in on your best prospects and donors. List them here. For additional names, make copies of this page or list on a separate page.

1.	14.
2.	15.
3.	16.
4.	17.
5.	18.
6.	19.
7.	20.
8.	21.
9.	22.
10.	23.
11.	24.
12.	25.
13.	

2. Study the list. Based on the names you see, assess whether there is an overall strategy that would enhance your organization's effectiveness and bring many of these people closer to your organization. Strategies might include serving on a board, committee, leadership council, or panel that includes a focus on TOP GIFTS™ fundraising. List strategy below, then indicate those who might be good candidates (by circling the number of the name above). Continue to add names to and delete names from your list.

Brief description of strategy:

3. To track progress on individual cultivation, decide on the tool(s) you will use. Create records/files for your top 25 to 50 individuals/groups. Record information on each prospect including his or her name, address, home and business telephone numbers, level and type of involvement with your organization, past giving history with your organization (if any), spouse's name, etc. Keep records of the date and action taken (phone call, visit, etc.), as well as thoughts on next step in cultivation/solicitation.

Tracking tools:

☐ Three-by-five cards   ☐ Files

☐ Excel spreadsheet   ☐ Calendar or planner

☐ Palm/computer software

TOP GIFTS™ WORKBOOK
Building TOP GIFTS™ Relationships

---

4. Identify friends and/or advisors of each individual/group who would be willing to assist you on a confidential basis. Determine what role(s) each could play (e.g., provide information, open doors, cultivate, assist in solicitation). Add friend/advisor name(s), phone number(s) to the file or record of your top prospects.

---

5. Develop personal cultivation strategies for each individual/group. As necessary, schedule actions on your calendar or planner.

---

6. Check to see if names are on your mailing list(s) to receive your organization's annual report, development newsletter, and other informational items. As you'll want to solicit each individual *in person*, if required by your mailing criteria, code for no direct mail solicitation.

---

7. Implement cultivation/involvement strategies and solicit (see next chapter). Record steps taken, including date of action. Consult friends/advisors to develop a profile of each individual's giving interests and, if agreeable, assistance in soliciting support for your organization.

---

8. At year-end—or more often if possible—review status of each prospect and plan actions for the coming year. Add or delete prospects, as needed.

Involvement

In most cases, personally ask.

Ask, and it shall be given you; seek, and ye shall find.

Matthew 7:7, Luke 11:9

"The reason people do not give is because they are not asked."

From a study conducted by the Gallup Organization
Official Fundraising Almanac

It's ironic; *of the time required to raise funds, the gift request itself represents only about 5 percent of the total.* In our eight-step TOP GIFTS™ process, asking for the gift is but one step. But it's the most important one. For, without it, your organization's dreams may never be realized. But don't take my word for it; a Gallup poll reveals that the reason most people don't give is because they are not asked!

In spite of this, asking for the gift in person can be a daunting task for staff members and top volunteers. Indeed, it may very well be the main reason why some fundraisers never advance beyond other types of fundraising. They are more comfortable with what they know . . . in direct mail, for example, by mailing to thousands of people, they can syndicate or minimize their risk. I'm likely to get *some* response, they think. If I asked in person, they believe, who knows what kind of response I'd get?

Overcoming Fear

After teaching more than a dozen half-day classes on asking for gifts in person, I can tell you *exactly* what most people fear.

"Why don't people like to ask for money in person?" I ask during the first five minutes of each class. In *every* class, the response at the top of the list is "rejection." The fear that the potential donor will say "No!"

"And what's the remedy?" I ask after compiling a list of reasons people are uncomfortable soliciting gifts. What's remarkable is the large number of ways people have for dealing with this one fear. Most responses fall into the category of "advance planning" or "doing one's homework *before* the solicitation to increase the chances of a gift being made." Here are some of the best responses:

- Learn as much as you can about the individual, his or her interests, and previous gifts, to be sure your project is a good fit;

- Research your organization's needs and opportunities so you'll be able to present them in the most interesting and compelling ways;

- Include two people in the solicitation: one person who has a close relationship with the individual, a second who can explain the project well;

- Make your own gift first so you can speak with conviction;

- Role-play your solicitation and, if two individuals are involved, determine who will ask for the gift and the amount being requested;

- Plan for objections and develop responses to those you can foresee so there are few surprises;

- Recognize that "no" may not mean the person is not interested. Instead, the prospect may be saying "I'm not able to give now" or "I need more time to complete a large gift."

These are all great ideas. But the response I love most was suggested by a librarian during the Free Library of Philadelphia's recent campaign. "I believe that your attitude is really important," she began. "Our campaign is about changing lives (actually the theme of the campaign). I'm giving someone the opportunity to do something really important. Each gift can open doors for students to enter new careers, to be happier and more successful in the future. Maybe, as a result of this gift, it will be the first person in this family who will go to college. This could be the most important gift that this individual makes all year. Hopefully, the individual I'm asking will see it that way. But if they say, 'No, I'm not going to give,' should I take it personally? No, not if I've explained our campaign well. Let me give you an example. If I go to a shoe store and try on a dozen pairs of shoes, but then decide not to buy one, do you think the salesperson goes home worrying about it? No, instead this person thanks me for visiting the store, because I might come back and he doesn't want to lose a sale in the future. Then, the salesperson gives his full attention to the next customer. That's the way I look at it. I'll do my best to ask for a gift, but I know that not every customer will be a big sale."

I couldn't have said it better.

What Does "No" Really Mean?

Few people are as effective in soliciting top gifts as Robert P. Thompson, a successful businessman, now retired, and a trustee and fundraising volunteer to several nonprofit organizations. Thompson's relationships with the people he calls on is so close that often he returns not only with a gift for the char-

ity, but with a personal gift as well. The individuals he calls on truly enjoy being with him. "I did have one gift request that initially was a real disappointment," he reveals. "This was a woman whom I had known for many years, and whose late husband had made gifts to the charity I represented. I asked her to consider a gift of three hundred thousand dollars for a project that would honor both her and her husband. I was turned down. I really thought she'd help in *some* way, so I asked if she would consider making this gift as a charitable bequest? Again, the answer was 'no.' I then told her how nice it was to see her and thanked her for her time. I thought keeping her friendship was more important than upsetting her by pressing for the gift."

Thompson's good judgment and manners were on target. Years later, this woman's attorney contacted the charity. As a result of Thompson's visit, this woman had reconsidered his request and changed her will to include the charity for one-third of the residue of her estate (the balance after all other distributions have been made). She had recently died and the charity would be receiving its bequest. The amount? More than eight million dollars!

Solicitation Tips

Major gift requests need to be tailor-made to each individual, business, corporation, foundation, or organization. Here are some guidelines to consider in your planning:

- *Case:* For people to give with passion, your needs or opportunities should be compelling. Create your messages so they resonate with the donor's interests, show impact, and fulfill his or her dreams as well as yours.

- *Leadership:* The higher the level of leadership you involve to ask for a gift, the more attention and respect you're likely to receive. While there are perhaps many people who can deliver your message, who can demonstrate that this project is important . . . that it's a priority for your organization?

- *Peers:* Look for the best connections, people who think like your prospect and can relate to his or her interests and needs. Business leaders understand other business professionals; physicians are often best at soliciting other physicians; faculty relate well to other faculty. Look within the prospect's circle of friends.

- *Location:* Solicitations can occur wherever you and the prospect feel most comfortable; at a time that is agreeable; and, as time allows. Some business leaders will allow you fifteen minutes maximum (his or her office might work best). Others may suggest a breakfast or luncheon meeting (reserve a quiet, private table, if possible). And still others may prefer to visit you at your organization.

- *Team Approach:* Whenever possible, I encourage the "buddy system," two people representing your organization. With two people, you'll have more expertise and greater depth. With two people, at least one person can be watching or listening at all times for clues to the prospect's reactions and interests.

- *Well Planned and Rehearsed:* Previous chapters focused on shaping your message into opportunities that inspire, and creating naming opportunities and membership programs. Based on your knowledge of your prospect, integrate your best ideas and approaches into planning for your presentation. Rehearse it to ensure that it conveys important points and can be relayed well within the time available.

Getting the Appointment

Generally, it's best to have the person who has the best relationship with the potential donor schedule the appointment. Depending on the relationship, this may be as simple as the individual making a phone call and asking for an opportunity to meet "to discuss a project at [name of organization] that may interest you. I'd like to have [name of official and title] join us, if that's okay with you." Another approach is to have the individual send a letter on his or her stationery with a similar message, which alerts the individual, "During the next few days, I'll be calling you to see when it is convenient to get together."

Formally Ask

When calling to set up the appointment, it's important that you or your volunteer not go into your presentation. Instead, the goal is to get the appointment. When you meet, you'll have an opportunity to make your case and answer any questions that arise.

No One Available to Solicit the Individual?

You may encounter times when either you are not able to identify a volunteer who knows your potential donor or, if they do, they say the relationship is "too close. I just can't be involved." How do you overcome this obstacle, and take the next step?

One solution is to involve top leaders of your organization, such as your president and a trustee, or the president and an experienced fundraiser. In some cases, the fundraiser or a consultant to your organization may be sufficient. If the person has high Connectivity, a sense of belonging with your organization (see chapter 8), he or she will be interested in, and open to, the meeting. What's most important here is that you present your case and ask for the gift.

Five Steps for Asking

While you'll want your visit to feel natural, you can prepare for it by organizing your presentation into the following five steps. This planning enables you to develop messages and strategies, and anticipate questions that may be asked. You'll want to be flexible, to encourage discussion and listen for his or her philanthropic interests.

1. The Opening

Within the time available, allow an opportunity to create or renew a positive relationship with the potential donor and representatives of your organization. This may be as simple as asking about the individual's hobbies, business, family, or other personal interests. If the person previously was involved with your organization, you might extend greetings from people he or she knows well, or compliment him or her on some past achievement. You could also present a small gift—a booklet on your organization, a cup with your logo, or another item that matches the individual's interests.

2. The Presentation

Briefly define the project you are seeking to fund and its benefits. For a campaign, this may be a statement such as, "During the past several months, you may have heard about our *Vision for the Future* campaign, which is designed to address the tremendous growth we're experiencing. The centerpiece of the campaign is a new facility which will not only address increased demand, but also position us as the premier business school [or hospital, museum, food bank, etc.] in our region." Then provide two or three key points about the project or campaign.

3. The Gift Request

Keep your request simple. "We're asking you to consider a gift of five hundred thousand dollars for the new facility. This gift could be paid over five years. In recognition of your support, we'd like to name the new main lobby and reception area in your honor. This is a really special and important gift to this campaign and we hope you will consider it."

Now pause, relax, stop talking. . . . Give the individual time to consider your request. Let silence be your ally.

4. Overcoming Objections & Resistance

Don't be afraid of objections; they are a natural part of the process, a clear indication that your request is being considered. Often, the individual is telling you the specific obstacle that needs to be overcome before the gift can be made. View any objection as helpful information. Let it be your guide. Be positive and courteous.

If you find resistance, be understanding but persistent. Convey the importance of the campaign and that, as a leader, his or her participation is needed for its success. See "Overcoming Objections" on page 261 for responses to some of the most common objections you may hear.

5. *The Closing*

Make it a positive visit by thanking the individual for his or her time and gift, if a commitment has been made. If not and more time is needed to consider your request, arrange for a follow-up visit or call (e.g., "Could we get together in about a week to see if you have made a decision? Would Thursday or Friday work for you?"). Or you may ask, "What are the next steps we can take?" Leave with the individual any printed pieces you have prepared about your campaign or, if there's interest, offer to send a personalized letter of request. Do not leave a pledge card. Instead, reinforce the message that you'd be delighted to visit again.

After the visit, send a letter to thank the individual for the opportunity to share information about your project or campaign. Briefly emphasize the importance of his or her leadership and how you look forward to answering any questions in the future. Follow up as promised.

Confirming the Gift

There are several ways to confirm the gift, ranging from:

- A simple pledge card ("I pledge $25,000 to be paid over the next five years, with the first payment to be paid prior to December 31, 2004"), to

- A letter of intent ("If I am financially able, it is my intention to make a gift of $5,000 per year for the next five years, starting in December, 2004. Although this is my intention, this is not a legally binding pledge . . ."); or

- A gift agreement, often prepared to name a building, create an endowment, or confirm details of a significant gift for other purposes. The agreement typically confirms the amount of the gift (and payment schedule for a pledge), how the gift and any income will be used, specific requests made by the donor, and recognition and its term ("The facility will be named the Costa Science Center for the life of the donor or fifty years, whichever is longer. If the research programs of Costa Science Center are relocated during that time, the replacement facility shall be dedicated and recognized as the Costa Science Center"). A well-drafted gift agreement can serve as a cultivation tool ("This agreement outlines some ways we would like to recognize you for such a meaningful gift . . ."), as a way to track and confirm details over an extended time period if you are negotiating details of the gift, and as a means of helping ensure that your organization will provide good stewardship. I keep our president and board chair informed during the gift discussions, then ask them to sign two original agreements (one for the donor, the second for our organization), after all the details have been confirmed.

Overcoming Objections	
Objection	*Possible Responses*
"I had a problem with your organization five years ago and I am still upset about it. Because of that, I'm not interested in giving to you now."	Apologize for the problem. Ask if you can look into it and get back to the individual. Place your gift request "on hold" until you can address the issue. *Or . . .* If your organization has new leadership responsive to complaints, indicate that your new president "would certainly want to address such issues. Would you be willing to meet with our president or her staff to describe what happened?"
"I'd like to give, but I can't. I live off the income from my stock."	If your organization offers a life income program (such as charitable gift annuities), suggest, "For many donors, there is a way you can make a gift and increase your income at the same time. Would you be interested in hearing more about it?"
"I have two kids in college" *or* "I just bought a new Mercedes." *or* "I just built a vacation home at the shore" "I really can't afford to contribute."	Stress the importance of his or her leadership, how it will help inspire others to give, or that there are a limited number of people who can make this project a reality. You are hoping that he or she can find some way to make this gift possible. *And/or . . .* Emphasize the pledge payment period. "This gift can be paid over three years. In some cases, payments can be extended to five years. Would this be of help to you?"
"I never make decisions without seeing something in writing."	"I understand. We can provide you with a description of the project and our request. I'd be happy to deliver it to you later today."
"I'm not really interested in giving to bricks and mortar. But I've always thought the school should have a program in international business. Have you ever considered establishing one?"	*If you are unable to pursue now:* "What a great idea. At this point, however, the school has had to prioritize in order to reach at least some of our goals. Were we to offer any new programs, we would need this new facility. Would you consider making a gift for the facility, which would better position the school to expand its programs in the future?" *If your organization is open to new ideas:* Ask what role the individual might be willing to assume in funding the new program. "Your idea sounds interesting. Have you reviewed it with anyone at the college? What was the response? Is this a program you would like to help underwrite?"

TOP GIFTS™ WORKBOOK
Asking for a Leadership Gift

Follow these eight steps to increase your confidence and success in securing top gifts.

1. Preparation is the key to success. Determine:

   Appointment
   Who will request the appointment and how request will be made (in person, by phone, letter, etc.):

   Solicitor(s)
   Individual with expertise about project or program:

   Individual with close relationship with potential donor (this person may also be setting up the appointment):

2. Determine the amount and purpose of your request. If you believe your potential donors would be interested in recognition, membership programs, etc., integrate these elements into your planning.

3. Have printed and/or video materials prepared and available (may include a pledge card, case statement, letter of request, sketch of new building or lobby, etc.). Determine how best to use them in your presentation.

4. Write out your presentation using "Five Steps for Asking" as a guide. Decide who will make what comments, and who will make the request. Role-play your presentation, being sensitive to what questions or objections may develop. Script how you would best respond to these concerns.

5. Make your own gift. If it is of a level that is inspiring, consider how you might use this information as part of the solicitation. If you have leadership donors who feel comfortable having their gifts made public, consider if revealing this information could help your solicitation.

6. Schedule the visit, rehearse the solicitation, and then organize any materials you plan to bring. Allow time before the visit so you are relaxed and confident when you make your call.

7. Think positively. Look to build the relationship as you make your gift request. If there are unanswered questions or a follow-up is needed, be service-oriented.

8. Send a letter of thanks for the donor's gift and/or the opportunity to share information about your project. Briefly reinforce the key points of your solicitation. If a follow-up call is required, make the call.

People love to be thanked. Recognize and show appreciation to top gift donors in ways that are meaningful to them.

"When you drink the water, remember the spring."

Chinese proverb

"Do what you do so well that people will come to see you do it again."

Walt Disney

You'll want to design recognition or appreciation programs for at least three groups of donors:

- The contributor(s) of your pacesetting gifts;

- Those who made leadership, major, and special gifts; and

- All other contributors.

The task is simple with some advance planning.

Special Recognition for Pacesetting Donors

Throughout this book, we have focused on the pivotal role of top gifts and the crucial role of the donor of the pacesetting gift . . . the individual, foundation, or organization that gives the largest gift. This gift sets a standard for others to emulate. It contributes significantly to the overall goal. It creates momentum. It is essential to success!

So how do we express our thanks? The answer is found in the values and the needs of this donor, and in the culture of your organization.

Many of the organizations profiled in *Dream Builders* have found ways to give special and added attention to their pacesetting donors. Often, this recognition is given prominence at an existing, high-stature meeting or program; at a new event organized to celebrate the success of a project and to honor contributors; or on several different occasions. Abington Hospital revealed its lead gift at a hospital board meeting, where the donor was given a standing ovation, and later in the year the hospital photographed him at a reception with eight nursing students who received full scholarships as a result of his family's generosity.

On the opening night in its new facilities, the Topeka Civic Theatre and Academy honored the donor of its largest gift, offered him an opportunity to say a few words, and then presented him with a small yet personal gift that displayed good friendship and humor (see the sidebar "The Little Tin Box" in chapter 1). Little League Baseball, in a touching surprise announcement, dedicated a stadium to honor one of its lead donors. Pepperdine University honored Blanche Ebert Seaver for her inspiring gift at a dinner attended by so many that it required two major hotels; her gift truly was a turning point in the university's future.

The Venerable Chair

Permanently linking an individual's name to a program, endowment, or facility often adds prestige, and demonstrates to the contributor that the gift is both lasting and appreciated. For many colleges and universities, the named endowed chair is one of the highest levels of recognition. It is a distinguished honor both for the individual after whom the chair is named and for the scholar who receives it.

The origins of the endowed chair can be traced to the Middle Ages, and perhaps even before, when monarchs, bishops, and the high clergy were seated in chairs, while others often sat on three-legged stools or benches. When a king or bishop awarded a lifetime grant to a teacher or professor, he often presented the honoree with a chair as a symbol of the academic stature the educator had achieved. Oxford and Cambridge Universities had endowed chairs in the 1400s and 1500s; Harvard established its first in the early 1700s.

Today, named endowed chairs are a sign of teaching excellence at colleges and universities throughout the world. As salaries and teaching costs rise, with increasing frequency a named endowed chair or professorship requires a minimum gift of $1.5 million to $2.5 million. The concept has been extended to endowed preceptorships for the most promising junior faculty, fellowships for graduate scholars and researchers, museum curatorships, as well as endowments for important staff positions throughout the nonprofit sector.

The names of pacesetting, leadership, and major donors can also be displayed in a prominent location at your organization (see the sidebar "Recognizing Dream Builders," pages 270–71)

These are historic gifts. As you get to know your best contributors, look for ways to show your organization's appreciation in ways that demonstrate their key role and are meaningful to them.

Honoring Leadership Donors and Other Contributors

The basis of this fundraising tenet, from all reports, is obscure. Some say its origins are Chinese, others point to religious roots. Thus far, I've heard no definitive proof of how it came about.

I'm referring to the *Rule of Sevens*, a fundraising precept that encourages you to "thank a contributor seven times before asking for the next gift." When I first heard about the Rule of Sevens more than twenty-five years ago, I wondered, with the pressures of a small development office, how I could organize my time to meet this standard. I was surprised to learn that I, like many other professionals, unknowingly measured up to this principle. As a result, our donors rewarded us with loyal and continued support.

Let's explore ways to say "thank you" to your donors, then create a donor appreciation plan that will be welcomed.

Letters of Thanks

Looking to create a lasting impression with top gift donors? Sure, you'll send a thank you letter. But why not invite other leaders of your organization to send a positive message as well? Unless your contributor insists on remaining anonymous, ask five or more prominent members of your organization (president, board chair, board member, dean or program chair, development council chair, etc.) to send a letter of thanks printed on business or personal stationery. Each should share, in his or her own words, why the gift is important, meaningful. You'll be surprised how many donors will say, "No one has ever done this before. It really left a great impression. Your organization really is special."

Meet the Student/Professional

For organizations funding scholarships, fellowships, chairs, and other positions, the recipient should be encouraged to write a letter of thanks and/or, for research or program positions, a progress report to the donor. Some organizations have the letters sent through the development office or school, which allows them to see and track the letters, as well as protect the confidentiality of donor information (e.g., home address).

Donors also may be invited to a reception, luncheon, or other event to meet recipients. This meeting can be quite powerful, as often it not only demonstrates that the gift was used as intended, but also creates a greater appreciation of the importance of the person and program that is being funded.

Groundbreaking, Hardhat Preview Tours & Dedication Ceremonies

If you are building or renovating a facility, you'll have ample opportunities to demonstrate progress. This includes inviting those closest to your organization—including your top gift donors—to programs such as a groundbreaking ceremony, hardhat tours during construction (be sure to review your tour plans with your construction site supervisor for safety), and/or a dedication. Depending on the scope and timing of your construction, there can be dedications of individual areas as well. When planning the program, determine which top official will briefly pay tribute to the donor(s) who helped made the facilities possible. If it is a named facility, offer special words of thanks to these individuals and determine if you will invite them to step up to the lectern to make their own comments. A small souvenir may be given to each participant (e.g., for a groundbreaking, a miniature shovel engraved with the facility's name and dedication date; for a dedication, a printed booklet showcasing the new facility, information about the pacesetting donor, history of the program; for a research facility, a test tube engraved with the facility's name and a flower to convey the promise of the future; etc.).

New Programs

Newly funded programs may also be dedicated with a lecture, dinner, or other occasion. To make the event memorable, consider inviting a noted professional, celebrity, and/or elected official to participate in the program.

Recognition Plaques & Displays

If your campaign or major and planned gifts program includes recognition plaques or a display, invite your donors to the dedication. Plan your program to include a presentation that thanks all donors, honors campaign leadership, and introduces one or more contributors making the highest-level gifts.

Donor Reports

Many organizations publish an annual report of donors, listing names by giving category and reporting on the year's progress. Top gifts donors may be highlighted in articles and photos. The report may be published initially to be distributed at an event, such as the dedication of a new facility.

An easy way to pass along a report to donors is simply to mail a copy of a favorable news story on the program or project funded, along with a brief note or letter that conveys appreciation for the donor's central role.

Press Release/Feature Articles/News Conference

The highest-level gift may command the attention of the news media. If so—and if the donor is agreeable to the publicity—prepare press materials and a photo.

Personal Calls or Letters

We've briefly discussed how a phone call to a new hundred-dollar or thousand-dollar donor can demonstrate that the gift is noticed and appreciated. Also consider sending a letter from your president (or other top official), once or twice a year, that provides an update on the progress and challenges at your organization. The letters can be scheduled in advance and, while planning your program, you can determine which donors will receive them (e.g., all donors who gave over a certain gift amount). With computers and word processors, a standard letter can be printed on your president's stationery with personal salutations, then hand-signed with an informal name (ex. "Ron" versus "Ronald R. Smith, III"). The letters may also be printed on stationery with your membership insignia for contributors who qualify for the membership group.

Awards

You can create and present an award each year that recognizes the best donor(s) for their leadership service and philanthropy. The award may be called the Philanthropist of the Year Award or the Trustees Distinguished Service Award, or it may be named after an individual or event in your organization's history. Design the award's piece to present to the honoree, and create a display to honor annual recipients. Give the award visibility in your publications. Although it is presented to only a small number of people, if orchestrated properly, many of your best donors will one day seek to be honored.

Events

Events may be organized to increase awareness of a new program, building, or service; launch your campaign or fundraising program; provide a membership benefit; thank contributors; or meet several of these goals. Determine whether you should expand an existing event or launch a new one to meet your goals.

Pins, Parking Cards, Discounts & Amenities, Other Signs of Appreciation

Encourage pride in your organization or for a membership group, by giving members a small lapel pin (with the group's logo), tie, or other small gift item. When conducting your interest survey (see workbook from chapter 6), test a few ideas to determine what potential donors would value most.

Some organizations have found that providing cards for free parking and/or discounts at gift shops or restaurants are also well received. Added conveniences or amenities are other ways of showing appreciation. Donors may use a special admission gate to enter a museum, theatre, or zoo; when hospitalized, donors to hospitals may receive greetings from the president (a rose in a bud vase and/or a get-well card). Determine what would be most valued by your current and potential top gifts donors.

Working Smarter

Evaluate existing reports, communication materials, and events and, if appropriate, weave them into your appreciation plan. If, for example, another department prepares a report or guide that you believe would interest your donors, ask if additional copies could be made available to you to mail to your donors. If not, offer to pay the cost of printing additional copies if the expense is reasonable.

Miscellaneous brochures on your organization's services may be assembled into membership packets with a welcome message from your president or executive director. Consider including information on how to make a planned gift (such as a bequest or life income gift) or a reply card to request this information.

Evaluate your organization's events, as well. An annual meeting of your trustees may be just the right forum for honoring your largest contributors.

Recognizing Dream Builders

A plaque or sign may be used to honor an individual con-tributor for a top gift, as seen in these views of a children's play area, and the Norman and Angelina Cooper Family Waiting Area (Duke University Children's Hospital).

Names also may be grouped for recognition, often by giving levels or membership categories. Recognition dis-plays can be designed to match the purpose, culture, his-tory, or another significant feature of the organization. These donor recognition displays designed and fabricated by Mitchell Associates are customized for the Richmond Ballet (graphic of ballerina), American College of Cardiology (forty-foot-long collage of science and medi-cine), Children's Hospital Trust/Boston (ten-foot-high chil-dren's book titled *The Story of Generosity*), Duke University Medical Center (wall-size mural featuring photographic treatment of Duke's gothic architecture; and a display with a landscape theme recognizing the Horizon Society) and the Upper Chesapeake Medical Center (waterfall and sculpture).

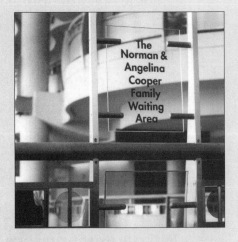

Thanks

TOP GIFTS™ WORKBOOK
Designing a Donor Appreciation Program

In chapter 6, we reviewed opportunities to encourage and reward your best donors. Now, let's focus on specific categories of gifts (pacesetting, leadership, others) to organize benefits and recognition plans.

1. **Recognition for Pacesetting Donor(s)**
   Identify the donor(s) of your largest gift amount, then list commitments made (e.g., naming a facility or program). Determine the interests of each pacesetting donor and how you can best recognize him or her (e.g., introduction at dedication ceremony, feature article in your publication, press release, etc.).

   Name of Pacesetting Donor(s)

   Recognition Plan

2. **Creating Categories for Leadership/Major & Other Contributors**
   Study your gift table to determine your levels of giving based on these guidelines.

   Leadership Gifts: Top 8 to 10 gifts representing one-third or more of your goal

   Major Gifts: Next 100 gifts (approx.) representing the second third or more of your goal

   Optional:
   Special Gifts: Remaining gifts representing 25% to 33% of goal

   Other Categories: List remaining giving level(s)

   Modify these categories, as needed, to correspond with your membership and solicitation programs. (Note: The names of these categories are for classification purposes only; you are welcome and encouraged to substitute the names of your own recognition levels, if you have established them.)

   Using the sample donor appreciation plan that follows as a guide, list each of your major categories or giving levels on the top row of the donor appreciation plan template below. List each giving category in its own shaded block (or, if you prefer, create a similar chart on a separate sheet).

3. List benefits you will provide in the left column of the donor appreciation plan template.

4. Review and refine your donor appreciation program with your development council or board. Seek final approval.

Next Steps?

Your donor appreciation plan can serve your entire development program. With this plan, you can chart specific responses for donors at each giving level, from your direct mail donors to those who make leadership gifts. The next page shows an overview of how Abington Memorial Hospital organized a donor appreciation program for its nursing initiative, followed by a template for creating your own plan.

SAMPLE
Donor Appreciation Plan
Nursing Initiative, Abington Memorial Hospital

Source/Gift Amount	Direct Mail	Membership	Special	Leadership & Major
Amount	<$1,000	$1,000+	$10,000+	$25,000+
Acknowledgments—Within 10 days				
Official thank you letter (sent within 48 hours)	✓	✓	✓	✓
Thank you letters from president, board chair, dean		✓	✓	✓
Phone call to first-time contributor (all gifts over $100)	✓ From director	✓ From director	✓ From vice president	✓ From VP & president
Ongoing Communications				
Annual donor report	✓ ✓ ✓ All donors			
2 newsletters/year				
Recognition & Memberships				
Name listed in annual report	✓ Over $100	✓	✓	✓
Name on plaque by membership group & level	✓ Over $100	✓ Chairman's Forum	✓ President's Council	✓ President's Council
Membership/ parking card		✓	✓	✓
Patient amenities		✓	✓	✓
Individual plaque				✓
Events				
Health education; financial seminars	✓	✓	✓	✓
Chairman's Forum Dinner		✓	✓	✓
President's Council Dinner			✓	✓
Dedication of nursing plaques				✓
Added Value				
Unexpected gift (during holidays)		✓ Selected by development staff		

TOP GIFTS™ WORKBOOK
Designing a Donor Appreciation Program

Source/Gift Amount				
Amount				

Acknowledgments

Ongoing Communications

Recognition & Memberships

Events

Added Value

Thanks

Keep your donors informed and involved. Report on—and celebrate—what you've accomplished together.

"Success leaves clues."

Anthony Robbins

A good giving experience is

the best cultivation for the next gift.

Anonymous

T ake a moment to reflect. Ask yourself these questions:

- Did you accomplish what you said you would with the gifts you received?

- Do your contributors feel a sense of accomplishment, as though their gifts have meaning and impact?

- Would you like the joy and accomplishments, as well as your donor recognition programs, to become the signature of your commitment to your donors?

- How can you make "a good giving experience the best cultivation for the next gift"?

For each of the organizations profiled in *Dream Builders*, stewardship is an ongoing process of informing top contributors of what the organization is doing with their gifts. Generally, the more personalized the stewardship program, the more donors appreciate it.

Five Ways to Design an Effective Stewardship Program.

1. Focus Your Stewardship

Design your stewardship program in two stages:

- First, create *systems or processes* that enable you to provide acknowledgments and reports to *all* contributors or, as your needs dictate, to target and communicate with specific groups of contributors. (Note: With increasing media attention, nonprofits may be required to communicate their effectiveness to nondonors as well, including government officials, watchdog groups, news reporters, etc.)

- Then, design and produce events, letters, reports, and other ways to communicate *that are focused on your top gift contributors.*

With a good coding system and today's fundraising software packages, it is easy to meet your first goal. As gifts are received, code donors in a unique way when they give to a specific campaign or project (e.g., all donors who give to your capital cam-

A Dream Come True

When stewardship is done well, it can have a positive and lasting effect on the donor, others interested in the organization's future, and the institution itself. Just ask Bruce Toll, co-founder of Toll Brothers, the largest builder of luxury homes in the United States.

"When I was younger, I remember attending the dedication of a new building at my local hospital," he told an audience of six hundred people. "I was so impressed that I thought, if I am ever able, one day I would like to attend a similar program. But this new program—and the new building—would instead be dedicated in honor of my parents."

His father, Albert Toll, was a Russian immigrant who by the age of twenty-four was a successful businessman and millionaire. During his business career, Albert developed more than one thousand homes, shopping centers, and luxury apartment buildings. Through many of these experiences, he taught his sons, Bruce and Robert, much about building and development. As a tribute to his guidance, when they started their company, Toll Brothers, they named him honorary chairman.

Bruce developed an appreciation for and expertise about his local hospital. Indeed, he and his brother served on its board, as well as key committees. They made other gifts, seeing their support launch new programs, improve peoples' lives.

Sylvia and Albert Toll

So when Bruce was asked to make a special gift to pay tribute to his parents, it was easy to say "yes." His parent had done so much for him and he remembered the dedication that was so special that he had attended many years ago.

Now, as he stood at the podium, a new patient care tower, the Toll Pavilion, was being dedicated in honor of his parents and the family's pacesetting gift. For both the hospital and for Bruce Toll, it was a dream come true.

paign are marked with a C in your computer's campaign or solicitation field). Thank you letters and campaign updates then can be readily produced and sent to all donors giving to that project. Your communications can be as simple as a brief note with a reprint of a favorable news article on a campaign project (e.g., the design of your new building winning a national award); taking a photograph (depicting the steel girders outlining the shape of the new building) and sending it to donors, or another form of mailing.

With good systems and practices in place, you'll have time for meeting your second goal—cultivating, recognizing, and communicating with your top gifts contribu-

Stewardship

tors. As one university official astutely told me, "Begin your stewardship with your thank you and cultivation, to see who is interested. You'll discover a core of individuals who are so interested that they don't give just one time, but they give repeatedly, more and more each time. It is here you want to focus your stewardship.

"Stewardship is the most obvious thing. It comes down to how much time are you willing to devote to this core group of individuals?"

2. Watch for Their Interests

For this core group with whom you want to keep in touch, report on the progress and achievements from their recent gifts, and watch for their giving motivations, as well as specific needs or projects at your organization that they find compelling. Organize your time, provide attention, and show interest. Let them know you consider them important, both as individuals and as leaders with your organization. Keep good records. An individual who indicates that "you really should consider building your endowment" may be a good candidate to make a leadership gift to a future campaign that has an endowment goal. Or perhaps this individual would contribute a planned gift (such as a current gift of real estate or other asset, a bequest, or a life income gift). One question I like to ask is, "What were you thinking when you indicated the need for an endowment?" A follow-up question might include, "Is there a way you might be able to help us address that need?" or, "Would you be interested in exploring ways that we could start an endowment program? Your gift could be the start of an exciting and important program."

3. Enlist and Educate Others

Make good stewardship a vibrant part of your culture. Development professionals at some organizations educate their faculty (colleges and universities), doctors (health organizations), trustees, and administrative staff about stewardship *well before the fundraising begins*. When approached to raise funds for a worthwhile project, development staff provide an overview of development communications—why it's important and how it's accomplished. If the trustee, faculty member, or doctor requesting support is too busy, development staff will draft the proposals and correspondence and maintain a tickler system (see below) to remind the individual of "next steps" in the development communications process. With their knowledge of donor motivations and interests, these development professionals serve as a resource and advisor, sharing information about each potential donor (matching interests with projects; suggesting gift amounts, possible recognition ideas, and other considerations), and offering suggestions and strategies to increase the likelihood of success.

Several studies show that a high percentage of top gift contributors, for example, like to be associated—and in direct contact—with the leadership of an organization. For a new professorship at a university, for example, a small dinner with the donor, the new professor, and the university's president would be a way to respond to this giving interest and celebrate this gift. A photograph could be taken of the contributor, professor receiving that professorship, and president, which would be presented to the contributor and, if appropriate, published in the alumni publication.

Several of the organizations profiled in *Dream Builders* have stewardship programs for endowed scholarships. Each year, the donor receives a letter with information about the scholarship recipient from the school, college, or university. In addition, the recipient is encouraged to write to his or her benefactor. In some cases, the university provides the student with sufficient information to not only write a letter, but also initiate contact with the donor so they may meet or perhaps have lunch together when the donor attends a class reunion or visits the campus for another reason. The result is that the gift becomes much more personal. Also, some colleges and universities provide class secretaries with lists of the named scholarships and their recipients, information which often is published in class notes. Invariably, donors talk enthusiastically with friends and neighbors about their contacts with their students, a real testimonial for the program.

4. Develop Records and a Tickler System

You'll want to create a central file for all correspondence to each of your major and planned gift donors, which becomes the *institutional memory* for such gifts. Maintaining good records in a central location gives you several advantages:

- You'll have a clearer sense of the donor's intentions (documented in proposals, letters, records of plaque wording, etc.);

- You'll be able to better coordinate and share complete information with the key people making regular contact with the donor;

- You'll have the basis for planning these contacts; and,

- When coupled with a system that provide you with reminders at predetermined times, often called a *tickler system*, you'll be less vulnerable to problems that can stem from staff turnover.

These records are a true asset for your organization.

The goal of a tickler system is to ensure ongoing contact between "key players" and the donor. A new arts center named after a pacesetting donor may want to design a tickler system that includes, at least twice each year, extending an invitation to a private reception with the organization's president and a visiting artist or performer. Other leadership donors may be invited to backstage tours. Immediately after each event or contact, development staff at the arts center write brief notes or reports on the activities and place them in its central files.

Designing a tickler system begins by determining how often you'd like to be in contact with your key donors, then scheduling actions that match or exceed the desired frequency. By organizing your stewardship activities to share the joys—and even the setbacks—of the uses of their gifts, you can bring your donors even closer to your organization.

5. An Integrated Approach

Meeting regularly with development staff and others whom you enlist in the stewardship process will ensure a coordinated and integrated approach. There can be benefits to extending your planning efforts to include professionals from other departments, such as public relations, facilities planning, management, and communications staff. If your organization has a separate public relations department, for example, through an open dialogue you can share your fundraising goals and stewardship needs to determine ways in which there is mutual benefit. A description of a new program prepared by your public relations staff may become the basis of your case statement, reinforcing key messages of importance to your organization. In return, you may be able to provide biographical information about the lead donor for a press release prepared by public relations staff. In some cases, a communications plan is prepared to identify key messages, actions, and responsibilities, as well as an implementation timetable.

Lessons from Successful Organizations

Good Recordkeeping Is Essential

Communicating your accomplishments begins with a clear understanding of the purpose and obligations of the gift, recording them clearly, and maintaining files that are available to you—and those who follow you—well into the future. In cases where there are restrictions on the gift and its income, or perhaps your organization has agreed to other conditions, you and your successors will want to be able to easily access key documents.

Here are several examples of the importance of good recordkeeping:

After joining one hospital, I noticed that records for the charitable bequests the organization had received were stored in several different locations, including the president's office, the finance department, and, to a lesser degree, the development office. I requested that we centralize and organize these records in the development office. My staff then created a file for each of the bequests.

One day, the development office received a call from our finance department asking if we knew anything about Beverly Weisman, whose grandmother, Sylvia Furman (names changed), had funded an endowed bed with a charitable bequest in her will. The hospital had received the bequest in 1948, and a provision of Sylvia's will indicated that, if the hospital accepted the bequest, her heirs would receive free care at our hospital. Beverly had delivered a baby, a boy, and she was asking the hospital to honor her grandmother's will. Should the hospital provide Beverly and her newborn son with free care?

Fortunately, with our new, centralized bequest files, we quickly found Sylvia Furman's will. Her granddaughter was correct. The will stipulated that Sylvia's heirs were entitled to free care. Good recordkeeping saved both the patients and the hospital from what might otherwise have been a stressful and possibly litigious experience.

Tom Marcus (fictitious name), a very generous donor and avid collector of impressionist paintings, made a large gift to his favorite museum to build a new wing for French impressionist art. During the discussions about the gift, the museum's director indicated that he was concerned that the museum may not be able to afford to maintain the new wing. Tom's response was, "Oh, you don't have to worry. I'll always be here for you." Although some of the museum's trustees thought it was "aggressive and unnecessary," the museum director asked Tom to sign a simple agreement indicating that he would pay annual operating expenses for the new wing, if requested by the museum. After Tom remarried, his interest in the museum waned and Tom was slow to pay the annual operating costs. Yet, with the agreement on file, the museum director was able to successfully prevail upon Tom to continue his support and, later, establish an endowment for the wing's maintenance.

Bequest files and gift agreements are great ways to create institutional memory for the top gifts you receive. Another area in which recordkeeping is important is in donor recognition. Consider this example.

A college was renovating its library and, unfortunately, no one informed the development or advancement office that the demolition of interior walls had begun. When development staff learned about the renovations, they donned hard hats and, working with the college's maintenance department, rescued thirty-five donor plaques dating from the early 1900s. Unfortunately, the walls of the library's reading room had already been removed and, with them, any plaques.

All was not lost. Previously, the development office had employed student interns to record the size, location, and wording of all plaques on campus. In some cases, photos of the plaques were taken. With these records, twenty replacement plaques for the library were ordered and later installed.

Whether you are a one-person development office or serve with a national, multisite development program, maintaining accurate records is essential. Princeton University has a separate office (the Office of the Recording Secretary) that maintains files on all donors and their gifts. This stewardship is clearly in the best interests of its donors and the university.

One-on-One or Group Activities?

Communicating progress to a donor may be one-on-one, consisting of meetings, phone calls, letters, and reports. You may also bring a group of donors together, which often reinforces a common purpose and a sense of shared joy. Or your stewardship plan can build interest and pride in accomplishment through a combination of personal and group activities.

Here are examples of good stewardship involving groups of donors:

Pepperdine University and the Trust for Children's Hospital (Boston): Presentations are made at meetings of leadership giving clubs, such as Pepperdine's university board and Children's Philanthropic Leadership Councils. Students are always on the agenda at Pepperdine, and researchers and physicians bring the latest progress in medicine to Leadership Council donors in small, informal group settings. Donors invariably hear that progress would not be possible without their help.

Abington Memorial Hospital: Each year, donors who have endowed full or partial nursing scholarships are invited to meet recipients of their aid. It's a way for the donor to both receive thanks and see the benefits of the gift realized. Recently, a letter was sent to leadership donors, informing them of the increased number of students entering the school (a direct result of their gifts and others).

Samaritan Inns: Accountability is a hallmark at Samaritan Inns; executive director David Erickson updates board members and donors regularly. A dedication and tour of its new facilities conveyed the importance of Samaritan's role in impacting the lives of the homeless.

Recognition Stewardship

As organizations change, so too do their programs and facilities. A research laboratory constructed with a gift in the 1950s may be outdated. The laboratory may be demolished to make way for a modern facility. What should be done with plaques in the existing facility? What are your responsibilities to donors?

One answer is to create an historic display of plaques in a visible location in your main facility or the replacement laboratory. A new plaque for the display may be inscribed with a message such as, "We remember. Our progress and success in research is a tribute to the generosity of generations of supporters. While changes in research may require new facilities and technology, we remain steadfast in our appreciation of those who advance our mission."

See the sidebar "Stewardship in Action" (page 288–89) for a display of historic plaques created for one organization.

Planned Giving Stewardship

Individuals who fund life income gifts and trusts with a charitable organization rely on the charity to invest their gifts prudently, and to ensure that the charity makes payments to beneficiaries in a timely manner. They also expect tax information to be sent early in the year and to receive regular statements on investment performance.

At Princeton University, the university's planned giving program recently provided a report on the performance of its life income gifts on the same day as its annual unitholders' recognition luncheon. At a time when financial markets were hard to predict, the university's investment performance demonstrated solid returns. Handouts presented statistics and charts for the charitable funds, and top university staff confidently answered questions.

Many organizations balance financial reporting with a reminder of how well their "social capital" is performing. This can be done by bringing your planned giving donors together to hear presentations by key leaders. Colleges may enlist successful alumni or university professors. Scientists and researchers may share their discoveries to donors of a research institute. Hospitals may recruit doctors, specialists, and wellness experts to address new advances in medicine.

Corporate, Foundation & Government Grants

Many corporations, foundations, and government agencies require annual and final reports as a condition of receiving a grant. Complete and return these reports before the deadlines. Program officers also like to receive status reports and to be informed when your project is delayed, if you are having difficulties meeting project goals, or if you need to reallocate funds in ways that vary from your proposal. This can be as simple as a phone conversation during which you define the problem and explore the remedies that your organization is considering. In some cases, the program officer may make suggestions, based on the experiences of other grant recipients.

To improve communications with trustees of family foundations, add their names and addresses to your organization's mailing list for publications and reports.

Advocacy

Relationships are resources that should be valued and protected. But, like any asset, they are at risk of loss or theft. If you hear a complaint from a top gift donor, among the possible responses are to:

- Ignore it;

- Indicate that it's "not my department" and try to downplay the seriousness of the complaint;

- Apologize and ask if it would be okay to look into the problem and get back in touch.

I believe the correct answer is the last one. *Apologize and ask if it would be okay to look into the problem and get back in touch.* While some organizations do not permit development staff to discuss service problems with donors, there are three reasons why I recommend it:

1. Your organization's reputation is at stake. The best time to resolve a problem is as quickly as possible after the problem has occurred. This gives you time to listen, apologize, gather information, and solve the problem when you can be most effective. In many cases, these problems are due to lack of communication and/or misunderstanding about information conveyed. Restoring the flow of information may be all that's needed.

2. Your donors really are friends of your organization and generally want to ensure your future and your best interests. If they are having a problem, you may hear comments such as, "Perhaps others are having similar experiences. We wanted

you to know so that you can correct it." If you are denied the opportunity to help resolve their problems, your organization does not receive the feedback it needs to improve. Equally important, you will most likely lose the friendship and support of a top gift donor.

3. Research repeatedly indicates that endorsements from family, friends, and peers are an important source for referrals, both for services and gifts. This is especially true for high-net-worth individuals. Likewise, a negative experience may prevent your organization from getting the referrals—and support—it needs to succeed.

Although it's not the main goal, don't be surprised if resolving service problems results in donations, too. One donor sent me a check for twenty-five thousand dollars as the first payment toward a hundred-thousand-dollar pledge, after I addressed a problem his wife had experienced with my organization.

Stewardship in Action

Here are several examples of good stewardship programs by the organizations discussed above.

1. Changes in facilities are inevitable for most organizations. At St. Christopher's Hospital in Philadelphia, Pennsylvania, donors to previous campaigns were remembered when plaques from facilities being replaced were grouped into this historic display by Mitchell Associates.

2. When a facility is named to honor the donor of a leadership or pacesetting gift, recognition and stewardship activities are many. One important responsibility that can be overlooked is to incorporate the donor's name into all references to the facility (in this case, Gerstadt Childcare Center, or the Gerstadt Center) for both print materials and the day-to-day life of your organization. Photos commemorate the facility's groundbreaking ceremony.

New Gerstadt Childcare Center Will Meet Crucial Needs
Abington Memorial Hospital's new Gerstadt Childcare Center is scheduled to open in Fall of 2003. The center will be built on a half-acre site just across Old York Road from the hospital's main campus. Designed with a residential look, the new center will be two stories tall and will provide a combination of full- and part-time care for approximately 150 children. The center will offer childcare for infants, toddlers, preschool children and kindergarten students, and will accommodate a variety of employee schedules – providing peace of mind for working AMH parents.

THE GERSTADT
CHILDCARE CENTER

SERVING THE EMPLOYEES
OF ABINGTON
MEMORIAL HOSPITAL

GIVEN BY
LOUISE & BILL GERSTADT
2001

3. Offering donors the opportunity to see the benefits of their gifts realized can have a profound impact. This may include a tour of a new facility before it is placed into service or, seen here, Mr. and Mrs. Fitz Eugene Dixon Jr. meeting their scholarship recipients at the Dixon School of Nursing of Abington Memorial Hospital.

TOP GIFTS™ WORKBOOK
Creating a Stewardship Plan

The goal of your stewardship plan is to fulfill your commitments to your donors in ways that share the spirit and joy of their philanthropy. Here are specific elements to be considered in your stewardship plan.

1. *Recordkeeping:* What data will you store on each top gift? How will you create and maintain records for these donors? Does your system allow you to schedule contacts with each of your top donors? Among your options:

   - Computer database: Some systems allow you to attach documents, such as gift agreements, and images

   - Paper files and calendars: Will all files be centralized? Who in your office will schedule contacts?

   - Other (list)_____

2. *Implementation:* Who in your organization must participate in carrying out the purposes of the donors' gifts? How will you enlist and involve staff in key decisions to move the program or project forward? Among the roles and participants in many organizations are:

   - Finance: Establishing a restricted account and making expenditures related to the gifts' purposes;

   - Public relations: Announcing the gift; may also be involved in signs, brochures, and communications materials for named programs or facilities;

   - Program chairs/deans: For research and educational organizations, the individuals who will carry out programs or projects related to the gift;

   - Financial aid officers: For awarding named scholarships;

   - Other (list)_____

3. *Frequency:* How often do you want to communicate with each of your highest-level donors?

4. *Communications and Reports:* Given the preferences of your donors and the culture of your organization, what are the best ways to provide these updates? These may include:

   - Meetings with leaders involved in the program or project being funded, your organization's top officials, and/or development staff;

   - Phone calls;

   - Letters and reports;

   - Other (list)_____

5. *Group Activities/Events:* In what ways can group activities or events help convey the impact and benefits being achieved through these gifts? What specific events should be planned? List those which offer the greatest potential benefit:

"It's not about a technique. It's about sharing a mission."

David Erickson, President
Samaritan Inns

"The best parachute folders are those who jump themselves."

Anonymous

This book has focused on sharing with you the steps, strategies, and techniques to help you become a dream builder for your organization . . . to help you understand both the roles and the synergies of a powerful vision, dedicated and capable leadership, and a focus on major and planned gift fundraising.

Leaders of the visionary organizations profiled in this book have echoed the views of Dr. Twink Lynch, a dream builder with the Topeka Community Theatre, who astutely advises, "I don't think you can become what you're capable of becoming, unless you dream of what's possible."

Call it a vision, a dream, a destination, or your horizon. As Drayton McLane Jr., vice chairman of Wal-Mart and owner of the Houston Astros once said to a group of fundraisers, "The real role of the leader is to define the future."

The role of a fundraising leader is not only to define the future, but also to make that dream a reality.

As a dream builder, take the first step by helping define your organization's future. Using techniques in this book, identify, enlist, and engage the leadership required to fund your dreams. Create "a seat at the table" at which they can become aware of your dreams and partner with you in mapping out the steps to make them possible.

An Invitation

In these final pages, I'd like to invite you to accept a second role—to share in the joy of giving. Your gift will establish you as a leader, serve as a model for others to follow, and add to your campaign's success. In the words of fundraiser and author Douglas M. Lawson, "Giving is the only way to find out what living is all about."

Describing his book *More Give to Live*, Doug Lawson says that, as fundraisers, we give our donors an opportunity "to participate in something that will give them back more than they give." Giving is a way to enrich our lives. You have everything to gain and nothing to lose, he says. He says that, as we give to change the world, we also change ourselves. We receive greater happiness and, with that joy, an opportunity to live longer, healthier lives.

A businessman who embodied these tenets was McDonald's founder Ray Kroc, who on his seventieth birthday made seven gifts of one million dollars each. Kroc believed so strongly in philanthropy that his legacy outlives him; at death (in his eighties), he left one billion dollars to the Kroc Foundation.

The joy of giving is seen in many of the leaders of the organizations profiled here.

"Every time I walk into our new community theater, I feel like a million dollars," says Dr. Lynch of the facilities she raised funds to provide. Then, jokingly, she adds, "Or at least like a hundred thousand," the amount of her family's gift to this campaign. Yet, listening to her talk about this special theater, it's clear that her joy and pride in this facility far exceed the amount she gave.

You too can share that joy by making your best gift to the project of your dreams.

A Personal Experience

I had this experience shortly after my wife and I made what was then our largest gift ever to Abington Memorial Hospital, for a new patient care pavilion. As a fundraiser, I had described the building's key role to our best potential donors literally hundreds of times. But the message had added meaning when I visited a close friend whose life was saved in our new emergency/trauma center. She had arrived at the hospital nearly comatose, but, after a harrowing experience, she was miraculously sitting up alert in our new critical care facilities. Today, I understand that my family's gift extends well beyond the dollars contributed. It saved the life of a friend and will save many more.

Is This a Moment When You Can Step Forward . . .

Doug Lawson says that when he meets with a potential donor, he often says, "In our lives, there are only a few opportunities to make a difference." He describes an opportunity of importance, then asks, "Is this a moment when you can step forward to make a difference in this world? We need you to join us, to be a part of this."

As you pursue your organization's dreams, why not also become the philanthropic leader that your organization needs? With your gift, you can help make the difference. In doing so, you'll be one step closer to realizing your dreams.

Contents

"Some people dream of success . . .

while others wake up and work hard at it."

Kevin Freiberg, Jackie Freiberg
Nuts! Southwest Airlines' Crazy Recipe for Business and Personal Success

"If you shoot for the moon and fall a little bit short, you wind up in the stars . . .

and that's not a bad place to be. I've always felt that that meant to set your sights high and

give 110 percent. And everything will turn out okay."

Joe Thiesmann
Quarterback for the Washington Redskins

Here are seven practical tips on starting a development program for a hospital, college, or community-based program. To encourage smaller organizations to establish a fundraising program, I'm using a modest, fifty-thousand-dollar goal. The same steps, however, can be used effectively for larger appeal programs. Finally, take time to test your highest giving level by conducting a donor interest survey (see chapter 6).

A successful annual appeal is the foundation of many development programs. It raises dollars for today's programs. It strengthens ties with friends who can help raise money for tomorrow's needs. It will reveal information about your donors and prospects for planning and evaluating future programs. Consider these seven steps for establishing—or reviving—your annual appeal:

1. Identify Your Best Prospects

Research shows that former contributors generally give when asked. If you don't have a list of former donors, ask the accounting department for records of contributors over the last five, ten, or fifteen years. Even nonprofits without a formal annual appeal receive gifts now and then. Ask your volunteers to check whether these donors still live in the area, then get updated mailing addresses with telephone numbers. The second major category of prospects includes those who 1) are interested in your organization, 2) provide services to it, or 3) benefit from it. Consider these groups when you compile lists of prospects:

- Members of your organization's board of directors, foundation, or development board,

- All employees of your organization,

- Support groups (for hospitals: volunteers, auxilians; colleges: parents, etc.),

- People you serve (for hospitals: patients or guarantors, members of the medical staff, participants of health education programs; colleges: faculty, alumni, participants of adult education courses, etc.),

- Businesses supplying goods and services (direct your appeals to the owner or manager), and

- Clubs and civic groups interested in your services.

Other prospects may include:

- Business and community leaders (attorneys, officers of corporations, members of bank boards, etc.),

- Banks (send your appeals to the president), or

- Local foundations that support general appeals.

You can also purchase the use of mailing lists, and even specify your criteria: income, home ownership, and the like. I believe it's best to learn as much as you can about your own donors and prospects before investing in someone else's list. Finally, as you develop your lists, select a code for each group (*BD* for Board, *PD* for Prior Donors) and assign it to each name in the group for easy reference, and to determine which groups give the most in any campaign.

2. Get to Know Your Donors and Prospects

If you've compiled a list of those who've given previously, appeal to them for renewed support. Meet members of each group to develop a donor profile—a composite of their interests and needs, how they view your organization, and the area they most want to support. As you meet with former donors, ask them:

- What they like—and dislike—about your organization;

- What needs of the community are unmet;

- What prompted them to give;

- How their previous gifts were acknowledged and if they were pleased with the process;

- What type of gift they prefer giving (unrestricted gift, gift for buildings or equipment, endowment, etc.).

In an interview with a physician who had once given, I learned that a group of community volunteers had organized an annual appeal that died due to a lack of commitment to fundraising by the organization. The doctor wasn't giving at the time of our interview because "no one asked me." He pointed out that when he gave previously he was seldom thanked, or else he received an impersonal, printed card that arrived weeks, sometimes months later. "I was never informed if my contribution did any good. Overall, I really didn't feet my gift even mattered to the hospital."

These comments and those of other doctors guided me through a number of successful annual appeals. I've learned to ask for support at least once a year; identify specific projects that, when begun, could be reported on readily to our contributors; use personal letters when asking for support and send personal, prompt acknowledgements; and constantly show how important each person's gift is and how much we appreciate the support.

3. Create a Development Team

Many organizations have created separate foundations to direct their fundraising. Foundations offer many benefits, the best being a separate board that has but one goal: raising dollars. If your organization doesn't see any value in forming a foundation, take heart. With the approval of your board of directors, you can create a development board or council to help you. Keep control over who is appointed to serve on it to ensure a good mix of community leaders. If your organization later decides it needs a foundation, so much the better; you'll have already begun to identify qualified leaders. (Many attorneys discourage having too many members serving on both the foundation's and hospital's boards of directors. Proceed with care.) Name at least one representative from each group you'll be soliciting to serve on your development council. Include your president or administrator.

To find the best candidates, ask former donors whom they would most likely listen to if asked to donate to your institution. Finally, once members feel comfortable working on the council, ask each to give you the names of ten or more people for your appeal list. Code them as VIPs.

4. Involve Your Development Council in Planning & Conducting Your Appeal

Council members who know what your organization needs, who understand fundraising, and who are asked to help plan your first appeal will share a concern for the campaign's success. Convene the council and have your president or administrator explain what needs are unmet and how an active development program could help your organization better serve its community. Share with the council facts from your donor profiles and encourage their comments. Explain ideas and programs used by organizations like yours, and ask them which would succeed in your community. Seek their advice on new programs you're considering. They represent the people from whom you'll be seeking support. Given the needs your administrator has outlined, what programs would they be most willing to support?

Do they like the theme of your appeal? Does your newsletter or brochure give information that encourages them and their associates to support your organization? Ask them if they would be willing to solicit their peers in person. If not, suggest they call or send personally signed letters. Listen. Plan. Revise. Offer the council ideas and leadership, but let it guide you to success.

5. Build for the Future

You are establishing a new tradition at your institution, so take time to ensure your first appeal lays a solid foundation on which you can build other successful programs. Seek to build support for your development program within your organization. Review with your president or administrator any proposals you're considering for the development council before you make your formal presentation. Discuss with your financial staff the contents of your appeal brochure, how you plan to process gifts, and other areas of mutual interest to ensure that you agree on a workable system. Evaluate techniques used by other organizations. Should you establish an honorary association for donors? Should you consider levels of giving? Should you offer a gift to encourage donations of $25, $100, $1,000, or more?

6. Establish a System for Soliciting & Acknowledging Gifts

The time to think about how to solicit and acknowledge gifts is before you send a single letter. A good plan should include answers to these questions:

- How will you solicit—by letter, phone, newsletter, brochure, the Internet, or a combination thereof?

- If you're using direct mail, how many mailings will you send? Who will write your letter? Will you use postage-paid business reply envelopes for the convenience of the donor? If so, do you have the necessary postal permit?

- Do you have a system that allows you to keep accurate lists of each appeal group, send mailings and reports on time, update your lists of donors and prospects easily, keep financial records, and produce recognition lists (if you've chosen that benefit for contributors)? If you don't have a computer (and I didn't for my first campaign), fundraising companies can provide appeal letters, acknowledgments, and reports on each code group. Interview these firms about services, costs, and schedules before you're knee-deep in contributions. How will you thank your contributors? A signed, personal letter of acknowledgment? A printed, hand-signed card? A simple receipt? A phone call from someone important in your organization? Who will sign your acknowledgments? Will the president of your board sign all of them—even for five-dollar contributions—or only those for gifts above one hundred dollars? Or one thousand?

7. Evaluate—Then Build on Your Success

What information will you need to evaluate this appeal and start next year's? How will the information be stored—on three-by-five cards, by an outside company's computer, or on your own system? Does your system let you select specific groups and their levels of giving, and can it expand as your lists of donors and prospects grow? With a good evaluation, much of the blood, sweat, and tears of your first annual appeal need not be repeated. Prepare statistical reports (see samples below) to help you measure the level of your success. A low response from one group may indicate you need to do more research or exert greater effort. In the example shown, you may need more representatives from VIPs (*VP* group), or you may want to personally

Annual Appeal Analysis

I. Response by Constituency

Appeal Group	Total # Gifts	Total Giving	Ave. Gift	% Response
BD	25	$10,000	$400	75%
DC	12	$3,000	$150	100%
PD	325	$11,375	$35	46%
VP	95	$5,225	$55	6%
ALL GROUPS	875	$50,000	$ 57.14	20%

II. Annual Appeal Donors by City/Town

Zip Code	Total # Gifts	Avg. Gift	% Response	% All Donors
00001	184	$75.23	23%	21%
00002	245	65.47	27%	28%
00003	8	18.01	5%	1%

III. Annual Appeal Response by Giving Level

	Total Donors	% All Donors		
$1,000 or More	11	13%		
$500 to $999	32	3.7%		
$250 to $499	60	6.8%		
$100 to $249	100	11.4%		
$25 to $99	222	25.4%		
$1 to $24	450	51.4%		

solicit this group next time. In part 3 of the analysis, since most gifts are under one hundred dollars, you may consider ways to encourage these donors to increase their giving to one hundred dollars or more. Finally, by comparing one year to the next, you can spot where you're progressing, and where you're losing support.

8. A Bonus

Although I promised seven steps to success, here's a bonus suggestion to save you time and effort. Call a development officer at a similar organization with a successful, entrenched development program (but, to be safe, not a group that's competing for gifts with you). Discuss ideas and programs for setting up a program at your organization. Ask questions and take notes liberally. Your investment in time will be well rewarded.

"You miss one hundred percent of the shots you never take."

Wayne Gretzky, Hockey great

"Outstanding leaders go out of their way to boost the self-esteem of their people. If people believe in themselves, it's amazing what they can accomplish."

Sam Walton, Founder of Wal-Mart

Three Roles for Trustees in Creating a Dynamic Planned Giving Program

1. Leadership
- Name a well-respected board member as planned giving chairman.
- Serve as advocates and solicitors.

2. Support
- Be the first to make planned gifts.
- Approve adequate funding for program.
- Remain open to new ideas.
- Keep apprised of program's status and progress.

3. Programs and policies
- Review and approve all programs involving long-term obligations or risk.
- Review and approve guidelines.

If your nonprofit organization or foundation is looking for ways to increase support for future programs, it might consider starting—or strengthening—a planned giving program. Offering contributors more flexibility in ways to give will help protect your fundraising program from recession. And, with planned gifts, you can build your endowment or reserves to better meet future needs. Without board commitment and support, however, a new planned giving program is likely to falter.

What Is Planned Giving?

Planned gifts are simply donations that require planning to complete; that is, they represent more than a check or pledge to your annual appeal campaign. In structuring planned gifts, the donor often brings in the services of one or more professional advisors, such as an attorney, accountant, estate planner, real estate broker, and/or insurance agent. An organization does not need to have a planned giving program to receive such gifts. For example, a donor could decide to include a charitable bequest to the hospital in his or her will without even consulting you or your staff. This happens quite often, and many organizations have received some very generous bequests over the years.

Types of Gifts

Among the most common forms of planned gifts are bequests, life income gifts, life insurance, and real estate.

Bequests

A donor can decide to leave your organization a charitable gift (or bequest) in his or her will. The estate receives a tax deduction.

Life Income Gifts

A donor can give a gift to some charities and, in return, be paid a lifetime income. The donor may name a second person to receive income for his or her life as well. Some life income programs operate like mutual funds in that the donor receives a portion of the income earned based on the number of shares he or she owns. (Because donations are "pooled," this type of program is called a *pooled income fund.*) Other plans are like annuities and make fixed payment amounts (called a *charitable gift annuity*). For larger gifts—generally one hundred thousand dollars or more—a life income plan can be tailored to the donor's needs through a charitable remainder trust. In all three plans, the charity receives the remaining principal and any appreciation after all income is paid to the beneficiaries. Finally, the donor is rewarded for being so generous (most charities require a minimum of five thousand dollars to fund a gift annuity or pooled income fund gift). In most instances, the donor increases his or her income, receives a charitable deduction for part of the gift (in the United States), and may receive some tax-free income. When the gift is funded with stock that has increased in value, the donor can avoid paying—or greatly reduce the amount of—capital gains tax, which is an added benefit.

Life Insurance

A donor can give your organization an existing life insurance policy that has cash value, or he or she may purchase a new policy that names the charity as irrevocable owner and beneficiary. If donors make annual gifts to cover the cost of their premiums, they may claim these costs as a charitable deduction.

Real Estate

Donors may give property to your organization in one of the following ways:

- They give their home or vacation property to your organization but reserve the right to live in it during their (or their spouses') lifetimes.

- They deed the property to a charitable trust that one day pays them income.

- They sell property to your organization at a greatly reduced price.

- They make an outright gift of property to your organization.

In the United States, all four options provide the donor with an income tax deduction, the amount of which is determined by an appraisal, the amount of benefit (or gift) to the charity, and other factors. Because individual donors may be subject to the alternative minimum tax and other tax provisions, it is always best that they review planned giving options with their tax advisors.

Why Establish a Program?

While a number of planned gifts are made without the charity's involvement, most people need to be informed about the opportunity to make such gifts before taking action. Surveys of annual giving programs have shown that many nondonors have never supported a charity because "no one ever asked me." You'll want to correct this shortcoming. You also need to alert potential donors as to the kinds of planned gifts your organization is prepared to accept.

Marketing planned giving and asking for the gift, then, are crucial to receiving the largest number of potential gifts. Finally, some planned giving vehicles—such as pooled income funds and gift annuity programs—are only available to donors when the charity establishes and administers them. It's important to consult with an attorney who specializes in charitable giving, as some states have laws regulating programs such as charitable gift annuities.

How does a donor benefit from such a program? Frequently, a prospective donor is interested in helping your organization while increasing his or her income. With a gift annuity, for example, the level of income is determined by age: the older the annuitant, the higher the income. For example, a sixty-year-old donor may receive 7 percent annually (Rates do change and are established by each charity. A membership organization, the American Council on Gift Annuities, offers guidance on what rates to offer); an eighty-year-old donor may receive 9.6 percent. These payouts are a benefit to older contributors on fixed incomes, and—based on projections by the American Council—your organization should receive at least half the original gift, often considerably more.

Another program of mutual benefit to the donor and a charitable organization is a gift of highly appreciated stock to the charity's pooled income fund. Because the charitable fund is selling the securities, there is no capital gains tax on the sale— enabling the fund to reinvest the securities for more income to the contributor. A donor who paid $4,500 for stock now worth $10,000 may have to pay $1,100 in capital gains tax (20 percent of the $5,500 gain) if the individual sold the stock. This would leave only $8,900 to reinvest. If the donor's new investment pays 5 percent, he or she will receive about $445 a year.

The same securities given as a gift to the pooled income fund would pay about $700, or 57 percent more than if the donor had sold and reinvested the securities. Assuming the contributor is seventy-two years old, he or she would qualify for a charitable deduction of nearly $4,100—providing a tax savings of more than $1,100 (28 percent income tax bracket).

Some contributors receive an added benefit by investing the tax savings in a savings account or a stock or mutual fund—or even making a later addition to the charity's pooled income fund. These benefits can be quite attractive.

There are numerous other examples. One of our more creative contributors is using a life income gift to meet future payment of estate taxes. He made a gift of highly appreciated securities to our pooled income fund and avoided all capital gains tax; now, he is using part of his income for premiums on an insurance policy designed to help pay estate taxes, which can be onerous. Most people are not aware that, for larger estates, the tax brackets range from 37 percent to 55 percent.

The Future of Planned Giving

The potential for planned gifts in the future is significant. Indeed, at least one fundraiser predicts that planned gifts in the future may equal or exceed annual gifts. During isolated years, I've personally seen planned giving eclipse annual support.

Fortune magazine describes wealth of those age sixty and over as "a social watershed" resulting in "the biggest intergenerational transfer of wealth in U.S. history."

Three reasons for establishing a planned giving program today are:

- Many of your donors are able to make such gifts today, enabling your hospital to secure this support before commitments are made to other charities.

- Planned giving offers potential donors more flexibility in ways to give that may make it possible for them to give more and be happier with the way they are giving. For example, some donors may find it difficult to make an outright gift of one thousand dollars, but would willingly give five thousand dollars for a life income gift, particularly if it increases their income and offers tax benefits. Other supporters will like the idea of making both outright and planned gifts because of their interest in the institution's well-being.

- Contrary to what some trustees may believe, planned giving can actually strengthen a fundraising program, particularly during a recession. Although some donors will decide to decrease their annual gifts during a recession, a planned gift can still be made since the donor does not lose needed income after making the gift. On the other hand, I have seen individuals who were considering a life income gift to charity decide not to complete these gifts; instead, they made large donations to the organization's annual fund seeking to get the largest tax deduction possible and support the charity.

Role of Trustees in Planned Giving

Planned gifts represent major gifts to an institution and, as such, require a major commitment. That commitment starts with your trustees.

Leadership

The degree of success for your organization's program may very well be tied to the volunteer leadership provided by trustees. Naming a planned giving chairman who has the respect of all trustees as well as of members of the community may help give a program added stature. Other trustees are needed to serve as advocates and solicitors.

Support

As with any new program or business, the startup phase is the most difficult. Trustees should be the first to consider making planned gifts. This will help build credibility and momentum and encourage others to follow their lead. At one organization, for example, during the first three years of revitalizing a planned giving program, one-third or more of all life-income gifts were made by trustees and former trustees. That has made all the difference!

Because planned gifts can be technical and promotion is needed to create awareness, trustees must approve adequate funding for legal counsel, marketing expenses, staffing, secretarial support, etc. And, just as medicine has specialists, the board must keep in mind that planned giving programs may need to have their own specialists available (such as an attorney, estate planner, and/or accountant). Although your organization's legal counsel may be skillful in personnel or employment issues, for example, the development staff needs to determine if this same firm has the knowledge, experience, and depth to prepare a charitable remainder trust. Some firms do, but many do not.

Finally, trustees can also support planned giving by having patience, understanding, and an openness to new ideas. Because planned gifts represent much larger contributions than annual fund donations, for example, the number of contributors may initially appear small, which is both normal and acceptable. In addition, the number and amounts of bequests often vary significantly from year to year. The planned giving chairman should provide the board with up-to-date reports on the progress of the program.

Programs & Policies

The board will need to review and approve all programs that place long-term obligations on the hospital (such as starting and accepting gifts to a pooled income fund, gift annuity program, etc.) or potentially place your organization at risk (e.g., gifts of real estate). In addition, the board will need to authorize one or more members of the development staff to carry out certain responsibilities—such as signing life income agreements, accepting and selling securities or real estate, and so on. Many boards also approve guidelines for planned giving options and suggested giving levels, based on recommendations from a development committee and staff.

Is Your Organization Ready?

In order to enhance the success of a planned giving program, your organization should have a well-developed annual giving program (a sign of commitment by a large number of supporters), a compelling reason or case for support, good public or community relations, and a true charitable mission. Because planned giving requires the development office to provide a high level of service, your organization will need to evaluate whether development staff has the time and expertise to take on the added responsibilities. If the administration is uncertain, consultants are available to audit the program. Finally, your organization needn't—and probably shouldn't—try to establish and promote all programs at once. In initiating planned giving, you will be introducing new ideas and options to your donors, which will take them time to understand. Unless you are hiring a seasoned planned giving officer to direct the program, you instead should focus on one program at a time, do it well, then add new options gradually.

By Jan Grieff

jgrieff@jgresearch.com

The following is a list of the top fourteen listservs for development professionals. These are online community bulletin boards that enable development professionals to correspond with each other regarding specific development issues, etc.

Instructions for subscribing to many of these listservs can be found at *www.charitychannel.com*. Click on "Forum Descriptions," which provides a list of community bulletin boards as well as detailed instructions for subscribing. Many of the other sites listed below use the same format.

Annual Giving . . . .*ANNUAL_FUND@CHARITYCHANNEL.COM*

Arts and Cultural Organizations . . . .*ARTS_GIFT@CHARITYCHANNEL.COM*

Development Officers . . . .*DEVOFFICERS@VAIL.AL.ARIZONA.EDU*

Nonprofit Issues . . . .*CHARITYTALK@CHARITYCHANNEL.COM*

Nonprofits and Public Relations . . . .*CHARITY-PR@CHARITYCHANNEL.COM*

PUBLIC-RELATIONS@LISTS.WAYNE.EDU

Online Fundraising . . . .*CYBERGIFTS@CHARITYCHANNEL.COM*

Planned Giving . . . .*GIFTPLAN@CHARITYCHANNEL.COM*

GIFT-PL@LISTSERV.IUPUI.EDU

Prospect Research . . . .*GIFTPROSPECTING@CHARITYCHANNEL.COM*

**Software, the Internet,
and Charities** . . . .*CHARITYSOFT@CHARITYCHANNEL.COM*

Sponsorships . . . .*SPONSORSHIP@CHARITYCHANNEL.COM*
University Relations and

Development Discussion List . . . .*LISTSERV@LISTSERV.KENT.EDU*

Women in Development . . . .*GEN-DEV@LISTSERV.UOGUELPH.CA*

Order additional copies of *Dream Builders* today

A must book for every professional fundraiser, volunteer and nonprofit executive

As a nonprofit leader, you can be the catalyst, creating the opportunities contributors of major gifts are seeking. In *Dream Builders* you'll find a complete plan to define and fund your organization's future. You'll discover how to progress from imagining fundraising possibilities to actually experiencing them.

Order extra copies of *Dream Builders* today to enhance your success. Present copies of *Dream Builders* to your best volunteers or use it to enlist, engage and excite your board members. *Dream Builders* also is an excellent tool to educate your staff in "best practices" in fundraising.

YES, I'd like _____ copies of *Dream Builders* for $47 each
plus $5.00 shipping for first book, $1 each additional book. Connecticut orders: Please add 6% sales tax.

E^3 Fundraising
PO Box 2402
Danbury, CT 06813-2402
203 796-0192
Or visit our website at www.e3fundraising.com

Name _____ Title _____

Organization_____

Address_____

City_____ State _____ Zip _____

Daytime phone _____ Optional: email address _____

Please charge my credit card:
Name (as it appears on card) _____

❏ Visa ❏ Mastercard Credit card number _____

Expiration date _____ Signature _____